MUHAMMAD ALI
JINNAH

MUHAMMAD ALI JINNAH

A Journey from India to Pakistan

J.B.P. More

NIYOGI BOOKS

Published by
NIYOGI BOOKS
Block D, Building No. 77,
Okhla Industrial Area, Phase-I,
New Delhi-110 020, INDIA
Tel: 91-11-26816301, 26818960
Email: niyogibooks@gmail.com
Website: www.niyogibooksindia.com

Editor: Priyanka Misra
Design: Shraboni Roy

ISBN: 978-93-86906-91-5
Publication: 2019

Printed at: Niyogi Offset Pvt. Ltd., New Delhi, India

CONTENTS

LIST OF ABBREVIATIONS

AICC	All India Congress Committee
AIML	All-India Muslim League
CWMG	*Collected Works of Mahatma Gandhi*
IAR	Indian Annual Register
INC	Indian National Congress
IOL	India Office Library and Records, London
JP	Jinnah Papers
NAI	National Archives of India, New Delhi
NMML	Nehru Memorial Museum & Library, New Delhi
NWFP	North-West Frontier Province
SWJN	*Selected Works of Jawaharlal Nehru*
TA	Tamil Nadu Archives
TP	*Transfer of Power*
UP	United Provinces

INTRODUCTION

In this book I intend to write about Muhammad Ali Jinnah, one of the prime architects of the Partition of India. The focus of this work will be on his life since birth to the various phases or avatars during the course of his political career until he launches the demand for Pakistan from Lahore in the year 1940.

I had worked on the controversial subject related to the Partition of India since 1999. I have collected a lot of material pertaining to the subject which has been published as a book under the title *Partition of India: Players and Partners* (2008). It was published by the Institute for Research in Social Sciences and Humanities, based in Nirmalagiri, Kerala. I have focussed on the crucial six to seven years that preceded the Partition of India. While working for this book, I had collected a large amount of authentic material related to Jinnah, his life, and his political role during the crucial years leading to the birth of the idea of Pakistan. It is this material that I intend to put to good use in the writing of life and political career of Muhammad Ali Jinnah until he raised the demand for Pakistan.

Writing about an enigmatic and controversial personality like Muhammad Ali Jinnah is not always an easy task. Much has been written on him both in India and Pakistan and also in the Anglo-Saxon dominated West. Generally, it is either written to praise him for his achievement of Pakistan within a short span of seven years, or it is written to deride him for having split India into two, on the basis of religion. In this work, my intention is neither to praise him nor deride him for his political achievements. I am neither an admirer of Jinnah nor am I his detractor. Instead, my intention is to look objectively at the life and political career of Jinnah in the light of the contemporary events which finally pushed him to raise the demand for Pakistan. This will be done on the basis of authentic evidences and recorded facts, paying the greatest attention to rationality and logic. Jinnah might have spoken many things on various issues during the course of his political life. But what is more important in Jinnah's life is not so much the words that he pronounced orally off and on, but what he actually did. In other words, I will dwell more on the real actions of Jinnah rather on his oral words, though the latter may sometimes have its own limited importance.

Muhammad Ali Jinnah is credited by almost everyone in Pakistan as the sole architect of Pakistan. In India too, the dominant view was that Jinnah and his Muslim League were responsible for the break-up of India. The Indian National Congress (INC) and its leaders also put the blame on the British colonialists for resorting to the 'Divide and Rule' policy to estrange Hindus from the Muslims. Some scholars think that the British pushed Jinnah to ask for Partition, while others maintain the contrary.

On their part, the British colonial authorities and scholars ranging from C.H. Philips to Francis Robinson usually asserted that as Jinnah and the Congress leaders were at loggerheads with regard to the future of India, Partition became unavoidable. Therefore they assert that the British, whose official policy was to maintain Indian unity, had no role in dividing India. A few among them thought that Jinnah was actually using the Pakistan slogan as a bargaining manoeuvre to extract more concessions for Muslims within a united India.[1]

It is obvious that most British scholars, if not all, conditioned by their national history and interests have a marked tendency to put the entire blame for the Partition of India on the Hindu and Muslim leaders as if the then British authorities had no role in bringing about the Partition. They had never raised an accusing or even a critical finger on any British leader or British Indian colonial authority for causing the Partition of India to happen. Therefore, for a neutral historian like me it will not be judicious to rely on them to give an accurate account of what happened for the Pakistan demand and the Partition to come about.

The protagonists of Jinnah, especially from Pakistan or of Pakistani origin see in Jinnah a man of impeccable character and indomitable will, combined with great political wisdom and acumen. They credit him for his extraordinary tactical moves, which to them were all part of a master plan. It is a matter of great pride for them to assert that Jinnah single-handedly braved top veteran Congress leaders like Mahatma Gandhi, Jawaharlal Nehru, C. Rajagopalachari, and Vallabhbhai Patel. He also courageously faced the British colonial authorities in order to achieve his Pakistan, which turned out to be the largest Muslim nation in the world and that too within a short span of seven years. For Aga Khan, the Imam of the Ismailis, Jinnah, the Gujarati Khoja, was the most remarkable man that the world had produced, far greater than Clemenceau, Lloyd George, Churchill, Curzon, Mussolini, and Mahatma Gandhi in strength of character and statecraft.[2] For the protagonists of Jinnah, it is simply impossible to imagine that Jinnah would have gone wrong in his calculations with regard to Pakistan.

Besides, the scholars from Pakistan generally did not accept the Indian argument of the 'Divide and Rule' policy of the British, for it belittled the stature of Jinnah and their belief in his brilliant strategy and tenacity in obtaining Pakistan, outwitting both the Congress leaders and the British. They would not even admit the existence of a combined Indian nationalism of the Hindus and the Muslims in British India. Instead, they saw in Jinnah an extremely skilful negotiator and expert constitutionalist right from the beginning.[3] For most of these scholars from Pakistan or of Pakistani origin, Jinnah was almost infallible in his words and actions and his strategy to obtain Pakistan was impeccable.

The position of the above scholars is understandable because they too, like the British, are conditioned by their national history and interests. They cannot take a position which would deride Jinnah or run him down in any manner whatsoever that may challenge the official Pakistani line—

Jinnah is the central figure in Pakistan and the Father of the Nation. The scholars will naturally have a strong tendency to interpret Jinnah's life according to their own national interests and predilections and run down all Indian leaders as no match to the intelligence and sagacity of Jinnah. So it will not be judicious to rely on these scholars to come out with a correct portrayal of the life and political career of Jinnah, which led to the Partition of India.

On the contrary, the detractors of Jinnah, especially in India, see in him a lean, wily and diabolic force, who used religion to split the common motherland into two. Many of them consider Gandhi as the personification of all virtues who fought till the end the division of the country. It is unthinkable for such scholars to question the integrity of Indian leaders like Mahatma Gandhi or Jawaharlal Nehru and put the blame on them for Partition. They too are conditioned by their national histories and interests. Therefore it is not judicious to solely rely on them to depict the correct happenings that brought about the Pakistan demand and Partition.

Many other Indian as well as Pakistani scholars hold that Jinnah was a nationalist until 1937 when he thought that Muslim interests and rights could be safeguarded within the framework of an united and federal India. They hold that this became impossible after the 1937 elections due to Congress policies in the provinces. We can include the names of scholars like Mushirul Hasan and A.G. Noorani of India, Sharif Al-Mujahid of Pakistan as also earlier British scholars and legislators Sir Percival Griffiths and Sir Reginald Coupland under this category.

These scholars put the blame squarely on the Congress leaders for Partition. In the process, they tend to overlook or neglect the role played by the British in the Partition of India. Therefore their ways of projecting the political career of Jinnah and the events that led to the Partition of India is not entirely reliable.

Pakistan, created by the British out of India in August 1947, consisted of two wings. The first was West Pakistan made up of the provinces of Sind, Baluchistan, North-West Frontier Province and the western part of Punjab province. It was a lengthy corridor State running from the Ocean northwards to the Himalayas, with no strategic depth and width. The second was East Pakistan, which consisted of the eastern part of the Bengal province. It was a congested marshy enclave, surrounded on almost all sides by the Indian Territory, and completely indefensible. In the name of Islam and as per Jinnah's wishes, both wings were united as one country although they were separated by more than thousand kilometres of Indian Territory.

Between 1970 and 1982, the crucial *Transfer of Power* papers, which was lying in the India Office Library and Archives, was edited and published in twelve volumes. It was during that period that Jinnah's papers were published too. That was quite significant because Jinnah, unlike his Congress counterparts, hardly wrote anything about his life or his long political career, in spite of being a British-educated lawyer like Jawaharlal Nehru or Mahatma Gandhi. In the light of new evidences and happenings in the subcontinent, these publications seem to have re-activated the interests of some scholars to re-examine the causes and events that led to the Partition of India and the roles played by the principal actors like the British, Jinnah, and the Congress leaders in this game of Partition.

However, Indian scholarship with regard to Partition and the role played by its various leaders did not vary much. Most of the Indian scholars held tenaciously to the view that Jinnah and British policy were responsible for the division of India. According to the historian Rafiq Zakaria, 'Jinnah ignored the fact that they (Hindus and Muslims) had lived together by and large, in peace and harmony for a thousand years'. He asserts that 'because of Jinnah, the Muslims find themselves out of place everywhere and at home nowhere'. The experienced American scholar, Stanley Wolpert who used the *Transfer of Power* papers to author a book on Jinnah in 1984 does not swerve from the official theory held in Pakistan that Jinnah was the sole architect of Pakistan. He had his own followers.[4]

But there were a few discordant notes which began to appear off and on which tended to heap the blame for Partition on the Hindu bias of the Congress leadership and portray Jinnah in a more positive light. One such study, though not penned by a professional historian, but by a jurist of Bombay of Parsi origin, was that of H.M. Seervai.[5] He had used the *Transfer of Power* volumes to elaborate his thesis.

Old British theories which held that Jinnah used the Pakistan demand as a bargaining counter to extract more concessions for the Muslims at the Centre in a united India were taken out of the cupboard and reformulated by some more recent scholars, like Ayesha Jalal, who was originally from Pakistan, but settled in the west. Given this background, we cannot expect them to be completely objective and impartial not just about Jinnah and his political career but also about the role of British in the Partition of India.[6]

Some scholars in India like A.G. Noorani were quick to favour such a thesis which minimized the role of Jinnah in the Partition of India, but also heaped the blame for the Partition on Hindu Congress leaders like Mahatma Gandhi, Jawaharlal Nehru, C. Rajagopalachari, and Sardar Vallabhbhai Patel. British scholars like Francis Robinson—who generally seem to be more sympathetic towards South Asian Muslims and who hold that Muslims have a historical and cultural identity uniquely different from their Hindu counterparts—were also quick to endorse Ayesha Jalal's thesis as it came as a god-send to cast most of the blame for the Partition of India on Hindu Congress leaders, who were all along accusing the British for pitting the Muslims against the Hindus and ultimately dividing India.[7]

In continuation with this line of thinking, very recently, Jaswant Singh, an ex-military man, politician, minister, and parliamentarian from Rajasthan, had brought out his own voluminous book on Jinnah where he tends to squarely lay the blame for Partition on Jawaharlal Nehru's authoritarian centralizing policies. He is critical of the entire top Congress leadership. He thinks that Jinnah was a nationalist and a constitutionalist who was pushed to demand Pakistan by the words and postures of the

Congress leaders. In the process, he ends up showering praises on Jinnah as a completely secular-minded person.[8]

Not just Jaswant Singh, but many scholars before him, both western and Indian/Pakistani were of the view that Jinnah veered towards the demand for Pakistan, only when he was neglected and was sidelined by the Congress leaders.[9] They hold that he was always an ambassador of Hindu–Muslim unity and a secular nationalist whose only desire was to protect Muslims' interests within the structure of a united India. They claim that Jinnah had never raised or supported any vivisection of India before the 1937 provincial elections. They assert that after the 1937 elections (in which the Muslim League was defeated), the Congress refused to collaborate with Jinnah and the Muslim League in the formation of Ministries, which naturally kept the Muslim League out of the corridors of power. Besides, they state that some Congress leaders like Jawaharlal Nehru and Maulana Abul Kalam Azad sought to belittle the importance of the Muslim League and destroy its very basis by their words and actions. Jinnah had no other alternative, except to react to this state of affairs where the Congress was condescending in its attitude towards him. It was this reaction that finally led Jinnah to demand Pakistan and not because he was a separatist at heart from the beginning.

My principal task, therefore, would be to explore if the preceding views and contentions of the various scholars—British, Indian, and Pakistani are true and are based on hard facts. If it is not true, I have to find out what was the grand strategy adopted by Jinnah right from the time he joined the Muslim League in 1913 that finally took him towards the demand for Pakistan in 1940. In the process, I also have to find out how far the Congress party and the British were responsible or were not responsible for Jinnah's demand for Pakistan.

Most of the books on Jinnah, and especially that by Ayesha Jalal, which were published after the secession of Bangladesh from Pakistan in 1971, do not give much importance to Jinnah's early life and political activities prior to the demand for Partition, that is, from the time he entered politics as a Congressman. Therefore my intention is to closely study the salient features of Jinnah's long life, especially his political life since he joined the Congress and reassess them on the basis of hard facts. I consider this absolutely essential to understand why Jinnah finally chose to demand Pakistan in the year 1940. This prompted me to write this book.

Human beings individually and collectively are ultimately responsible for their actions and their historical evolution since time immemorial. We cannot put the blame on Providence or some sage or ideology or evolving material conditions and escape responsibility. That is why it is necessary for the historian to stand outside all ideologies, cultures, beliefs, or social and material conditions and look into the past facts of an individual or a society with clear eyes. I intend to unravel the life and political career of Jinnah, until he demanded Pakistan, with this objective detachment of mind.

Besides, in the course of this study, I will also find out what was the role of charisma in Jinnah's life that ultimately led him to demand Pakistan. I will also delve into the contention in some quarters, spearheaded by scholars like Paul Brass that Jinnah manipulated Islamic symbols in order to mobilize the Muslims in support of his demand for Pakistan and find out the truth about it.[10] We have a whole school of Cambridge scholars, starting from Anil Seal to C.J. Baker and David Washbrook, who assert that ideas, ideologies, and principles were never the motivating factors behind the national movement or the separatist movement of the Muslims; and the individuals and interest groups at the local, provincial, and national levels involved in such movements. They argue that they were the results of patronage, factional quarrels, and ambitions and the quest for power, profit, prestige, and social standing, within the political institutions established by the British. So in this study of the life of Jinnah, I also have the task of finding out how far these assertions were true or not true as far as Jinnah and his demand for Pakistan were concerned.[11] All this will be done through a critical study of the life and political career of Muhammad Ali Jinnah until the time he raised the demand for the division of India, into India and Pakistan.

I must affirm once again that I am neither for nor against Jinnah. Neither am I for nor against the Congress and its leaders or the British colonial authorities. Instead, in the course of this study, my singleminded intention is to focus on hard historical facts related to Jinnah's political life. These facts will of course be backed by adequate evidence and logical arguments. But before going into all this step-by-step, it is necessary to delve into the salient features of Jinnah's ancestry and early life starting from his birthday, which might have a bearing on his late entry into Indian politics and the evolution of his political life and standpoints until he raised the demand for Pakistan. This will, of course, be done by taking into consideration the social, economic, and political context in which Jinnah evolved.

HISTORICAL BACKGROUND

SOCIO-POLITICAL CONTEXT

Before going into the salient aspects of the birth and early life of Quaid-e-Azam Muhammad Ali Jinnah, it will no doubt be worthwhile to be aware of the socio-political and historical context in which he comes into existence and evolves. Jinnah belonged to Islam, a religion that came to India from West Asia through invasions and trade. Islam was born in Arabia in the seventh century. By the beginning of the eighth century an army of the Islamized Arabs penetrated northwest India as invaders, conquerors, and rulers. They were followed by the Islamized Turks who established the Delhi Sultanate in the Gangetic Plains around the twelfth century. The Turks were succeeded by the Islamized Mongols or Mughals, who made India their homeland. Afghans and Persians also penetrated India.

During the Arab, Turk, Afghan, Persian, and Mongol rule, many Indians from different castes converted from Hinduism to Islam due to various reasons. These Indian converts did not completely mix and mingle with the Arabs, Turks, Persians, Afghans, and Mongols. The latter who belonged to the 'white' or fairer stocks were collectively known as Ashrafs (foreign conquerors). The local Indian converts largely of darker complexion who made up for more than 90 per cent of the Muslim population of India were relegated as lowly 'Ajlafs (local converts)' by the Ashrafs of prestigious foreign descent.[1] However, during more than seven centuries of Ashraf Muslim rule in India, Hindus of all castes were considered as second class citizens in their own lands. They were nothing more than *dhimmis* (tolerated infidels). The Ajlafs were not *dhimmis*. They shared the same religion Islam with the Ashrafs. This seems to have led many Indian Ajlafs to consider themselves as associated somehow with the ruling classes of foreign origin, which they were not actually, historically and racially.

There is a wrong conception in historical circles and popular imagination especially among the Muslims of south Asia that the British inherited their Indian empire from the Mughals. As a matter of fact, the British never fought and vanquished the Mughal emperors. Instead, they conquered India by vanquishing the Nawabs of Bengal, the Mysore Sultans of indigenous descent and the Maratha and Sikh confederacies, who largely divided the Mughal Empire between themselves during the eighteenth century. In 1757, Bengal came under British rule after the defeat of its Nawab at the Battle of Plassey. In 1799, Tipu Sultan of Mysore was defeated by the English and his territories in southern India came under British control. It was only in 1818 that the Marathas were decisively defeated by the British and all their territories in western, central, and northern India passed into British hands. The Sikhs were finally defeated in 1849 and Punjab was amalgamated with British India. It is noteworthy to mention that during the eighteenth century, the Sufi reformer Shah Waliullah (1703–1766) had asked the king of Afghanistan, Ahmad Shah Abdali to invade India in 1761 and relieve the Muslims from the domination of Maratha Hindu infidels. Ahmad Shah Abdali did invade India. He routed the Marathas and went back to Afghanistan, not realizing that the weakening of the Marathas would subsequently pave the path for the conquest of India by the British.[2]

With the defeat of Tipu Sultan, the Marathas, and the Sikhs, English East India Company rule became well established in India. Persian was still the official language in many parts of India during that period. In the 1830s, the British decided to abolish Persian as the official language in India. They replaced it with English and some vernacular languages. This was a severe blow to the prestige and influence of the Ashrafi Muslims throughout India. The introduction of modern secular education in English during that period was seen by the Muslims in general and the

Muslim elite consisting of former rulers, princes, nobles, aristocrats, and zamindars in particular, as a convenient tool to extirpate all Muslim influences and undermine Muslim cultures and religion. As a result, from the very beginning the Muslims shunned western modern education. In due course of time, Muslim and Hindu discontent with British rule grew by leaps and bounds.

The discontent resulted in the Great Indian Revolt of 1857 which sought to overthrow British power in India and enthrone the ageing Mughal Bahadur Shah Zafar as Emperor of Hindustan in Delhi. That was a monumental watershed in modern Indian history. Both Muslims and Hindus participated in this revolt, which was spearheaded mainly by the Muslim feudal nobility and the *taluqdars* (landlords), along with their Hindu allies. The British used all means at their disposal including some of their new-found Indian allies like the Sikhs, Gurkhas, Pathans, and the Sepoys, and even some migrant Muslim aristocrats like the Aga Khan in order to suppress the revolt. They did succeed in it, but not before they indulged in one of the bloodiest massacres in the annals of world history in which several lakhs of Indians, both Hindus and Muslims perished. The Muslims bore the brunt of British wrath. Emperor Bahadur Shah was put on trial for treason at Delhi. He was exiled to Burma where he died a miserable death in the year 1862. The British officer William Hudson shot his sons Mirza Mughal, Mirza Khazir Sultan, and grandson Mirza Abu Bakr at the *Khooni Darwaza* (the bloody gate) near Delhi Gate.[3] The British were convinced that it was the Muslims and not the Hindus, who wanted to overthrow British rule and retrieve their lost power and prestige.

Of course, the revolt brought down the curtains on the English East India Company rule in India. The Government of India Act of 1858 dissolved the company and transferred its ruling powers directly to the British Crown. A new India Office was created in London with a Secretary of State for India to formulate future Indian policies. The Governor-General of India under the company became the Viceroy of India, with his capital at Calcutta in the Bengal Presidency or Province.

British policies in India from at least the time of the Queen's proclamation of November 1858, created a situation where Indians were forced to look more and more to the government for their material progress and welfare. Such dependency was particularly striking in education, employment, and related fields. In short, the State started regulating the lives of the people.

The Despatch of 7 April 1854 definitely accepted the education of the entire people of India as State duty. Similarly, in the matter of employment the British had committed themselves to employing Indians of all 'races' and creeds in the services, freely and impartially.[4] Through the Act of 1861, the British established provincial legislative councils and a Central Legislative Council. But the Act did not provide for the election of Indians to the Councils. They were nominated by the Viceroy and their role was purely advisory.

At that time, British India was made up of the Princely States and the Presidencies. There were six Presidencies in all—Madras Presidency, Bombay Presidency, Central Provinces, United Provinces, Punjab, and Bengal. The Hindus were a majority in most of these Presidencies. The Muslims were slightly more numerous in the Punjab, Bengal, and to some extent in the United Provinces. In 1886, Burma was conquered and made a province of British India. In 1893, after two bloody wars with the Afghans, the British entered into an agreement with the Afghan king and drew a line called the Durand Line which cut through the Afghan homelands. The eastern part called the North-West Frontier Province (NWFP) as well as the eastern part of Baluchistan became a part of British India. The peoples of this region in their great majority did not belong to the traditional Indian stock. The NWFP was made part of the Punjab province while Baluchistan became the Chief Commissioner's province. The Durand Line served as the Line of Control or frontier between Afghanistan and British India. Thus Afghanistan, reduced in size, became a buffer State between British India and the expansive ambitions of Russia towards the Indian Ocean.

In the year 1871, William Hunter's book depicted the backwardness of the Muslims of Bengal. Thenceforth the government remoulded its policies towards the Muslims in general all over India. It issued instructions to the provincial governments to take the necessary steps to promote education among them. Muslims were singled out for special and preferential treatment in the educational and employment fields. Separate electorates on the basis of religion were also permitted in some areas for Muslims by the British in Punjab. This measure naturally awakened the political consciousness of the Muslims on the basis of religion. Top British colonial authorities and administrators had always maintained since that period that there was no Indian nation or Indian people; and that India was a mere geographical expression like Europe or Africa.[5]

It was the British who had endowed India with a certain political and administrative unity, which had never existed in the past. They also introduced the modern system of secular education which was the key to government employment. The education system brought about the professional class. They also promulgated the land reforms which created a class of landlords.

MODERN MUSLIM STALWARTS

During that period, there were two important Muslim personalities who seem to have played a significant role in the evolution of the Muslim community of India, especially in the political and social fields. They had not taken part in the Great Indian Revolt. One was Sayyid Ahmad Khan who was born in Delhi in the year 1817. The other was the Persian-speaking Aga Khan who came as a refugee to India during the nineteenth century. The first one was a Sunni Muslim, while the second was the Imam of the Ismaili Nizaris, a miniscule sect among the Shias.

Sayyid Ahmad Khan's ancestors are known to have come from Arabia, passing through Afghanistan to India during the reign of Mughal emperor Akbar. His ancestors and family were part of the Mughal nobility. In the year 1842, the Mughal Emperor, Bahadur Shah conferred upon

Sayyid Ahmad Khan the titles of *Javad-ud Daulah* and *Arif Jang*. But the decline of the Mughal Empire seems to have forced Sayyid Ahmad Khan to join the civil service of British India as a jurist. During the Great Indian Revolt, he failed to rally behind the Mughal emperor. Instead he remained loyal to the British and even saved many English lives during the revolt. After the revolt, he penned a booklet where he traced the causes of the revolt to the faulty British policies. This work was translated into English and was welcomed by many British colonial administrators including the Viceroy Lord Canning. In the year 1860, Sayyid Ahmad Khan wrote an essay about the 'Loyal Mohammedans of India'. During that period Sayyid Ahmad Khan believed that Hindus, Muslims, and Christians formed just one nation.[6]

During the course of time, Sayyid Ahmad Khan was convinced that the Muslims had no other alternative but to reform themselves on rational lines and take to western education. On 9 January 1864, he founded the Scientific Society of Aligarh. In 1869, he visited England. Very much impressed by the visit, he wrote: 'All good things, spiritual and worldly, which should be found in man, has been bestowed by the Almighty on Europe and especially on England—.'[7]

After his return to India, in the year 1870 he initiated the journal, *Muhammadan Social Reformer*. Given the abolition of Persian as the official language in the 1830s by the British and its replacement by English, Hindi, and the vernaculars, Sayyid Ahmad Khan shifted his allegiance to Urdu and worked for its promotion as the cultural language of Indian Muslims and opposed Hindi tooth and nail since 1867.[8]

He pioneered modern scientific education among Muslims, by founding the Muhammadan Anglo-Oriental College in Aligarh in the year 1875. The College enjoyed British patronage. The young Englishman Theodore Beck, who held similar views like Khan was appointed as thePrincipal of the College. Sayyid Ahmad Khan was much older to Theodore Beck, but still both felt the need to develop western education among Muslims. Khan incessantly worked for the cooperation of the Muslims with the British authorities, exhorting them literally to be loyal to the British Raj. As a reward, the British government awarded him the Order of the Star of India in the year 1869. He went to England to collect it. In 1878, Sayyid Ahmad Khan was nominated to the Viceroy's Legislative Council by the Viceroy Lord Lytton. However, Sayyid Ahmad Khan's activities did not suit the taste and liking of the orthodox traditional Muslims like the ulemas of Deoband seminary, founded in 1867. Even the pan-Islamist Jamal-al-din Afghani who viewed the British designs with suspicion, condemned Sayyid Ahmad Khan as a 'stooge and sycophant of the British and asked the Indian Muslims to take pride in the contribution of Hindus to the advancement of humanity'.[9]

It must not be forgotten that when Sayyid Ahmad Khan spoke of Muslims, he often meant only those of Ashraf origin, who were the descendants of former rulers and conquerors of India. He wrote: 'The Muhammadans are not the aborigines of this country; they came in the train of the former conquerors—'[10]

It is quite obvious from the above that Sayyid Ahmad Khan had never included the indigenous converts to Islam in his definition of Muslims or *sharif* culture, in spite of them constituting about 90 per cent of the Muslim population of India.[11] But with the fast evolving scenario where the idea of democracy was looming its head in the political horizon of India, Sayyid Ahmad Khan seems to have had no other alternative but to adapt to the changing situation. That is why he chose to promote Urdu, a popular language of the Muslims as a sort of lingua franca for all Indian Muslims, instead of choosing Persian, which was the language of the nobility and the Ashraf class of people until lately.

During the Viceroyalty of Lord Dufferin, the INC was founded in Bombay on 27 December 1885 through the efforts of Allan Octavian Hume, an Englishman. He was the general secretary of the Congress until 1892. The first session of the Congress was presided by W.C. Bonnerjee, an Indian Christian. The Congress grew up as a political organization to which all Indians irrespective of caste and creed could adhere to.

However, there were only 2 Muslims out of the 72 delegates who attended the Bombay foundation of the Congress. In the second Congress Session held in Calcutta, there were only 33 Muslim delegates out of 431. Syed Ameer Ali, who had established the National Mahommadan Association in Calcutta in 1878, had refused to participate in this session. The third Congress Session held in Madras was presided by the prominent Muslim barrister from Bombay, Badruddin Tyabji, a Sulaimani Bohra by birth. There was no Hindu, who presided the Congress Sessions until its seventh session.[12]

In the early years of its existence and at least until the beginning of the twentieth century the Congress was a very moderate organization, affirming its loyalty to the British, and petitioning or asking off and on for some power and petty reforms in the political, economic, and administrative fields. As time went on, the Congress asked for elected councils and recruitment for the services through examinations. In Bengal, there were modernists and educationists like Nawab Abdul Latif (1828–1893) and Syed Ameer Ali (1849–1928), who like Sayyid Ahmad Khan stood aloof from the Congress.

The Congress stood for greater representation of Indians in the various institutions created by British. It was obvious to men like Sayyid Ahmad Khan that in any British-created institution or political organization or democratic form of government in India, it would be the Hindus who would dominate by virtue of their numbers. So in 1886, Sayyid Ahmad Khan organized the All India Muhammadan Educational Conference in Aligarh, to promote modern education and the political unity of Muslims. In 1888, he founded the United Indian Patriotic Association to further promote cooperation between the British and the Muslims, and also between Muslims from all over India. Many Muslim associations of various parts of India were affiliated to it. Hindus opposed to the Congress were admitted as members of this association.

In a speech delivered at Meerut on 14 March 1888, Sayyid Ahmad Khan pleaded that the British should remain in India forever so that peace might prevail between the two nations—the Mohammedans and the Hindus. The same year, Sayyid Ahmad Khan was knighted by the British government for his activities and the following year he received an LLD *honoris causa* from the University of Edinburgh. Thus, as pointed out by Francis Robinson, Sayyid Ahmad Khan was promoted by the British as a leader of the Muslims, in spite of his unorthodox views and postures, which was in variance with those of the majority of the Indian Muslims.[13]

On the other hand, Theodore Beck was opposed to anything that could weaken British control over India. He too like Sayyid Ahmad Khan felt that the Congress would undermine this control. He expressed his fear about the Congress in a letter that he wrote to Sayyid Ahmad Khan on 7 May 1888. In another letter dated 30 March 1890, that he addressed to Khan, he wrote: 'I think it is very necessary for us to prove to the people of England in the most unmistakable way that the Mohammedans are opposed to it (the Congress).'[14] These two letters prove that there was some sort of understanding between Sayyid Ahmad Khan and Beck in their desire to oppose the Congress. There is no doubt that Beck very much influenced Sayyid Ahmad Khan's views with regard to his opposition to the Congress.

Theodore Beck declared in the *Aligarh Institute Gazette* that the principle of democratic representation in India should be opposed as it was not suitable to this country. In 1890 a petition was submitted on behalf of Beck and signed by 50,000 persons—chiefly Anglo-Indian officials and Muslim landlords—to the British parliament, stressing that democratic institutions were unsuited to India as there were different communities inhabiting it. Sayyid Ahmad Khan's views, of course, matched with that of Theodore Beck. It was during that period that the high ranking British Indian civil servant, Sir John Strachey observed: 'There is not and never was in India, no Indian nation, no "people of India".' On his part, the British historian, Sir John Robert Seeley wrote that India was 'a mere geographical expression like Europe or Africa'.[15]

In the year 1892, the Indian Councils Act was adopted by the British. This Act provided for the principle of popular representation by nomination as the basis for the Constitution of the legislatures in India. The Indian representation always retained its advisory and consultative character. This Act also gave the Muslims the right to separate representation, without any Muslim organization asking or agitating for it.[16]

In 1893 Sayyid Ahmad Khan, most certainly under the influence of Theodore Beck founded the Mohammedan Anglo-Oriental Defence Association of Upper India. Only Muslims and Englishmen could become its members. Theodore Beck was one of its active council members. He, along with a son of Sayyid Ahmad Khan, formulated a scheme in 1896 which demanded parity in representation for Muslims not only in the Imperial and provincial councils, but also in municipal and local bodies, where the Muslims constituted 25 per cent of the population. It was also suggested in the scheme that Muslim members of the various councils must be elected only by Muslims. So it is not totally out of place to conclude that Theodore Beck was largely the brain behind the idea of separate electorates for Muslims, which laid the groundwork for the political separatism of the Muslims. The Viceroys Lord Dufferin and Lord Lansdowne were particularly supportive of the idea of separate electorates. Though Sayyid Ahmad Khan had previously thought that Hindus and Muslims constituted one nation, later he revised his position and said that Hindus and Muslims belonged to two different nations.[17] However, he never proposed the political division of India on religious lines. Instead he wanted British rule to continue. That was also the wish of Beck.

Sir Sayyid Ahmad Khan passed away in the year 1898. He was a fervent loyalist till the end of his life. He opposed democratic institutions in India, in which Muslims will be reduced to a minority. He was no doubt the originator of the two-nation theory. He was always suspicious of the Indian National Movement and believed that the Muslims will be better off under the British Raj. He wielded a great influence on the political orientation of the Indian Muslims, especially the educated elite even after his death.

The field of political and other activities of Sir Sayyid was in the United Provinces. But he was influential in other provinces too. There was a certain Muslim awakening in other parts of India too like Bengal, Madras, and the Bombay Presidency during that period. In Bombay, it was mainly due to Muslim personalities like Badruddin Tyabji and the Aga Khan. Both were Shias. In the year 1881, the Muslim National Association of Bombay was founded by the Aga Khan. Aga Khan was the leader or Imam (Pope) of the Ismaili Nizaris who were known as Khojas in western India.

The Khojas were basically Shias and therefore, were not considered to be a part of the mainstream and orthodox Muslim community of India, the Sunnites. The Gujarati word 'Khoja' was actually derived from the Persian word 'Khwaja'.

The Khojas have a long history behind them. Tradition holds that they were originally Hindu Lohanas of Gujarat and were converted to Islam by Pir Sadruddin during the fourteenth century. They were found mainly in Gujarat, eastern Sind, and even in Maharashtra. They accounted only for a few million. They were a sect called Ismaili Nizaris among the larger community of Twelvers Shias or the Isna'Ashari. Unlike the Isna'Asharis who believed in the Twelve Imams as successors to the Prophet, the Ismaili Nizaris and Khojas believed in the spiritual leadership and Imamate of the Aga Khan. He was the living Imam for the Khojas, while the Isna'Asharis believe in a hidden Imam who will return at the end of this earth.[18]

Aga Khan was a Turco-Mongol title; Aga in Turkish meant 'lord' while 'Khan' simply meant 'chief'. It was attributed by the Shah of Persia, Fath Ali Shah Qajar in the year 1818 to the 46th Nizarite Imam, Hasan Ali Shah, who is believed to have descended from Ali, the son-in-law of the Prophet Muhammad and Fatima, the daughter of the Prophet. The original home of the Nizaris was Egypt from where they had fled to Iran earlier. Hasan Ali Shah was actually a descendant of a prince of Fatimid Egypt known as Nizar.[19]

Hasan Ali Shah alias Aga Khan I married the daughter of the Shah of Persia. He was appointed governor of Mahallat in Persia. As the former claimed to be the living Imam on earth, the Shah of Persia revoked the title of Aga Khan and sentenced him to death. The Aga Khan, with some of his cavalry fled towards Afghanistan and India, seeking British protection, when they were trying to expand their empire towards India and Afghanistan.

In the First Anglo-Afghan War during 1841–42, the Aga Khan and his cavalry came to the help of the British General William Nott in Kandahar. The Aga Khan also came to the help of Sir Charles Napier when he embarked upon the conquest of Sind in 1843, which paved the way for its annexation by the Governor-General Lord Ellenborough. After the conquest of Sind, the British attempted to subjugate the neighbouring Baluchistan. The Aga Khan once again helped them militarily and diplomatically. He advised various Baluchi chieftains to submit to British rule. For his services in the conquest of Sind, he was granted an annual pension of £2000 by the British. During that time, the Aga Khan himself entered Sind from Afghanistan with his horsemen.

He came to Bombay in February 1846. By 1849, the Aga Khan established his headquarters in Bombay. During the Great Indian Revolt of 1857 which sought to overthrow British power in India and enthrone the ageing Mughal Bahadur Shah as Emperor, the Aga Khan and his men came to the rescue of the British and played their role in the crushing of the combined revolt of Hindus and Muslims. The Shah of Persia sought his extradition from British India. But the British went out of their way to protect the Aga Khan and establish him on a high pedestal in India. The services rendered by the Khan were considered as very crucial services to the English under difficult conditions. The British reciprocated by granting a pension for the Aga Khan and honouring him with the title 'His Highness'. He was treated as a prince by the British colonial authorities since 1877. He also became the only religious leader, who was conferred a gun salute by the British.[20]

Nevertheless, the Aga Khan who practically came as a refugee to India, after having been driven away from his native Persia, had in India—especially in Gujarat and Sind, which were parts of the Bombay Presidency—his Khoja followers. The Khojas accepted the Imamate of the Aga Khan. Their ancestors had been converted to the Khoja sect since the penetration of Ismaili Pirs or missionaries from Iran to Gujarat in the twelfth century. The Ismaili missionary, Pir Sadruddin is believed to have converted the Lohanas, a bania caste of Gujarat and given them the name *Khoja*. Pir Sadruddin was even attributed Hindu names like Sahadev or Harichand. The Ismaili Khojas followed many Hindu customs and traditions. They presented Adam as *Vishnu*, Prophet Muhammad as *Mahesh*, and Pir Sadruddin as *Brahma*. The most revered book of the Khojas was the *Dasavatar*, dealing with the ten incarnations of Vishnu, the last one being Ali. It was Pir Sadruddin who compiled the first *du'a* (prayers) for the Khojas which was in vogue until 1954 when the Aga Khan replaced it with an Islamic version in Arabic. It was he who instituted the *jamatkhanas* (Assembly and Prayer Halls) for the Khojas.

Hasan Ali Shah was the Aga Khan from 1818, until his death in 1881. He was succeeded by Aga Khan II who was born in Mahallat (in Persia) towards 1830. He founded the Muslim National Association of Bombay in 1881. Its members were mainly Bombay Khoja businessmen. He died four years later in Pune, and was buried at Nejaf in Iraq, near the tomb of Imam Ali. The mantle of the Aga Khan fell on Sultan Mohammad Shah (1877–1957) when he was just eight. He became the 48th Imam of the Nizari Ismailis and the Khojas. He grew up as a short-statured man. Mahomed or Muhammad Ali Jinnahbhai and his ancestors were born into the Khoja sect, of which the Aga Khan was the lord and chief. It was a very special sect, hardly recognized as an Islamic sect until recently.[21]

It is quite obvious that apart from the personalities and their activities recounted above, there were two ideas that were gaining ground in British India. One was the idea of democracy and the other was the concept of the Indian nation. Both were western ideas, to which Indians were never accustomed to in their long history. Indians like Sayyid Ahmad Khan and the British like Theodore Beck and John Strachey looked upon these ideas with suspicion. Being an Ashrafi Muslim, Sayyid Ahmad Khan was worried that in any democratic set-up, the Hindus would ultimately predominate in politics and administration by virtue of their numbers. Similarly he feared that in any democratic united Indian nation, the Muslims will be permanently subjected to the Hindus. He like Theodore Beck was conscious that these two ideas were intimately and inseparably associated with power. Therefore for men like Sayyid Ahmad Khan, who belonged to the class of elite Muslims and who had ruled India for several centuries before the British, was left with no other alternative but to resist those ideas, which were thought to be progressive. It was under these circumstances that the idea of two nations was born and the idea of separate electorates for Muslims came into existence. Thus it is clear that ideas however progressive they may appear to be, due to its association with power have a natural tendency to divide and separate. So rather than putting the blame squarely and hastily on men like Sayyid Ahmad Khan as the originator of Muslim separatism, as is done by many Indian nationalists, it is necessary first to ponder over the role played in society by ideas and ideologies, which are invariably associated with power, unlike the contentions of some Cambridge scholars like Anil Seal, David Washbrook, and others. Therefore it becomes necessary to admit the fact that the very ideas of democracy and the Indian nation, associated with power, spawned the counter-ideas of 'two nations' and separate electorates, also associated with power. It cannot be otherwise because most ideas and ideologies if not all, being disconnected from facts or being based on illusory concepts, possess the natural inborn quality to divide and separate, preparing the ground for endless conflicts between men.

FROM JINNAHBHAI TO JINNAH

EARLY LIFE

Mahomed Ali Jinnahbhai's life starts with a controversy for we do not know when exactly he was born. According to the school register of Sind Madrasatul Islam, he was born on 20 October 1875. But there are other claims that Mahomed Ali was born in 1870 or even in 1876.

There is also a doubt regarding Mahomed Ali's place of birth. Generally it is admitted that he was born in the coastal town of Karachi in Sind. However some claim Jerruck as his place of birth. Mahomed Ali himself had not given us any precision regarding his date and place of birth.

Neither has he given us any precision regarding his origin and ancestry. There are those who want to invest Jinnah with a glorious ancestry and high status. They intentionally trace his origin to Iran so that he can be included as one among the Ashraf Muslims of India. This not being really tenable, others tend to find a Rajput origin to his ancestors. They claim that Jinnah was a descendant of a Rajput, converted to Islam who married an Ismaili Khoja girl of Gujarat. In this way, they try to identify Jinnah with the warrior castes of India of a higher status. But even this does not seem to hold water. There are others who claim that he was descended from Hindu Bhatias. There is no evidence for this either. So in the present juncture, I think it is more reasonable to hold that Jinnah descended from the *bania* converts of the Hindu Lohanas. According to Saleem Qureshi, Jinnah was a Muslim of recent origin, that is, his family had been Muslim since only three generations.

Whatever the truth, Jinnahbhai seemed to have been born into a fairly wealthy Gujarati Khoja family at Paneli village, in the small princely state of Gondal in Kathiawar. His father's name was Jinnahbhai Poonja. He seemed to have prospered in business in Karachi, though his grandfather was of a more modest origin. His mother's name was Mithibhai. He had three brothers and three sisters—Rahemat, Maryam, Ahmed Ali, Shireen, Fatima, and Bandeh Ali. Mahomed Ali or Muhammad Ali was basically a Gujarati belonging to the Ismaili Khoja community. He grew up speaking Gujarati at home. Later when the family moved to Karachi, he seemed to have learnt some Cutchi and Sindhi. According to Bolitho, the official biographer of Jinnah, Jinnah lived within the confines of two rooms at the first floor in Newnham Road, Karachi, along with his parents, brothers, and sisters. At birth, he was known by his pet name 'Mamod', meaning 'small and weak'. Nobody knows for sure if Mamod regularly attended the Quranic classes that all Muslim children were supposed to attend, where they learnt the basic tenets of Islam. Mamod was not trained to read the Quran in Arabic during his early years. As a result, he did not have a sound religious grounding. However, as a kid his head was shaved off at Hassan Pir's dargah at Ganod near Paneli. Hassan Pir was an Ismaili missionary from Iran. This was followed by a grand feast.[1]

At six, Mamod was taught Gujarati at home and at nine he went to the Sind Madrasatul School. It seems then that an aunt of Mamod, known as Manubhai Peerbhai, who lived in Bombay took him under her care. She was instrumental in getting him admitted first to Gokuldas School and later to the reputed Anjuman-i-Islam School of Bombay. But as the boy was not serious in his studies and preferred wandering with his friends in the posh British-built areas of south Bombay and on the beaches rather than attending classes, his father took him back to Karachi and enrolled him in the Sind Madrasatul Islam, which was a high school. He studied for about three and half years there. Then he was enrolled in the elitist Christian Mission High School of Karachi, affiliated to the University of Bombay.

His name was given as Mahomed Ali Jinnahbhai and his date of birth was given as 20 October 1875 in the Sind school register. In Karachi too, the boy's wayward attitude seemed to have continued. He was never known to be bright in his studies. However, he seems to have been literally subjugated by the British Christian values and the atmosphere prevailing in the school, that he on his own anglicized his name in the school register by simply dropping the 'bhai' in his name. He probably thought that 'bhai' was old-fashioned and antiquated. He was thenceforth known as Muhammad Ali Jinnah at least in the school. It seemed that he even arbitrarily changed his date of birth to 25 December in the school register to coincide with the birth of Jesus Christ. Whatever the truth regarding this was, it seemed his passport carried 25 December 1876 as his date of birth.[2]

It was however quite clear by then that Muhammad Ali Jinnahbhai did not have a sound religious education, even of the Khoja variety. His father seemed not to have bothered about it very much. Jinnahbhai never prayed daily or fasted during Ram'zan. Besides, he never performed the Haj. In fact, as far as I know, there is no record to prove that he was interested in performing the Haj. In short, he was not brought up in a religious atmosphere or temperament. We do not know how far he was conscious that the Aga Khan was the head and the living Imam of the Khojas Ismaili sect to which he belonged by birth.

JINNAHBHAI IN LONDON

Muhammad Ali himself is never known to have expressed his desire to continue with his higher studies. It was his father, probably on account of his wealth and the prodding of some of his British business friends, who decided to send his son to England to study law. Muhammad Ali was hardly sixteen then. Mithibhai feared that in London he might marry some 'white' girl. So before he left for London, he was married off to a fourteen-year-old Khoja girl called Emibhai, who happened to be a distant cousin. Three days after his marriage, he left for London by ship. He traded his traditional Khoja dress—a long coat and the Aga Khani cap for western suits, which fitted him quite well. He thus bid goodbye to Indian dresses for quite sometime. We do not know if Muhammad Ali's marriage was consummated before he left. Nothing is known of it.

In London, he first worked as an apprentice in a shipping company at Threadneedle Street in London. Later he took to study law. Impressed by the immensity of London and its cold climate, Muhammad Ali seemed to have felt very lonely and miserable in the beginning. He very soon got used to the British way of life, language, and manners. It seems that at one time he even toyed with the idea of converting to Christianity. He had a number of British friends. He frequented British theatres and clubs where it is likely that he would have consumed British food and alcohol, although he had never written anything about it, as far as I know. Anglicized to a considerable extent in his manners, he was offered a job to act in an English theatre company. His father put his foot down. So he refused to take up the job. That was probably one of the last occasions when he listened to his father. Tall, lean, and fair, and elegantly dressed like a British gentleman, he looked exactly like the Aga Khan when somebody took him by mistake for an Englishman. During his stay in London, he stayed as a paying guest with Mrs Page-Drake. It seems that Page-Drake's daughter was fond of Muhammad Ali, but Muhammad Ali never reciprocated.[3]

Of the four Inns and Temples of Court in London, Muhammad Ali chose Lincoln's Inn to pursue his law studies in 1893. In the Lincoln Inn's Admission Register for 1893, Muhammad Ali's name is given as Mahomedalli Jinnahbhai of Karachi. Jinnah assumed wrongly that Lincoln's Inn was named after Abraham Lincoln, the great American President, whereas it was actually named after the fourteenth century King's Sergeant of Holborn, Thomas de Lincoln. According to Hector Bolitho and G. Allana, the same Muhammad Ali seemed to have claimed later in his life that he joined Lincoln's Inn, because he saw the name of Prophet Muhammad among the great law-givers of the world engraved at the entrance of the Inn. But in his speech at the Sind Bar Association after Independence, Muhammad Ali Jinnah had claimed that he joined

Lincoln's Inn because he saw a fresco in the Great Hall of the Inn portraying the image of Prophet Muhammad along with the other great law-givers of the world. Rafiq Zakaria maintains that there was no such painting of the Prophet in the Inn and that it is all a concoction of Pakistani scholars. But the present author visited Lincoln's Inn and obtained confirmation that the Prophet had been painted by Watt along with other law-givers using his friends as models. It is quite obvious that Muhammad Ali Jinnah had been oblivious or ignorant of the basic fact that the representation of the Prophet in any form was prohibited in Islam and that it was blasphemous in Islam to portray the Prophet in such a manner. He was not conscious of his error even in the 1940s when he delivered his speech.[4] In normal circumstances, as a Muslim he should have objected to the portrayal of the Prophet's image in the fresco. But he never did that. Instead he took pride in the portrayal and gave that as a reason for joining Lincoln's Inn. Such instances demonstrate without an iota of doubt that Muhammad Ali's grounding in certain aspects of historical and religious knowledge was inadequate.

JINNAHBHAI BECOMES JINNAH

In the beginning of the year 1895, Muhammad Ali applied for permission to gain access to the British Museum Library. He obviously made a wrong declaration then to the Librarian that he was not under 21 years of age. He also declared his name for the first time to the librarian as M.A. Jinnah. But in the Lincoln Inn's register his name was still Mahomedalli Jinnahbhai. He did not like this longish, old-fashioned, and traditional Indian name much. He wanted to anglicize it badly. So on 14 April 1896, just before he was called to the bar, he requested the masters of the Bench of Lincoln's Inn to change his name from Mahomedalli Jinnahbhai to just M.A. Jinnah. He occulted Mahomed Ali under the initials M.A. and cut off 'bhai' from Jinnahbhai so that it became just Jinnah. After some hesitation, his request to shorten his name as M.A. Jinnah was granted. In the course of this study, I will use this name to refer to Mahomedalli or

Muhammad Ali Jinnahbhai, as it has been chosen by Jinnah himself. The shortened name 'Jinnah' meant 'wing' in Arabic and 'lean' in Gujarati.[5] But Jinnah was never aware that such meanings to his name existed.

Having anglicized his name, M.A. Jinnah perennially let himself to be influenced by British ideas and values like democracy and liberalism. He was particularly attracted towards liberal statesmen like William Gladstone, Joseph Chamberlain, and John Morley. He frequented the library of the British Museum and Hyde Park. Thus within four years of his stay in London, he became a near-perfect British gentleman, both inwardly and outwardly. His ancestral religion, traditions, and culture took a backseat in his life during that period.

In spite of his Anglicization, for the British M.A. Jinnah was still an Indian and a Muslim. Jinnah himself knew this factor. This seems to have pushed him towards other Indians in London at that time like Dadabhai Naoroji, the 'Grand Old Man of India', who belonged to the INC. It seems that while he was still in India, he was overjoyed by the election of Dadabhai Naoroji to the House of Commons in 1892. Dadabhai Naoroji was a Parsi—a descendant of Zoroastrians who had fled from Persia to Gujarat in India when Islam penetrated Persia. The Parsis had adopted Gujarati as their mother tongue, though they kept their religion. Jinnah himself being of Gujarati Khoja origin, did not find it very difficult to strike a good relationship with Dadabhai Naoroji, who was neither a Muslim nor a Hindu, but an ardent Parsi Indian nationalist. He was more at ease with Indian nationalists like Dadabhai of Parsi origin than with the others during this period. However, it can be admitted that he was introduced to Indian politics and nationalism in London through his acquaintance with Dadabhai Naoroji. His connection and predilection for the Parsis, who were as westernized as himself in many ways, was to continue in his life. It is noteworthy that during that period, the Bombay Congress was dominated by Parsis like Dadabhai Naoroji, Pherozeshah Mehta, and Dinshaw Wacha.[6]

After qualifying as a barrister-in-law at Lincoln's Inn in April 1896, M.A. Jinnah returned to India in May. At that time, M.A. Jinnah declared in a petition to Lincoln's Inn that he had attained the age of twenty-one years. This attests that his year of birth was 1875.[7] By that time, that is, while he was away in London, his mother and even his young wife Emibhai had passed away. He was hardly in his twenties then. He did not decide to live with his father in Karachi or practice law in the Karachi court. At that time, his father was heartbroken and sick due to loss of his wife and also financial losses in his business. But there is no indication that Jinnah cared much about such things. Jinnah was no comfort to his father at that time. Instead, he decided to settle down in Bombay in a very modest accommodation. He never seemed to have thought of remarriage. He had never frequented any 'white' girl in London, as earlier feared by his mother.

Jinnah was equipped to face the world with his Law degree, thanks to his father. While in London, he had perfected his language as well as his legal and oratorical skills. This, he thought, he could put to good use in the Bombay bar, rather than in Karachi. He seemed to have struggled for a couple of years in Bombay, before he set up private practice.

It is worthwhile to note at this juncture that Jinnah being a Gujarati Khoja never really tried to master Urdu, which was growing to become the cultural language of a great number of Muslims in India. He spoke very bad Urdu. He never seemed to have been attracted by Sir Sayyid Ahmad Khan's pleas in favour of Urdu as the cultural language of the Muslims of India. Nor did he subscribe to his view that Muslims stood to gain by being loyal towards the British. He did not also subscribe to Sir Sayyid's fear that if unadulterated democracy was introduced in India, Muslims will be made into a permanent minority. Nor did he think that Hindus and Muslims belonged to two different nations following Sir Sayyid. He would not subscribe to the unorthodox religious views of Sir Sayyid either. This was obvious because Sir Sayyid was a Sunni Muslim, while he was a Khoja Shia. Sir Sayyid was never a role model for Jinnah. Instead, one could say at this juncture that he was secular-minded in the western sense, with no thought of mixing religion with politics. Being westernized in his dressing sense, food habits and thought, there was no question of Jinnah playing the role of a reformer like Sayyid Ahmad Khan. He was never cut out for that.

Besides, Jinnah mainly due to his penchant towards British culture, never really associated himself with his mother tongue, Gujarati, although he spoke rather fluently. Instead he switched over to English, the language of the colonizers for all practical purposes.

Jinnah's father having lost everything in Karachi came to Bombay with his family and stayed in a small two-room tenement in Khoja Mohalla. But as Jinnah was unhelpful, he moved away to Ratnagiri, far away from Bombay. Jinnah never seemed to have maintained any intimate or regular contact with the members of his father's family, except his younger sister Fatima, who came to live with him subsequently.

In 1897, just after returning from London, Jinnah joined the Anjuman-i-Islam of Bombay. Anjuman-i-Islam was established by some Bombay Muslims as a progressive institution for the education of Muslims and their social upliftment. It was then led by Badruddin Tyabji, who was a judge of the Bombay High Court. Tyabji was a Congressman who sought to redress the backwardness of the Muslims through the organ of the nationalist Congress. Jinnah naturally came under his influence.

Anjuman-i-Islam was the first Indian organization which Jinnah adhered to, in spite of his relationship with Dadabhai Naoroji. Badruddin Tyabji, who was of Arab ancestry and belonged to the Sulaimani Bohra sect, was the first Indian barrister who took his Law degree from London in 1867. He was an early leader of the Congress party and was nominated to the Bombay Legislative Council in 1882. He was also the first Indian to hold the post of Chief Justice of Bombay. By joining the Anjuman-i-Islam, while he was still an Ismaili Khoja, Jinnah made known his interest with regard to the welfare of the Muslims. He also proved by this act that he was not a camp follower of the Aga Khan to whose sect he belonged by birth.[8]

In the late nineteenth and early twentieth centuries, a minority among the Khojas converted to Twelver Shi'ism or the *Isna ashari.* Jinnah had never taken the religion of his forefathers seriously. But he was one among the converts. He himself had never clarified the reason for his conversion. It appears that he wanted to get away from the overpowering authority of the Aga Khan. There was no chance for him to outshine the Aga Khan, as long as he remained an Ismaili. His decision to leave the Ismaili sect and join the bigger Shia group of Twelver Shi'ism opened up new possibilities for him in Indian public life. Technically speaking he no more owed allegiance to the Aga Khan, though he remained a Khoja and Shia. However, there is no indication that Jinnah frequented the *Jamaatkhanas* (Khoja mosques) or any other mosque regularly for prayers during that period or earlier.[9]

In any case, M.A. Jinnah did not belong to the upper echelons of Indian Muslims society like Sayyid Ahmad Khan or the Aga Khan or even Badruddin Tyabji or Ameer Ali.[10] He was rather drawn from a more modest Indian indigenous background, with no particular standing or prestige. As a result, during the early period of his public life he was not in a position to be considered to be among the 'natural leaders' of the Muslims, who were the Ashrafs of foreign origin. This may possibly be one of the reasons which would have pushed Jinnah since his stay in London towards non-Muslim stalwarts like Dadabhai Naoroji, who were more nationalistic and non-sectarian in their attitude and approach rather than towards the Muslims stalwarts of Ashraf origin, who still considered themselves as superior to the indigenous Indian Muslims of lower status and were generally more loyal to the British.

ENTRY INTO POLITICS

THE NATIONALIST PHASE

During that period, the Bombay Congress was dominated by Parsi stalwarts. Naturally Jinnah renewed his contact with Parsi leaders in Bombay. He came under the influence of Sir Pherozeshah Mehta, also known as the 'Uncrowned King of Bombay'. His acquaintance with Badruddin Tyabji continued. When a Committee was formed to oversee the coronation ceremony of King Edward VII, Jinnah and Badruddin Tyabji participated in it.

In the year 1904, Jinnah was elected to the Bombay Corporation. In the same year, a session of the Congress party took place in Bombay. Sir Pherozeshah Mehta was the chairman of the Congress Reception Committee. Jinnah participated in this session. He assisted Mehta. It was then that the Bombay Congress decided to send a delegation to London under Gopal Krishna Gokhale, in order to plead for a greater share for Indians in the administration and to enlighten the British on Indian affairs. Pherozeshah Mehta made Jinnah part of this delegation. But Bal Gangadhar Tilak, the other firebrand Congress leader objected to it. He gave Jinnah's inexperience as the reason for his objection. Besides, he seemed to not have relished the fact that Jinnah belonged to the Mehta–Gokhale group. During that period Jinnah came in close touch with Gokhale, although both Gokhale and Tilak were Maharashtrian Brahmins.

In 1906, Jinnah formally joined the Congress party. In the same year, he was re-elected to the Bombay Corporation. Jinnah resigned immediately after in order to bring in his mentor Mehta into the Corporation by seeking the annulment of the election. He was not successful in this as he lost the case. Later in the year when Dadabhai Naoroji came to India to attend the annual Congress Session at Calcutta, Jinnah seemed to have been very helpful to him. He even acted as secretary to him for sometime during that period. During the conference it appeared that Jinnah took more interest in Muslim affairs like wakf and reservations. It is understood that he even opposed the resolution for reservation of seats in the legislatures and administrative services for 'educationally backward classes'. Essentially due to his contacts with Sir Pherozeshah Mehta, Dadabhai Naoroji, Badruddin Tyabji, and Gopal Krishna Gokhale, Jinnah grew up as a moderate in Indian politics. The Parsi leaders and Gokhale saw politics as different from religion unlike Tilak. This suited Jinnah's temperament very well.[1]

In 1900, when A. McDonnell introduced Hindi in the United Provinces, Nawab Mohsin-ul-Mulk formed the Urdu Defence Academy. In 1901, Lord Curzon, the Viceroy of British India, created a new Muslim-majority province by dividing the North-West Frontier areas, inhabited predominantly by Pathans, from the rest of Punjab.[2] The creation of the new province was largely on the basis of language and ethnicity. The division of the Punjab province did not face any significant opposition either from the Congress or from the Muslims. During the same year, Lord Curzon had offered the Aga Khan, who was just 24 then, a seat in the Bombay Legislative Council.

Lord Curzon had always held that there was no such thing as 'Indian nation'. Following the institutionalized official policy of separate treatment for Muslims since the last quarter of the nineteenth century, he decided to divide the Bengal province into two in 1905. He created a separate province of East Bengal and Assam out of Bengal. Incidentally it had a Muslim majority. He cited administrative reasons for the division; however, it became quite apparent that for the first time a big province with a clear Muslim majority was created by the British. Many Muslims, led by Nawab Salimulla, the zamindar of Dacca, came out strongly in support of the division. It is understood that the Nawab was first opposed to the Partition, but was eventually won over by British through the grant of a loan of £100,000 at a low rate of interest.

However, there was stiff opposition to the division from the Bengalis, especially the upper-class Hindus and some Muslims. They accused the British of trying to divide the Indians on the basis of religion. The hitherto benign Congress party took the side of the Bengalis and accused Lord Curzon of sowing seeds of discord between Hindus and Muslims. As a Congressman, M.A. Jinnah too took the side of the Bengalis. Thus, what was a purely Bengali communal problem became a national communal problem due to the interference of many non-Bengali Congress leaders like Bal Ganghadhar Tilak and Lala Lajpat Rai, in Bengali affairs. M.A. Jinnah was just a budding second-rank politician at that time and nobody ever took his opposition to the division of Bengal seriously.[3]

It is however obvious that Lord Curzon by his single act of dividing Bengal on religious lines, and creating a new Muslim province, without the Muslims really demanding it or agitating for it, had heightened the Islamic consciousness of the Muslims in Bengal and in the rest of India. As a consequence, Muslim personalities of the provinces where the Muslims were in a minority like in the United Provinces and Bombay began to search forcefully for ways to offset their minority status and safeguard their interests. They feared the brute majority of the Hindus, who would dominate by virtue of their numbers in any representative body. Among those, who were in the forefront of this search, was the Aga Khan of Bombay as well as Nawab Mohsin-ul-Mulk, a Shia associate of Sir Sayyid Ahmad Khan who had earlier been conferred the title of 'Nawab' by the Nizam of Hyderabad and was then the Honorary Secretary of the Mohammedan Anglo-Oriental College of Aligarh. It was simply impossible for them to demand partition of the Muslim areas in every province of British India like in Bengal. The ultimate idea that they fell upon to ward off Hindu domination, both in the provinces as well as at the Centre, was the idea of separate electorates, conceived earlier by Theodore Beck and endorsed by Lansdowne and Dufferin, in order to have a share in the evolving power structure. They wanted the creation of separate electorates for Muslims, where Muslims alone would elect Muslim representatives to the various legislative bodies. Thus the idea of separate electorates for Muslims became associated with the power for the Muslims, especially for the elite among the Muslims, belonging mainly to the landed aristocracy right from the beginning. Idea and power are neither opposed to nor disconnected from one another, as asserted by some Cambridge scholars like Anil Seal or David Washbrook; rather, they go hand in hand.

The British on their part did nothing to dissuade the growth of this idea. Instead, they aided and abetted its growth, in order to create a Muslim counterweight to the Congress. Thus the demand for separate electorates was a fallout of British policy dividing Bengal on religious grounds. The partition of Bengal led to the radicalization of a section of the Congress party under leaders like Bal Gangadhar Tilak, Bipin Chandra Pal, and Lala Lajpat Rai and the exacerbation of the division of society on religious lines. It gave rise to the Swadeshi Movement, especially in Bengal, which involved the boycott of British goods.

A moderate faction of the Congress led by Gopal Krishna Gokhale and Sir Pherozeshah Mehta, and to which Jinnah belonged, pleaded for constitutional reforms. But the extremist faction, led by Bal Gangadhar Tilak, wanted *Swaraj* or autonomy and favoured boycott. Tilak was the first Congress leader who had used religion to mobilize the masses in the 1890s itself by organizing the Ganesh festival and the Shivaji cult in Maharashtra. Another extremist leader from Bengal, Aurobindo Ghose asserted that the groundwork of Indian nationalism and the composite culture of India were undoubtedly Hindu. The Aga Khan, realizing the dangers of Congress radicalism, on no account wanted India to dissociate from Great Britain. Instead, he sympathized with the stand of the moderates which included Jinnah and drew the ire of Tilak and his followers. The British of course were against Tilak's extremism, which demanded self-rule for India.[4]

During the autumn of 1906, Lord Minto, the new Viceroy was in his summer retreat at Shimla. Following Lord Curzon and his predecessors, Lord Minto too cultivated the friendship of the Aga Khan. He considered the Aga Khan as a strong mediating hand.[5] He received a deputation of over fifty elite Muslims of India, comprising of Nawabs, *taluqdars*, landlords, maulvis, Khan Bahadurs, Khans, Maliks, and other influential men in Shimla. Most of them were of *Ashraf* origin, that is, descendants of Muslims who can trace their origin to Afghanistan, Persia, Arabia, and west or Central Asia. It also included some who were assimilated as Ashrafs due to their wealth, status, and social standing. They were the 'natural elite' of the Muslims of India. Under the reforms contemplated by the British, they did not want to be subjected to the Hindus, who were subjects of the Ashraf rulers during the pre-British days. Naturally, the deputation devised means to offset this impending domination.

The deputation was headed by none other than His Highness the Aga Khan, who was just 29 then. Some of the other prominent members were Syed Mahdee Ally Khan or Nawab Mohsin-ul-Mulk of Aligarh, Nawab Viqar-ul-Mulk of Moradabad, Moulvi Rafiuddin Ahmed, Nawab Sardar Ali Khan of Bombay, Hakim Ajmal Khan of Delhi, and Khan Bahadur Mian Muhammad Shafi of Lahore. Nawab Salimullah of Dacca was not able to accompany the delegation due to illness. There was no question of including Jinnah in the delegation, although he was a moderate Congressman. He was still an Ajlaf of a lower status, in spite of his education and profession. Besides, he had defied just a few years back the Aga Khan, who was as young as himself, by abandoning his Ismaili sect and authority altogether.

The demands of the delegation were embodied in the Shimla Memorandum. Another Ashraf, Nawab Imadud-doulah Imad ul-mulk Moulvi Sayyid Husain Bilgrami, who was a trustee of the Muhammadan Anglo-Oriental College, seems to have been the author of the Memorandum. The Memorandum demanded separate electorate for Muslims to safeguard the political and other interests of the Muslims. They also insisted that Muslim representation should depend not on the number of Muslims, but on their 'historical and political importance' and the value of contribution that they made or make to the defence of the British Empire. The members of the delegation believed that the Muslims had a special past as they were the ruling power before the British. They also thought that they had a special destiny as Muslims, with superior ideals, traditions, and beliefs, completely different from their Hindu counterparts, which qualified them for a special treatment in the political field.

But it was overlooked that the great majority of the Muslim population of India, probably more than 90 per cent of which were Ajlafs, were the descendants of mostly lower-caste Hindu converts to Islam, with almost no political power in India. M.A. Jinnah was one among them. However, it was the minority Ashrafs of foreign origin, who considered themselves as superior among Muslims and posed themselves as the 'natural leaders' of the Ajlafs, who too like the Hindus were subject to their ancestors in the past.[6]

The Muslim delegation consisting mostly of Ashrafs, while claiming to speak for all the Muslims of India, in the name of Islam, wanted desperately to protect, in the process, their elite interests. They wanted not only to stave off impending Hindu domination, but also not to be subjected to the Ajlafs, who were considered to be inferior to them by birth, status, past history, and wealth. However, they were less and less vocal about it. This is because the idea of democracy was gaining ground in Indian politics during that period, which was highly favourable to the Ajlafs due to their preponderant numbers.[7]

We do not know exactly why, how, and who chose the young Aga Khan to lead the delegation. According to the Aga Khan's own admission, it was a collective effort initiated by him, along with Nawab Mohsin-ul-Mulk and Syed Ameer Ali of Bengal, who were all Ashrafi Shias. Besides, Lady Minto as well as Sir Valentine Chirol had affirmed that it was the Aga Khan who engineered the Muslim delegation to offset Hindu ascendancy, which would have a destabilizing effect over British rule. Further, there is clear evidence that Mohsin-ul-Mulk, the political heir of Sir Sayyid Ahmad Khan as well as some other Muslim leaders kept in close touch with the Viceroy's private secretary, Dunlop Smith and the

Lucknow Commissioner Harcourt Butler through Principal Archbold of Aligarh College. Some historians have found the first draft of the Muslim Memorandum in Harcourt Butler's private papers. This suggests that British officials had a hand even in the drafting of the Muslim Memorandum. There is also a letter by Lord Minto's private secretary Dunlop Smith to Nawab Mohsin-ul-Mulk wherein it is suggested that the 'Muslims should seek representation by nomination rather than by election'. It has also been admitted by some British officials that separate electorates was 'a work of statesmanship' which will keep the 62 million Muslims from seditious Congressmen opposing British rule. During that period, the British were more favourably disposed towards the Muslims as a counterpoise to the growing Indian nationalism. For instance, the Secretary of State Morley had pressed Lord Minto to sanction Rs 14 lakh loan to Nawab Salimullah of Dacca as 'a political matter of great importance'. Of course, Jinnah never seemed to have been aware of this collusion between some top people of the British Indian establishment and certain members of the Muslim elite like the Aga Khan and Mohsin-ul-Mulk.[8]

The Aga Khan still had his roots in west Asia or rather Persia, though born in 1877 in Karachi where his grandfather Hasan Ali Shah and family had sought refuge earlier. It is doubtful if he considered himself fully as an Indian, as his ancestors migrated to India quite lately. He was happy to hear that he looked like a prosperous Englishman. It has also been reported that he spent more time in his luxurious suites in the Ritz Hotel of London and his several homes in France than at his princely estate in the elite European Bombay suburb of Malabar Hill. When he died, he did not wish his mausoleum to be built in India (where he was born); instead, he wished that the mausoleum be built in Aswan in Egypt. This shows his extra-territorial loyalty. Besides, he did not belong to the Sunni confession, to which most Muslims of India belonged. He did not even belong to the majority Twelver group of Shias to which Jinnah then belonged. Instead, he was the leader and Imam of the small group of Khojas, who were not even considered as true Muslims during that period.[9]

Nevertheless, the stark fact was that he led the delegation. Why did suddenly the Aga Khan, of Persian descent, who was until then the leader of the miniscule Ismaili Khoja sect, don the garb as representative of the Muslims of all British India, both Sunni and Shia? There is no doubt that the British had been constantly involved in the raising of the status of the Aga Khans among the Muslims of India, since they fled Persia during the nineteenth century. The British had even granted them a princely pension for their loyalty and past services. This alone seemed to have been enough for the Aga Khan to qualify as the leader of the delegation. The British were bound to respond favourably to the demands of the delegation because it was being led by His Highness the Aga Khan, a time-tested ally of the British, whose ancestors had very much helped them in the past to conquer and subdue the turbulent northwestern parts of India and also quell the Great Revolt of 1857.[10]

At that time, there was at least one Muslim, who was not yet prominent as a political leader, who daringly questioned in harsh terms the representative character of the Muslim delegation, which as we know consisted mostly of Ashrafs. He was a young barrister in his thirties. M.A. Jinnah, who collaborated with Congress moderate stalwarts was not an Ashraf. Theoretically he was an Ajlaf, that is, of lower birth, status, and wealth. But the Aga Khan or Nawab Mohsin-ul-Mulk or the other prominent Ashraf dignitaries never bothered to invite M.A. Jinnah to be part of the delegation. This might have hurt Jinnah's growing ego to some extent. The Aga Khan wrote later in his *Memoirs* that Jinnah, a distinguished Muslim barrister from Bombay was not only the doughtiest opponent of the Muslim delegation's memorandum but also of his friends and himself. However, there were also some Ashraf personalities who were opposed to separate electorates. One of the most prominent among them was Badruddin Tyabji, who died in London in August 1906. The passing away of Tyabji cleared a crucial deck for Jinnah to emerge as the spokesman of the Muslim wing in the Congress party.

Lord Minto did not turn down the demands of the Muslim delegation led by the Aga Khan. Instead, contrary to the claims of Jinnah, he considered the delegation as representative and was overtly sympathetic to their demands and even went to the extent of justifying them. This came as an encouragement to the delegates to pursue, still further, their separatist path. The Aga Khan in his *Memoirs* had claimed that he had never had a sympathetic hearing from the Congress leadership with regard to the grievances and problems of the Muslims and accused it of relying on third-rate Muslims from Madras and Bombay to represent the Muslims.[11] Thus it is clear that at least for the Aga Khan Muslim leaders from Bombay like M.A. Jinnah were 'third rate' Muslims.

All this was happening at a time when there was no representative form of elected government, although the British had announced their intentions to create representative institutions since the 1880s, especially through the Indian Councils Act of 1892. Besides, the Congress party was not yet saddled with any form of power. But many members of the Muslim delegation with the likes of the Aga Khan, Syed Ameer Ali, and Nawab Mohsin-ul-Mulk in the lead seem to have thought that the only way to carry forward their demands was by establishing a political party. Already in Bengal, the Nawab of Dacca Khwaja Salimullah had floated the idea of forming a Muslim All India Confederacy.[12]

In the same year, precisely in December 1906, Muslim delegates from various parts of India met at Dacca, the capital of the newly created East Bengal province, during a session of the All India Muslim Educational Conference, founded by Sir Sayyid Ahmad Khan and whose the then secretary was Nawab Mohsin-ul-Mulk. The location of the conference in Dacca was no doubt most appropriate, because East Bengal had an absolute Muslim majority. It was principally convened by none other than Nawab Sir Khwaja Salimullah of Dacca, the main protagonist of the division of Bengal. The leading lights of this conference were generally of Ashraf descent or those who have been assimilated. Some of the most prominent among them were Nawab Viqar-ul-Mulk, the Aga Khan III,

Syed Ameer Ali, Hakim Ajmal Khan, Maulana Mazharul Haque of Bihar, and Sir Mian Muhammad Shafi of Punjab. It is believed that Mohammad Ali, Shaukat Ali, and Syed Wazir Hasan were present at Dacca during the foundation of the conference, though their names do not figure in the list of the founders, members, or office-holders. During the conference, a Muslim political party known as the All-India Muslim League was founded, in order to protect and promote Muslim interests in a future India. The conference resolved 'to promote among the Mussalmans of India, feelings of loyalty to the British Government…'. It came out against the *Swadeshi* movement and the boycott of British goods. It also pressed for separate electorates for the Muslims. In fact, it called upon the British and relied upon them to safeguard and promote the special interests of the Muslims within a united India.

The All-India Muslim League was a sectarian party right from the beginning, as it was meant exclusively for the Muslims. It nevertheless signalled the entry of Muslims into national politics on the basis of religion. The foundation of this party and the development of Muslim separatist scenario were the immediate byproducts of Lord Minto's endorsement of the Muslim delegation's demands. Incidentally, the first president of this all-India Muslim party was the Aga Khan—the Khoja leader and Imam—who always had a good rapport with the British rulers. Mohsin-ul-Mulk and Viqar-ul-Mulk became the joint secretaries of the League in 1906. The Aga Khan along with other Muslim princes and Nawabs like the Nawab of Arcot financed the League in its early years. During that period, the British officials and rulers had customarily relied upon such Muslims as the Aga Khan, Syed Ameer Ali, and the Raja of Mahmudabad, who happened to be Shias, as interpreters of Muslim society and politics.[13]

Although the All-India Muslim League was founded in Dacca in the Bengali Muslim-majority eastern province, the head office of the League was located first in Aligarh, in the United Provinces, a Muslim-minority province, which was nevertheless the heart of Muslim India, historically and culturally. Then from the year 1910, the head office was shifted to

Lucknow. The Raja of Mahmudabad (1878–1931), owner of the rich estate of Mahmudabad in Oudh, financed the Muslim League during that period.[14] This shows the influence wielded by the Muslim stalwarts of the UP on the All-India Muslim League right from its inception in Dacca. The Constitution of the League was framed at the Karachi session of the League in December 1907, presided by Sir Adamjee Peerbhoy. According to this Constitution, there was a permanent president of the League, who was none other than the Aga Khan.

On 10 November 1907, Pherozeshah Mehta organized a meeting of the Central Standing Committee of the Congress in his palatial residence in Bombay. Jinnah attended this meeting. During that period, Jinnah was working in Mehta's chambers. At the annual Surat session of the Congress that followed, there was a formal and violent split in the Congress party between the moderate faction led by Pherozeshah Mehta and Gokhale and the extremist faction led by Tilak. Tilak and his extremist followers were disowned by the Congress party thenceforth. Jinnah participated in this session as a moderate, but passively. It was during this session that Jinnah got acquainted with Tilak.[15]

Jinnah was also present at the meeting when the extremists led by Tilak were expelled from the Congress. In the same year, Bal Gangadhar Tilak was arrested for sedition. A case was foisted upon him. Jinnah was a moderate in politics. Theoretically he was opposed to Tilak. Nevertheless, he filed an application for bail on behalf of Tilak. He argued on the lines that it was not sedition for an Indian to demand freedom and self-government in his own country. Jinnah's bail application was rejected by Davur, an Indian judge of the Bombay court. Tilak would not allow Jinnah to defend his case, even though the latter did not want to charge him any fees. Probably he still thought that Jinnah was inexperienced. Jinnah emphasized that Tilak was more intent on establishing that the Anglo-Indian Press was guilty of defaming India and the Indian people, rather than to secure his release. So Tilak defended himself in the court. He was sentenced to six years of rigourous imprisonment for sedition by

Davur. From September 1908 to about the middle of 1914, Tilak was in a jail in Mandalay. Davur was knighted by the British for sentencing Tilak. Jinnah was unhappy and refused to attend the dinner hosted in honour of Davur. At that time, M.A. Jinnah had set up a lucrative legal practice in Bombay. However, he is not known to have been a very skilled lawyer. His close associate, Mohammad Karim Chagla had attested this fact.

It is quite surprising to see Jinnah, the moderate, aspiring to defend Tilak, the extremist who had been disowned by the Congress. We do not know if his mentors, Gokhale and Mehta approved of this action. But the fact remains that defending Tilak would have given Jinnah a huge publicity in government circles and among the masses, which naturally would have boosted his legal and political prospects and ambitions still further. According to Jinnah's own admission, Tilak was known to be communalistic in his early days. In spite of this, Jinnah had desired to defend Tilak. This showed, for the first time, that Jinnah was capable of changing his conviction and striking his own path in politics if that suited him.[16]

In the year 1909, the Indian Councils Act created an expanded Imperial Legislative Council, consisting of 60 members, of which 27 were to be elected. The Act formally instituted the policy of separate treatment of the Muslims in the political sphere by the right to Muslims to elect their representatives—the right to elect their representatives by separate electorates, the right to vote in general electorates, the right to 'weightage' in the legislative bodies, followed by the demand put forward by the Muslim delegation of 1906 and the All-India Muslim League. The franchise was extended, but it was still extremely narrow, based on property and education. Thus the idea of separate electorates was given a legal form. In this way, the British laid the foundation for the political separatism of Muslims in India. The Muslim delegation did not have any mandate from its population. They were not elected by the Muslims to represent them, as noted by Jinnah. They were largely self-appointed members belonging to the cream of the Muslim society. There was no mass agitation of Muslims for separate electorates, for the British to fear Muslim unrest. In fact, the British feared Hindu extremist terrorism during that period, but they deliberately chose to concede this crucial demand. Henceforth, it was on this separate foundation, provided by the British, that Muslim politics was bound to evolve. By conceding separate electorates, the British sought to recognize the All-India Muslim League under the Aga Khan as a representative organization of Indian Muslims, which could be used as a counterpoise to the recalcitrant Congress. It undermined to a great extent whatever possibilities there were for joint Hindu–Muslim political action. In one deft constitutional move, the Congress was cut down to size. Its largely Hindu leadership could hardly do anything about it. They had to swallow the bitter pill of separate electorates, although they disapproved of it.[17] They were no more in a position to rise in revolt against the separate electorates for Muslims as it was the case when Bengal was partitioned on religious lines. Jinnah himself did not want to take the lead against separate electorates in spite of the fact that Badruddin Tyabji was no more. But one of his mentors, Gopal Krishna Gokhale had endorsed separate electorates for Muslims right from 1909 onwards. However; Jinnah seemed to have been in two minds with regard to separate electorates during that period. Sometimes he spoke in favour of it and at other times he was against it, probably due to Congress pressure.[18]

But very soon by December 1909, probably encouraged by the stand of Gokhale, M.A. Jinnah seemed to have made up his mind to contest the election to the Imperial Legislative Council from Bombay, not from a general constituency as one would expect, but from an exclusively Muslim constituency. He was pitted against the President of the Muslim League of the Bombay Presidency, Moulvi Rafiuddin Ahmed (Barrister-at-Law). The latter was a member of the Shimla Deputation in 1906 and a founder of the Muslim League in Dacca. Jinnah won the election as a Congressman, but not before the idea of separate electorates had sunk into his mind, due to the visible advantages that it could procure for the Muslims. The Imperial Council included a large number of Europeans and Indian loyalists. It had no real power. But Jinnah seemed to have taken an active part in the deliberations of the Viceroy's Executive Council. He played a significant role in the legitimization of the Muslim religious endowments, the Waqf. In the Viceroy's Council he rubbed shoulders with tall Congressmen like Dinshaw Wacha, Srinivasa Sastri, Tej Bahadur Sapru, and Madan Mohan Malaviya. In December 1910, at the session of the Congress party, Jinnah moved a resolution deprecating the proposal for extension of the principle of separate electorates to municipal and local bodies. At the same time, he left himself in a loophole by affirming that the resolution reflected his personal views and not the views of the community. By this, he seemed to suggest that the Muslim community wanted separate electorates, although he may not want it.[19]

Given the continued opposition to the partition of Bengal primarily by upper class Hindus and the threat of revolutionary terrorism, the British revoked the partition in 1911. At the same time, they announced the shifting of the capital of British India from Calcutta to Delhi, the imperial capital of the Mughals, as a sort of consolation to the Muslims, who then constituted about a quarter of the total Indian population. Many Muslims did not relish the revocation of the Partition. They thought that their interests were no safer in British hands. Besides, the very next year in 1912 the provinces of Bihar and Assam were carved out of Bengal. That put an end to Bengal being the centre of gravity of Indian politics. Strangely the Congress chose not to agitate against the partitioning of Bengal into three provinces, which eventually gave the Muslims a slender majority in what remained of the Bengal province. Even Jinnah, Nawab Salimullah, and the Aga Khan (the then President of the All-India Muslim League) preferred to go silent on this issue. The Aga Khan even exhorted the Muslims not to agitate against the revocation of Partition.[20]

In the year 1911, Turkey confronted Italy in Libya. This was followed by the Balkan wars. Britain refused to give a helping hand to Turkey. But Turkey being the seat of the Caliphate and the Ottoman Empire, the sentiments of Indian Muslims were deeply affected. Some rising young leaders of the Muslim League like Mohammad Ali Jouhar (1878–1931) of west Asian descent and his brother Shaukat Ali, Syed Wazir Hasan, Hasrat Mohani, and T.A.K. Sherwani of the United Provinces, Zafar Ali Khan of the Punjab, and Fazlul Huq of Bengal who came to form the 'Young Party', were particularly perturbed.[21]

Besides, in the year 1914, when the First World War broke out, the Turkish Sultan chose to ally with Germany in its war against Britain, which pitted Britain against Turkey to the great displeasure of the Muslims of India. Further, the British supported the Arab revolt of 1916 against Turkish rule. Many Indian Muslims like Mohammad Ali and Dr M.A. Ansari were not happy with it as it endangered the sanctity of the Muslim holy places. The Ali brothers and Zafar Ali Khan were interned in their hometowns during the duration of the war.[22] Unlike the members of the 'Young Party' like the Ali brothers, Jinnah preferred to keep low profile with regard to the fate of Turkey and the Muslim holy places. He did not want to be in the bad books of the British by adopting a confrontational approach like Mohammad Ali and go to jail.

JINNAH JOINS MUSLIM LEAGUE

In the year 1912, Syed Wazir Hasan (1874–1947), a Shia by faith like Jinnah, became the secretary of the Muslim League. This signalled the capture of the League by the 'Young Party' members. They were not titled zamindars, except for the Raja of Mahmudabad, the Shia aristocrat of the UP. They did not belong to the upper echelons of Muslim society. They were mostly employed in the services or in the professions.[23]

Strangely in the year 1911, Jinnah did not attend the annual Congress Session. Instead, in 1910 and 1912, Jinnah attended the Muslim League annual sessions. In the Muslim League Council meeting held at Bankipur on 31 December 1912, with the Aga Khan in the chair, the Constitution of the League was modified to include self-government within the British Empire as one of the prime aims of the League. This modification was pushed through by none other than Syed Wazir Hasan.

The old guard of the League like Nawab Viqar-ul-Mulk resisted giving up the loyalist stance. Jinnah was present during this meeting upon invitation, and he seemed to have thrown his lot with the young elements of the party. Jinnah pointed out at the session that the system of self-government on colonial lines was not feasible for India. He congratulated the League for going ahead, even of the Congress, in the formation of the ideal of self-government. Replying to Viqar-ul-Mulk, who mentioned that the time had not come for attainment of self-government, Jinnah said, 'Nobody asked for it to be given tomorrow or the day after. It was the goal and ideal of the nation and might be attained say a century later.' Apart from the resolution for self-government, other resolutions passed during the session included the promotion of the political and other rights of the Muslims and Hindu–Muslim unity. The resolutions were supported by Maulana Mohammad Ali Jauhar.

At the Lucknow session of the League held two months later, Jinnah was once again present. During this session the AIML placed on record its sense of gratification at the passing of the Muslim Waqf Validating Act, 1913 which restored to Indian Muslims the full benefit of their personal law with regard to the religious institution of Waqf. The League while recognizing the great services rendered by Honorable Syed Ameer Ali and Shibli Nomani in the matter, congratulated Jinnah especially for his skilful piloting of the Waqf Bill (tax-exempt Muslim endowments) in the Imperial Legislative Assembly. In the same year, the Viceroy appointed Jinnah as a member of the Imperial Legislative Council. Jinnah participated assiduously in the deliberations of the Council and spoke on various issues.[24] Neither the Aga Khan nor the British had any reason to be happy about the League drifting away towards a nationalist agenda. Under these circumstances, during the course of the year 1913, the Aga Khan, a loyalist of the first order, decided to resign from the presidency of the All-India Muslim League. Even Syed Ameer Ali resigned from the League.

In April 1913, M.A. Jinnah went to Britain with Gopal Krishna Gokhale. He stayed there for six months. He addressed a meeting of

Indian students at Caxton Hall in London and founded the London Indian Association during his stay there. In London he happened to meet Mohammad Ali and Syed Wazir Hasan, Secretary of the Muslim League, who were there on a deputation with regard to the destruction of a portion of the mosque in Kanpur. Mohammad Ali had maintained that the purpose of their visit to London was also to explain the Indian Muslims' point of view and their situation in India and abroad. It is generally admitted that Mohammad Ali and Syed Wazir Hasan persuaded Jinnah to join the Muslim League; it is strange that two young members of the UP belonging to the lower echelons of the Muslim society had decided to rope in Jinnah as member of the League. The Ashrafs of the old guard like Mohsin-ul-Mulk or the Aga Khan would not have done this. Jinnah, who until then never held any official position in the Congress party, felt the invitation to join the League attractive for his future political prospects. After returning to India, Jinnah formally enrolled himself as a member of the League towards the end of the year; but he continued to be a member of the Congress. Neither the Congress party nor Pherozeshah Mehta or Gopal Krishna Gokhale objected to this dual responsibility of Jinnah; instead, Jinnah was hailed as the ambassador of Hindu–Muslim unity by Gokhale himself. In return, Jinnah affirmed that his loyalty to the Muslim League would not mean disloyalty to the larger national cause.[25]

Probably leaders like Gokhale thought that Jinnah would act as a bridge between the Congress and the League. The Congress dropped its opposition to separate electorates and even moved a resolution seconded by Jinnah during its session in Karachi at the end of the year 1913 welcoming the League's adoption of self-government as its ideal. Later during the Agra session of the League Jinnah opposed separate electorates, asking the members to postpone the decision on it for one year, knowing fully well that the League members were not in a mood to accept it. During that time, Jinnah proposed a measure of Council Reforms by which one-third of the Viceroy's Indian Council Members would be elected by the members of the Indian Central and provincial legislatures. In May 1914,

Jinnah was part of a Congress delegation to London. They unsuccessfully tried to obtain the opening up of the Council of India to at least three non-official Indians, elected by the Imperial and Provincial Councils. But all this cannot mean that Jinnah was an unadulterated nationalist; in case his demands were conceded, he would have most probably seen to it that Muslim interests were safeguarded adequately.[26]

What was forgotten in the process was that Jinnah had decided to sail the Indian political waters with one leg in the Congress boat and the other in the Muslim League boat. Though Jinnah did try to bring the two boats together and sail smoothly, it was going to be an impossible task in the continuously evolving political situation. It is simply out of place to consider Jinnah as a non-sectarian nationalist at this juncture, as some like Sarojini Naidu and more recently Jaswant Singh would want us to believe. This is because Jinnah had one leg in the Muslim League boat and his nationalism was subjected to the protection and promotion of Muslim interests since at least the time he joined the Anjuman-i-Islam in 1897.

The Aga Khan noticed that since the revocation of the Partition of India and Turkey's wars, some young members of the League wanted the party to adopt a more radical nationalist line against the British. He was, of course, referring to M.A. Jinnah, Syed Wazir Hasan, and Mohammad Ali. He warned the British of the impending dangers. He wrote in the *Edinburgh Review* of January 1914, advising the government to abandon the policy of separating Hindus and Muslims and to rally the moderates of both the creeds, so as to provide a counterpoise to the radical nationalist tendencies of young India, both Hindus and Muslims.[27]

Towards the middle of 1914, Tilak was released from prison. He had mellowed down completely in six years to the point of becoming a moderate. Contrary to his earlier radical position against the British, that time he came out openly in support of the British war efforts. In fact, the Congress as well as the Muslim League supported Britain in war. Jinnah too rallied behind Britain. Everyone hoped for some political reforms in the process. But radical young people of the Muslim League of which Jinnah was a member now, were unhappy that Britain had declared war against the Turkish Sultan and Caliph. They tended to be sympathetic towards Turkey. Already in 1913, the 'Young Party' of the League, especially the Ali brothers, were involved along with Abdul Bari's Farangi Mahall, the Ulama School of Lucknow in the setting up of the *Anjuman-i-Khuddam-I Kaaba* to protect the Muslim holy places. Abdul Bari helped Mohammad Ali's Red Crescent Fund to raise funds to support Muslim holy places and the Khilafat. On their part, Zafar Ali Khan and Dr Mukhtar Ahmed Ansari (1880–1930) were leading a medical mission to help Turkey in the Balkan wars. In 1914, the Raja of Mahmudabad, together with Abdul Bari tried to dissuade the Turkish Sultan from allying with Germany against Britain.[28] It would have been awkward for the highly westernized Jinnah to find himself in the company of people in the League like the Ali brothers who wanted to defend the Muslim holy places and the Caliphate. Generally he seems to have steered clear of such pan-Islamic activities during that period, as it was being sponsored mainly by the Leaguers of the United Provinces, the heart of Muslim India, where his influence counted for very little during that period.

In the year 1915, three significant things happened that pushed Jinnah further into the arms of the Muslim League and catapulted him as a leader of Muslims and Leaguers. First, was the return to India of Mohandas Karamchand Gandhi (1869–1948), a Gujarati *bania* and a Kathiawari barrister like Jinnah, after 21 years in South Africa, where he had developed and practised the art of *Satyagraha* or non-violent agitation against the colonial government. Gokhale, Jinnah and others welcomed Gandhi to Bombay in January 1915. Jinnah had already met Gandhi in London in 1914. A garden party was organized by the Gujarati Sabha of Bombay, in honour of Mr and Mrs Gandhi. Jinnah, being a prominent personality of Bombay and a Gujarati like Gandhi was invited to preside over the party. Jinnah attended the party, dressed impeccably in his western clothes. He addressed his welcome speech in equally impeccable English, in honour of Gandhi, on behalf of Bombay and India; and dwelt on the necessity of cooperation between the Muslims and the Hindus even in the garden party as if he wanted to impress upon Gandhi, who was just a new entrant into Indian politics. The garden party was not an appropriate place to raise communal issues. Gandhi, dressed in typical Gujarati attire, replied in Gujarati. He simply chose to skirt the communal issue and ignored Jinnah's plea because he still did not know the ins and outs of Indian politics as it was evolving then. Instead, he thanked Jinnah for presiding a Hindu gathering. He also did not miss the occasion to mildly admonish the previous speakers which included Jinnah for speaking in English in a Gujarati gathering.[29] Jinnah did not respond. Gandhi would have no doubt been puzzled by the presence of Jinnah in the gathering as the latter had one leg in the Congress and another in the Muslim League at that time.

Gandhi never hid the fact that he was a Hindu, right from his stepping back into India. He was proud of his ancestral religion and culture and even the caste system. He proclaimed that one should remain in one's religion and reform the defects in it and not run away from it. He simply did not believe that religion had nothing to do with politics; he considered that politics divorced from religion was like a corpse only fit to be buried. In short, he wanted to drive western civilization out of India and denounce it as 'Satanic Civilisation'.[30] But what one seems to forget quite often is that these were Gandhi's personal views. He had never sought to get all his views accepted as the official policy of the Congress party.

Jinnah did not appreciate right from the start Gandhi's views and his mixing religion with politics, in spite of the fact that he was then a member of a sectarian religion-based party too. Jinnah never hid the fact that he was a Muslim. He always wanted the 'two great sister communities' to cooperate and unite for the sake of self-government, where Muslim interests would be adequately protected at all levels. As for separate electorates for Muslims, he maintained that it had been settled by the Indian Councils Act 1909 and the question was no more open for discussion.[31]

Though Gandhi was educated in London, he was still very much an 'Indian' in his dressing sense, thought process, and mannerisms, unlike Jinnah who was westernized in many ways. He also spoke most often in his mother tongue Gujarati or in Hindustani, whereas Jinnah conversed most of the time in immaculate English. Jinnah never appreciated Gandhi's style of functioning, and his penchant for reaching out to the common people, who had been excluded from voting by the British Act of 1909.

Secondly, during that period, Jinnah had engaged with Gokhale to evolve the 'Gokhale scheme', which provided a governor for each province with a Cabinet of six—three Indian and three European members. The scheme wanted the Executive to be responsible to the Legislative, the services to be provincialized, with the Viceroy and his council having only a nominal control. But in February 1915, Gopal Krishna Gokhale, one of Jinnah's mentors passed away. Jinnah considered him as India's 'great political rishi'. Jinnah, for reasons we do not know, did not carry forward Gokhale's scheme. In the same year in November, his other mentor Pherozeshah Mehta also passed away. Dadabhai Naoroji who was extremely old also passed away two years later. Tilak, due to his past association with extremism and his old age, was not in a position to don the mantle as the undisputed leader of the Congress at that time. He and his group were still out of Congress. Tilak seemed to have approached Jinnah with regard to his re-entry into the Congress. A deal may have been struck. In December 1915, when both Gokhale and Mehta were no more, a resolution was finally passed at the annual session of the Congress in Bombay with the objective of admitting extremists into the Congress. The Muslim League Session also took place side-by-side with the Congress for the first time.

Thirdly, the Ali brothers were interned under the Defence of India Act in May 1915. They were released only towards the end of the year 1919. Their internment cleared the way for Jinnah to obtain certain ascendancy in the Muslim League and play a role in the Congress–League rapprochement. In a letter written by Mohammad Ali to Syed Wazir Hasan from his internment at Lansdowne on 26 September 1915, he asked the latter to put forward four resolutions for discussion during the forthcoming session of the AIML Council. He even asked to show these resolutions to Dr M.A. Ansari, M.A. Jinnah, and Maulana Mazharul Haque (1866–1930), a rich landlord of Bihar. Haque was one of the founders of the Muslim League in 1906 and a veteran Congressman of Bihar. The resolutions wanted a political status for India equal to that of the self-governing colonies, adequate representation of Muslims in the evolving political situation, recognition of all the legitimate claims of India as a whole, while safeguarding, at the same time, all the legitimate rights and interests of the Muslims. They also wanted the holding of a joint conference of the Congress and the League delegates at Bombay prior to the next sessions of these two organizations. Jinnah was most certainly aware of these resolutions devised by Mohammad Ali. In the light of the above, Mohammad Ali seems to be right in claiming that the League Session at Bombay took place along with that of the Congress Session due to his brother's and his suggestions. Maulana Mazharul Haque presided this session to bring about a joint meeting of the Congress and League leaders in order to adjust future political relations between Hindus and Muslims. Mohammad Ali expected Jinnah to join the session which the latter did. He held the following regarding Jinnah:

> I hope Mr Jinnah would soon come back to us. I may mention that an infidel becomes a Kaffir and a Kaffir becomes an infidel; likewise when Mr Jinnah was in the Congress, I was not with him in those days, and when I was in the Congress and the Muslim League, he was away from me. I hope someday we would reconcile.

Mohammad Ali finally claimed that it was due to the efforts of the President, Maulana Mazharul Haque and that of Jinnah as well as that of Maulana

Hasrat Mohani (1875–1951) that a rapprochement was brought about between the Hindu and Muslim leaders in Bombay which was to bear fruit in the following year at Lucknow. During the League Session at Bombay a Committee of 71 members was appointed, representing all provinces, in order to formulate and frame a scheme of reform in consultation with other political organizations.[32] Thus it is clear that Jinnah was not the only one involved in bringing about a Congress–League rapprochement; it was a collective effort with Maulana Mazharul Haque in the lead.

Meanwhile Congress had entered a period of transition and there was a power vacuum in the party during that period. Jinnah though close to Gokhale and Mehta, was not in a position to stake the claim for leadership of the Congress party, as he already had one leg in the Muslim League. He probably sensed that the Hindu-dominated Congress party will not accept him as a leader; he had never positioned himself as a leader above communal considerations like Badruddin Tyabji, acceptable to the majority Hindus. It was equally difficult for him to stake his claim for leadership in the Muslim League, where there were many other leaders like the Ali brothers, who would have never accepted the leadership of Jinnah.

However, it was during the years of transition and power vacuum in the Congress in 1915–16, that the Home Rule Leagues were founded by the theosophist Annie Besant, based in Madras and Tilak in Maharashtra. Tilak once again landed himself in trouble due to some of his speeches on Home Rule at Belgaum and Ahmadnagar which was deemed as seditious. M.A. Jinnah and four others defended Tilak before the District Magistrate of Poona. But the Magistrate directed Tilak to put bonds valued at Rs 20,000 in security for good behaviour for a period of one year. Tilak appealed against this in the Bombay High Court. M.A. Jinnah and Erulkar were his counsels. Jinnah argued that the Home Rule Movement had never been objected by the government authorities and it was neither illegal nor unconstitutional. This time Jinnah's defence was adequate and he won the case. This naturally drew Jinnah closer to Tilak. Jinnah thenceforth was full of admiration for him.

Jinnah subsequently joined the Home Rule League, after the internment of Annie Besant in 1917, along with Jehangir Petit, one of his Parsi acquaintances. He became the president of its Bombay chapter. He participated in a protest meeting against the internments, along with Tilak, Syed Wazir Hasan, and Jehangir Petit. During that period, the President of the Bombay Provincial Congress Committee was Dinshaw Wacha, another Parsi friend of Jinnah. The Home Rule League wanted Dominion status for India within the British Empire. Jinnah too wanted the same, with a further instalment of political reforms. He along with Surendra Nath Banerji signed a statement which committed them to the Lucknow Congress resolution and the demand for Home Rule. At a joint meeting of the All India Congress Committee and the League Council, it was decided to send a deputation consisting of Jinnah, Wazir Hassan, Sapru, Srinivasa Sastri, and may be C.P. Ramaswamy Iyer to England to explain to the British public the general situation in India and promote the scheme of reforms adopted at Lucknow. At the sessions of the Congress and the League held side-by-side in Calcutta in December 1917, the Raja of Mahmudabad who presided the League Session asserted that the Muslims were ready to sacrifice for the country as much as for Islam.

During the public farewell to Tilak on 25 March 1918, Jinnah spoke highly of Tilak. When Tilak rose to speak, he was greeted with loud cries of 'Vande Mataram'. Jinnah never raised the slightest opposition to such 'religious' cries in a public meeting. During that period, Jinnah came out in support of the *Satyagraha* Movement of Gandhi in Gujarat and even pleaded for the release of the Ali brothers. When Tilak's passport was cancelled in 1918 which prevented him from proceeding to London, Jinnah was among those who protested vehemently. He even signed a statement along with Tilak and Besant demanding self-government so that they might cooperate in the war effort. But unlike Tilak who preferred to walk out of the War Conference called on 10 June in Bombay—for being prevented from speaking in favour of *Swaraj* by Governor Willingdon—Jinnah simply took his seat after making his speech. He told Willingdon:

'You must make the educated people feel that they are the citizens of the Empire and the King's equal subjects, if you wish to enable us to help you to facilitate and stimulate recruitment.'

A public meeting was held subsequently in Bombay, with Gandhi in the chair. Jinnah participated in this meeting. Gandhi protested against the behaviour of the Governor in the War Conference. On 11 December 1918, a memorial meeting was organized by the citizens of Bombay in the Town Hall for the departing Governor Lord Willingdon. Jinnah along with others was in the Town Hall to register their protest against honouring Willingdon. In the scuffle that ensued, Jinnah is believed to have been roughly handled. To commemorate this event, funds were collected from Hindus, Muslims, and Parsis and a memorial hall was built in the Congress House compound. It was named as 'Jinnah's Memorial People's Hall'. Annie Besant inaugurated it. However, Gandhi wrote to Jinnah, Besant, and Surendra Nath Banerji that a Home Ruler must save the Empire in order to approach *Swaraj*. They did not endorse Gandhi's view. Gandhi became a Recruiting Sergeant for the First World War. He believed that *Swaraj* could be won by participating in the defence of the empire.[33] Jinnah was probably unaware at this juncture that Gandhi was making his presence felt in the Congress and it was bound to increase in future, especially due to the absence of Tilak who made his way to London.

UNITED PROVINCES MUSLIMS' INTERESTS AND THE LUCKNOW PACT

In October 1916, 19 members of the Imperial Legislative Council presented the Viceroy Lord Chelmsford a memorandum demanding a reform of the constitution. Immediately the Muslim members came forward with a number of demands like the creation of separate representation for Muslims in the Punjab, fixing the numerical strength of the Muslim representation in the Provincial and Imperial Legislative Councils, and safeguards against legislation affecting Muslims, their religion, and culture. Jinnah, who was a member of the Council and a signatory of the memorandum, jumped earnestly into the fray to find a solution to the Muslim demands.

On 21 October 1916, the Bombay Provincial Political Conference was held at Ahmedabad. Jinnah presided the conference and spoke in favour of the memorandum of the 19 elected members. It was on this occasion that Sarojini Naidu described Jinnah as the Ambassador of Hindu–Muslim unity. She described him as 'tall and stately, but thin to the point of emaciation, languid and luxurious by habit'.[34] She however never gave thought to the simple fact that the same Jinnah who was advocating Hindu–Muslim unity, was also at the same time straining his nerves to see to it that Muslim interests were not sacrificed at the altar of this unity.

At a joint conference of the League Reforms Committee and the All India Congress Committee presided by Surendra Nath Banerji held at Calcutta on 17–18 November 1916, a 'Reform Scheme' was adopted. It was Fazlul Haq and not Jinnah who conveyed the contents of this Reform Scheme to Mohammad Ali in custody. We have already seen that the Hindu–Muslim rapprochement at Bombay was due to the Ali brothers, Maulana Mazharul Haque, and Maulana Hasrat Mohani of Lucknow. Jinnah joined this group only later. In December 1916, the 'Young Party' members within the League decided to elect M.A. Jinnah as the President of the party at the League Session held along with the Congress annual session at Lucknow, in the United Provinces, where Muslims were a minority. Jinnah sported a red *fez* during the session. The Lucknow session was attended by 2,301 delegates. Extremists like Tilak and Khaparde were seated side-by-side with moderates like Rash Behari Bose and Surendra Nath Banerji. Gandhi was also there. Among the Muslims the most prominent were Jinnah, the Raja of Mahmudabad, and Maulana Mazharul Haque. It was a session dominated by the Muslim leaders of the UP who were hell bent upon protecting and promoting the interests of the Muslims, especially in the minority provinces. Jinnah hailing from the Muslim-minority province of Bombay, where he was

President of the Home Rule League, seems to have shared the worries of the UP Muslims in the evolving political scenario. Jinnah also being a member of the Congress had already opened negotiations with some Congress leaders like Tej Bahadur Sapru, Motilal Nehru, and Madan Mohan Malaviya of the UP had thrashed out an agreement, which aimed to obtain Dominion status for India within the empire. The agreement focussed more on the protection and promotion of the interests of the Muslims of the Muslim-minority provinces, especially the UP. In this he seemed to have been very much inspired by the earlier resolutions of Mohammad Ali. From the Muslim League's side, apart from M.A. Jinnah, A.K. Fazlul Huq (1873–1962), a lawyer of Bengal was also one of the key negotiators of the Pact. He was one of the founders of the Muslim League at Dacca. He served as President of the League from 1913 till 1919; at the same time he was a member of the Congress.[35]

By the Pact, the Congress including Tilak recognized Muslims' right to separate electorates while demanding representative government elected on a broad franchise. But the Muslims, especially of the Muslim-minority provinces, obtained many generous concessions from the Hindus both in the Central and provincial Legislative Councils. In the Punjab, they were to get 50 per cent of the Indian seats, in Bengal 40 per cent, in the United Provinces 30 per cent, in Bihar 26 per cent, Bombay 33 per cent, and Madras 15 per cent. Although the Muslims secured more representation in the Legislative Councils than their share in the total population in the Muslim-minority provinces as in the United Provinces and Madras, yet in the Punjab and Bengal, Muslims were given a lower share than what was warranted by their population. Thus, the Muslims were not in a majority in any province, not even in the Muslim-majority provinces of Bengal and the Punjab.[36]

It was quite obvious that the Pact was dictated more by the interests of the UP Muslim League leaders like Syed Wazir Hasan and the Raja of Mahmudabad in particular and the Muslims of the Muslim-minority provinces in general. It would seem, at this juncture, that Jinnah had succumbed to the pressures wielded by the UP Muslim leaders, who were largely responsible for making him the president of the League Session in order to promote their provincial elite interests.[37] It is also quite obvious that the Congress, which was open to all Indians including the Muslims had gone a long way to meet the demands of the League Muslims through the Pact.

The signing of the Pact prompted some Congress stalwarts like Sarojini Naidu to shower encomiums on Jinnah as the 'embodied symbol of the Hindu–Muslim unity' and as a 'great-hearted Prince of Indian Nationalists'. Naidu even called him as the 'Muslim Gokhale'. Others thought, he was Gokhale's heir. Even Tilak hailed the Pact and wanted to give the Muslims all that they wanted, for the sake of a united front against the British. Thus Tilak repaid Jinnah for his role in getting him back into the Congress. However, Gandhi, the new entrant in Indian politics did not evince any interest in the Pact. Jinnah obtained a certain all-India stature through this Pact. Jinnah even used threatening words against the critics of the Pact. He said:

> Do you think that in the first instance it is possible that the Government of this country can become a Hindu Government? ... If 70 million Musalmans do not approve of the measure which is carried by a ballot box, do you think that it could be enforced or administered in this country? (Cries of 'No') ... Therefore I say to my Musalman friends: Fear not.[38]

It is clear from the preceding paragraph that Jinnah was convinced that the Hindus cannot govern the country without the cooperation of the Muslims. What, of course, was forgotten in the process was that Jinnah had negotiated the Pact in his capacity as President of the Lucknow session of the Muslim League, an exclusively Muslim party. Besides, he had ruled out any merger of the League with the Congress even before the signing of the Pact. Another factor which seems to have been completely ignored by many historians from Pakistan, especially Riaz Ahmad is that the

Lucknow Pact was not due to the efforts of Jinnah alone, but a collective effort, inspired primarily by the Ali brothers, and in which other Muslim stalwarts like Maulana Mazharul Haque, Hasrat Mohani, and Fazlul Huq had played significant roles.

Of course, we cannot expect Sarojini Naidu and those who write history on the basis of her accounts, to be aware of the roles played by these gentlemen, who owed allegiance both to the League and to the Congress. Jinnah simply followed their footsteps in politics. But in the end Jinnah ignored their contributions towards the conclusion of the Lucknow Pact. Earlier he had altered his conviction and accepted separate electorates for Muslims benefitted from it.

The Pact was denounced by the old guard of the League, who were mostly loyalists. Sayyid Husain Bilgrami, the author of the memorandum of 1906 was not happy with the emphasis on self-government in the Pact and feared that it would lead to Indians being ruled by men 'of very low birth like Mr Jinnah'.[39] It is true that from the point of view of the Ashraf class of Muslims like Bilgrami, Jinnah being a descendant of Gujarati Lohana converts and was the first *ajlaf* to make inroads into the top leadership of the League, undermining the 'natural leadership' status of the Ashrafs. Others of the Ashraf class like Nawab Ali Chaudhuri and Sir Abdur Rahim of Bengal, who were members of the Muslim deputation in 1906, as well as Mian Mohammad Shafi of the Punjab denounced the Pact for disregarding the 'political importance' of the Muslims and the principle of weightage for Muslims conceded by the 1909 Act.[40]

Therefore, the old guard of the Muslim League and also the Muslim aristocracy were at variance with not only the younger elements in the League, but also the Lucknow Pact. Some others like Maulana Hasrat Mohani attacked Jinnah for his lack of knowledge of the Quran and the *Hadiths*. They accused him of being an agent of the Hindus. They said he neither looked nor behaved like a Muslim nor did he speak their language, and wondered how could such a Muslim speak on their behalf. Jinnah hardly followed Muslim customs and traditions during that period and even much later. Besides, he spoke in English most of the time. His close associate of those days Mohammad Karim Chagla had recounted in his book *Roses in December*, how Jinnah relished eating pork sausages. The old guard of the League ended up forming a new All-India Muslim Association in opposition to Jinnah's party.[41]

The Pact was not advantageous to the Muslim-majority provinces of the Punjab and Bengal, which were nevertheless peripheral provinces. The Pact was perceived with suspicion by the Muslim leaders of these two provinces as catering to the interests of the Muslim-minority provinces; Jinnah was considered as their spokesman especially in the UP. Jinnah was at the service of Muslim elite interests of the minority provinces, as he demanded more council seats for this class, much above the Muslim share in the total population. He was never known to be preoccupied with the problems of the large majority of the Muslim masses, especially their backwardness and poverty. His demands on behalf of the elite interests of the minority provinces were not conducive to the Muslim elite interests in the Punjab and Bengal. That is why the All-India Muslim League failed to strike strong roots in these provinces where provincial Muslim parties saw the light. Jinnah had to struggle for years to get himself accepted as the leader of the Muslims of these provinces. Fazl-i Husain of the Unionist Party of the Punjab, which was an alliance of the Sikh–Hindu–Muslim landed gentry, would never want to submit to Jinnah's dictates until his death.

With regard to the Congress Session at Lucknow in the year 1916, the upcoming leader of the Congress, Jawaharlal Nehru conceded that 'the Congress had always clung to a national basis, but in effect it was predominantly a Hindu organization because of the overwhelming majority of the Hindus in it'.[42] However, there was nothing in the Lucknow Pact which officially recognized the Muslim League as the only authoritative spokesman of the Muslims of India. As admitted by Jinnah himself, the League was 'the chief representative of the Muslims of India'. He never claimed that it was the only representative of the Muslims of

India. His legal mind would not permit that. Similarly the Congress was the chief representative of the Hindus of India according to Jinnah. In his presidential speech on 30 December 1916 at Lucknow, Jinnah who had in 1906 dismissed the Muslim League as unrepresentative, now sang a different tune and claimed that the party was founded for 'the retention of Muslim communal individuality, strong and unimpaired in any constitutional re-adjustment that might be made in India in the course of its political evolution.'[43] In any case, the new breed of leaders gathering around Gandhi like Jawaharlal Nehru, Rajendra Prasad, C. Rajagopalachari, Vallabhbhai Patel, and Gandhi himself never accepted the League as the only representative of the Muslims. More than anyone else, Jinnah knew that. Neither did the British have any reason to do that as the League and the Congress had actually joined hands through the Lucknow Pact, as warned earlier by the Aga Khan, to present a united front to the British.

The Lucknow Pact was made possible because of a leadership vacuum in the Congress which was undergoing a transition period, caused mainly by the death of Gokhale and Mehta. Gandhi was still not very much in the picture. Jinnah seems to have made use of this opportunity to strike a deal with lesser leaders of the Congress like Tej Bahadur Sapru. He also had the support of Tilak, who is believed to have played a role in the framing of the Pact. The Congress was under no pressure to negotiate a settlement with Jinnah on the communal issue. But still it did negotiate mainly due to the double role played by Jinnah and some other Muslim leaders like Maulana Mazharul Haque. By concluding the Lucknow Pact with Jinnah, the Congress seemed to have raised Jinnah's status in Indian politics and among the Muslims in general. It conveyed the message to everyone including the British that the League was still the most important political organization of the Muslims and that the Congress had recognized it. It even set a precedent that in any future negotiations on communal issues, the Congress had to deal with the Muslim League and Jinnah.

JINNAH FALLS IN LOVE

Probably while Jinnah negotiated the Lucknow Pact or after that, he had time to fall in love with Rattanbai or Ruttie, a Parsi girl, 24 years younger to himself. She was born on 20 February 1900. We have already seen that Jinnah had many westernized Parsi friends in Bombay. One such wealthy friend was Dinshaw Petit, a leading Bombay businessman. Jinnah frequented the Petits and other Parsis at the Parsi club quite often. Jinnah was also a frequent guest of the Petits. They had a beautiful daughter called Rattanbai. Though he was married before he left for London in 1892, he never lived with his wife as she passed away while he was in London. Since then he is not known to have befriended anyone of the fair sex. He was already 41, but still charming enough to befriend young and vivacious Rattanbai or Ruttie, as she was fondly called.

The Petits never minded Jinnah befriending their daughter. But when Jinnah announced his intention of marrying Ruttie to Dinshaw Petit during 1916–17, all hell broke lose. Ruttie defied her parents and married Jinnah on 19 April 1918 in spite of severe opposition from them. She was never destined to see her father again. The Shia aristocrat, Raja of Mahmudabad, who had by then become a close friend of Jinnah, signed the marriage contract on Jinnah's behalf. The ring which Jinnah gave to his wife on the wedding day was a gift by the Raja. Jinnah spent his honeymoon at the Raja's house in Nainital.

Ruttie nominally converted to Shia Islam before marriage and went to live with Jinnah in his house in Bombay at Mount Pleasant Road. She took the Muslim name Maryam, which she never used. Jinnah never objected to it. They had a daughter by the name of Dina in the month of August 1919. She was Jinnah's only daughter. She was born in London where Jinnah had gone to give evidence before the Joint Select Committee of the Parliament on the Montagu Bill.

Ruttie sometimes participated in Jinnah's political activities. She was there when Jinnah protested against Governor Willingdon in Bombay. Ruttie even assisted Jinnah in the protest against the farewell ceremony organized by the citizens of Bombay to Lord Willingdon. It must be remembered at this juncture that Jinnah had a previous misunderstanding with the Willingdons, when they were invited to dine with them. Ruttie had worn a revealing low-cut dress for the dinner. Lady Willingdon made it obvious that she did not approve Ruttie's style of dressing. But Jinnah was unhappy with the remark of Lady Willingdon and abruptly left the dining table along with Ruttie, deciding never to return again to the Governor's Residence. Jinnah's social life during that time seemed to have been mostly with his wife's Parsi friends.

Later Ruttie went to Shimla with Jinnah where the latter attended the Indian Legislative Assembly. Ruttie even dabbled with Annie Besant's Theosophical Society for some time. Jinnah never objected to it. Instead, when Jinnah found time, she went with him to spend some time in Kashmir.

The years 1918–19 were a pleasant interlude in Jinnah's political career. This was at a time when the First World War ended and the Muslim League had gone almost out of action. By 1919, the League's membership was a mere 777. Besides four out of the six League council meetings was adjourned for lack of quorum.[44] Jinnah seemed not to have cared much about the dwindling fortunes of the League during that period when he was romancing with Ruttie. Ruttie had even accompanied Jinnah to the famous Nagpur Session of the Congress held in late 1920.[45] Politics always remained the first love of Jinnah. Ruttie learned about it very soon when she was left to languish, while Jinnah plunged headlong into the thick of politics during the 1920s.

BIDDING ADIEU TO CONGRESS

On 5 August 1917, Jinnah was elected as the first President of the Muslim Students Wing of Bombay. On 20 August 1917, the Secretary of State for India, Lord Montagu declared in the House of Commons that his Liberal Party intended to gradually take India towards responsible self-government. Montagu himself came to India in November 1917. Jinnah met him on several occasions to press for reforms on behalf of the Home Rule Leagues, the Congress, the Muslim League, and also in his individual capacity. Lord Montagu was full of admiration and praise for Jinnah's sterling qualities. However, Jinnah stressed for reforms sometimes in the most inappropriate of the places like during the War Conference held at Delhi by Lord Chelmsford on 30 April 1918, in support of British War efforts. He had also brought up this topic during the garden party organized in honour of Gandhi in 1915 on his return from South Africa. In the Calcutta Congress Session presided by Annie Besant, Jinnah seconded a resolution for self-government.[1] During that period, the Aga Khan proposed to separate Sind from the Bombay Presidency and amalgamate it with the North-West Frontier Province and Baluchistan to form the Indus province with Quetta as capital. But nobody including Jinnah paid heed to it.[2]

This was followed by the *Montagu–Chelmsford Report* of 1918 and the Government of India Act of 1919, which created a bicameral system at the Centre, with a Council of State and Legislative Assembly. At the provincial level a system of dual government (dyarchy) was founded with enlarged provincial Councils and an extended electorate of about 3 per cent of the population, based on a property qualification, the payment of land revenue in the rural areas, of income or house tax in the towns, and some special qualifications like the possession of a university degree. Some departments like education, agriculture, local bodies, and health were transferred to the provincial councils and its ministers; while the other departments like finance, and law and order were reserved subjects for officials and governors who enjoyed a veto. The Legislative Assembly consisted of 145 members of which 105 were elected and 40 nominated. The total members in the Council of State were 60 of whom 34 were elected and 26 nominated. The total proportion of Muslim seats was fixed in accordance with the Lucknow Pact.

Separate electorates were maintained for the Muslims and extended to the Sikhs in the Punjab, the Europeans, the Anglo-Indians, and the Indian Christians. Moreover, the Muslims in the minority provinces got some weightage, but not in Punjab and Bengal where they were in a majority. These measures were also, no doubt, inspired by the Lucknow Pact. Under the Act, indirect election was replaced by direct election, and the proportion of elected members in the provincial councils was raised to at least 70 per cent. There was however no talk of conceding Dominion status to India in the Act of 1919 as demanded by the Lucknow Pact or the Home Rule League. But provision was made for the institution of a statutory commission after 10 years to examine the working of the new constitution and advice on further self-government.[3] The 1919 Act confirmed that democracy would be introduced in India in small doses from the above. Only 3 per cent of the population was enfranchized by the Act. Consequently an elite voting system, based on property, qualification, and income was devised, providing only for elite participation in politics and the race for political power. Thus, the idea of democracy that the British sought to introduce in India was framed in such a way that it always favoured the rich and the privileged, while the large mass of the population were simply left out or had no say in the governance of the country.

These developments seemed to have been enough for Annie Besant to become almost a moderate and loyalist. By September 1918, Tilak went away to England, leaving the field clear for Gandhi to try out his *Satyagraha* experiments in India. A section of the Congress under Surendra Nath Banerji agreed to accept the Mont–Ford Reforms. The Bombay Home Rule League under the Presidency of Jinnah became inactive. Besides, in the Delhi session of the Muslim League held in December 1918, some radical politicians like M.A. Ansari—who was active in the Home Rule League of Delhi, supported by Farangi Mahall's Abdul Bari—captured the League from moderates like Syed Wazir Hasan and the Raja of Mahmudabad, who wanted to work in the 1919 reforms, and steered it towards Gandhi. After a meeting with Gandhi in mid-March 1919, Abdul Bari himself came out in support of Gandhi's agitation against the Rowlatt Act, which curbed civil rights. Jinnah along with others like Surendra Nath Banerji, Madan Mohan Malaviya, and the Raja of Mahmudabad wanted to postpone the introduction of the Rowlatt Bill. He even thought that the 1919 reforms were not substantial enough for Home Rule, though much that had been demanded by the Lucknow Pact had been granted by the reforms and he had reasons to be happy about it. But then he decided to raise his pitch a bit and asked for a little more. He stood thenceforth for some form of dyarchy in the Centre and for autonomy in the provinces, where Muslims' interests will be safeguarded. He was never someone who was above communal considerations, in all his demands for more political concessions or for self-rule.[4]

Jinnah watched with bewilderment the spectacular rise of Gandhi in Indian politics—who was just six years elder to him—with his new methods of non-violent agitation called *Satyagraha*. Gandhi called for an all-India *hartal* (strike) on 30 March and 6 April 1919 to protest against the Rowlatt Act, which restricted civil rights. Gandhi toured the whole of India to mobilize the masses for the hartal. Hakim Ajmal Khan was one of the leaders of the agitation in Delhi. This new form of non-violent agitation on a national scale attracted the general mass more and more towards Gandhi and the Congress. A new form of defiance against British rule was developing. Jinnah too resigned from the Viceroy's Council to protest against the Rowlatt's Act.[5] But nobody took note of it.

On 13 April 1919, General Dyer ordered his troops to open fire on unarmed civilians in an enclosed ground in Jallianwalabagh in the Punjab. 379 people were killed. This created a furore all over India. It was in this background that the Amritsar Congress Session took place. Motilal Nehru presided the session. It was attended by M.A. Jinnah, Madan Mohan Malaviya, Annie Besant, Tilak, C.R. Das and M.K. Gandhi. But the Rowlatt Satyagraha had set the stage for Gandhi to launch the Non-Cooperation Movement, which involved the boycott of the councils, colleges, courts, and government jobs. By 1919–1920 Gandhi's supremacy in the Congress had become unassailable. The Congressmen who wanted to work out the reforms like Tej Bahadur Sapru and M.R. Jayakar had to leave the party to form the National Liberal Association. Surendra Nath Banerji too was in favour of the reforms. Tilak's followers and the Bengal group under C.R. Das and even Motilal Nehru were not strong enough to counter Gandhi.

Besides, during that period, many of Jinnah's colleagues in the Muslim League like Mohammad Ali and Dr Ansari were more interested in the fate of Turkey and Khilafat and were drawing themselves closer to the Congress to confront the British. Mohammad Ali, who became a Maulana from that period onwards, led a Muslim delegation to Paris in March 1920 to plead for the retention of the Caliphate and the Turkish Sultan. In Bombay, the Central Khilafat Committee was formed to fight for the Turkish cause. The Ali brothers had embarked upon a confrontational course, by calling for hartals and non-cooperation since the All India Khilafat Conference held at Delhi on 22–23 November 1919 which gave birth to the All India Khilafat Committee. In this they had the support of Maulana Abul Kalam Azad, Hakim Ajmal Khan, Asaf Ali, Hasrat Mohani, Abdul Bari, and Dr M.A. Ansari.[6]

The twelfth All-India Muslim League Session took place in Amritsar during 29–30 December 1919 and on 1 January 1920 in a hall known as 'Vande Mataram'. Among those present were M.K. Gandhi, Motilal Nehru, Madan Mohan Malaviya, M.A. Jinnah, and M.A. Ansari. The Ali brothers entered the hall with the cries of 'Allaho Akbar'. Mohammad Ali thundered: 'There was no government except the Government of God'. Jinnah declared that the League was concerned with the political consolidation of the Muslims.[7]

On 19 January 1920, a Khilafat Deputation met the Viceroy at Delhi. Among the signatories and supporters were M.K. Gandhi, M.A. Jinnah, Madan Mohan Malaviya, M.A. Ansari, Hakim Ajmal Khan, Abdul Bari, Hasrat Mohani, and the Raja of Mahmudabad. A month later on 18 February 1920, Jinnah, being a Khoja, was invited to preside the annual Social Gathering of the *Young Khoja Brotherhood* of Bombay. In his speech, Jinnah said:

> ...the Khoja community could not be divided from the rest of the Mahomedan community. In the past whether in municipal matters or Legislative Councils the representatives of the Mahomedan community were mostly Khojas because of their position and education....

He further asked the Khojas to wake up and not be clannish. The publication of the Treaty of Sèvres on 14 May 1920 which confirmed the dismemberment of the Ottoman Empire radicalized still further the Khilafatists who stood for the retention of the Turkish Sultan and the Caliphate. At a meeting at Calcutta held on 7 September 1920 in the presence of Gandhi, Jinnah considered the treaty as a death warrant while Gandhi branded it as 'crime against humanity'. But Jinnah did not come out openly in favour of the Khilafat. Nether did he endorse Gandhi's non-cooperation unequivocally, following the Ali brothers, though he denounced the post-war reforms and the Rowlatt Act.[8]

All the preceding events led to the joining of hands of the Congress under Mahatma Gandhi and the Khilafatists led by the Ali brothers, and the joint launching of the Khilafat and Non-Cooperation Movements against British rule, which involved surrendering of titles, boycotting of the legislatures, schools, courts, and foreign goods. The Congress and the

Khilafatists boycotted the elections held in November 1920 under the 1919 Act to the provincial councils and the Central Legislature. Mohammad Ali seems to have thought during that period that the Khilafat Committee was the representative organization of all Indian Muslims. Only a third of the electorate voted, which is a very small number of the elite voters. This brought to power Fazl-i Husain's Unionist Party in the Punjab and the Justice Party in Madras. The former party was an alliance of the Hindu, Sikh and Muslim landed gentry of the Punjab, while the latter party was an exclusively non-Brahmin elite party of zamindars and merchants.

Maulana Mohammad Ali and Hasrat Mohani like Shah Waliullah in the eighteenth century were not averse to the invasion of India by the Amir of Afghanistan and asked the Indian Muslims to join the Afghans in the fight for Islam. But when thousands of Muslims primarily from Sind and the NWFP tried to enter Afghanistan which was *Dar-ul-Islam*, in order to flee the 'impious' Raj of the British, they were stopped by the Afghans. By 1920, it became evident that Afghanistan, a neighbouring Muslim country would not admit Indian Muslims into their country.[9] That was the first setback to the pan-Islamic Khilafat Movement and Islamic solidarity; Khilafat agitation continued in full swing in India.

Contrary to Gandhi or even Maulana Mohammad Ali, Jinnah was never a charismatic mass leader. He remained highly westernized and never knew how to connect with the general public. He had never led any agitation against the British for self-government or freedom. His role was limited to passing resolutions and devising pacts and schemes for a measure of self-government, but never for outright independence. He had never gone to prison. His support to the Turkish cause was also much muted. Jinnah realized that Gandhi, who entered Indian politics about a decade later than him, was stealing the show in Indian politics right under his nose.

On the Muslim side, Maulana Mohammad Ali was looming larger than ever, overshadowing other Muslim leaders including Jinnah during that period. In the provinces like Punjab and Bengal, provincial-based

Muslim parties came into existence due to the 1919 Reforms Act of enlarged Councils, which restricted the role of the League as an all-India party. But Jinnah could do nothing as he was still having one leg in the Congress and the other in the League, with no mass following. Jinnah at this juncture found that he was unwanted and politically isolated. The League itself had lost steam in Indian politics. Naturally Jinnah reacted. First he withdrew from the Home Rule League along with 18 others like Jayakar, Kanji Dwarkadas, and K.M. Munshi, on the pretext that Gandhi, who had become the President of the Home Rule League, had changed the League's object from Dominion status to *Swaraj* and its name to *Swaraj Sabha* during the Home Rule meeting of 3 October 1920, attended by Motilal Nehru and Ali brothers. In fact, on 22 September 1920 Gandhi had promised *Swaraj* in one year through peaceful means. But Jinnah wanted *Swaraj* through constitutional means; unlike Gandhi, he wanted to maintain the British connection with India.[10]

However at the meeting of the Bombay Congress Provincial Committee held on 28 November 1920, 20 members were elected for the All India Congress Committee. Among them were M.K. Gandhi, M.A. Jinnah, M.R. Jayakar, and Vallabhbhai Patel. In his speech at Fergusson College of Poona, Jinnah forcefully came out against Gandhi's Non-Cooperation programme of boycotting schools and colleges, Councils, and foreign cloth.[11]

Later in the year, Jinnah decided to leave the Congress probably because he was unable to counter the hold of Mahatma Gandhi on the Congress and the masses, and his preference for the Ali brothers. The Ali brothers turned against Jinnah due to his opposition to Khilafat and his preference for constitutional means at the Nagpur session of the Congress in December 1920, which was attended by 14,000 delegates. M.A. Ansari moved a resolution at the Nagpur session affirming League's support for non-cooperation, in the presence of Jinnah. The session was attended by a great number of Muslims who supported the Ali brothers and Gandhi, but not Jinnah. During his speech at the session, Jinnah, dressed in his usual impeccable western attire, was shouted down several times by the vast multitudes, for not mentioning Gandhi as 'Mahatma Gandhi' and Mohammad Ali as 'Maulana Mohammad Ali'. Jinnah maintained that Gandhi and Mohammad Ali cannot obtain *Swaraj* by peaceful methods. He challenged them by saying: '...you will never get your independence without bloodshed' and asked him (Gandhi) to call off his movement.[12]

We do not know at this juncture what Jinnah meant when he asserted that independence cannot be got without bloodshed. It is simply incomprehensible that Jinnah who was reputed to be a constitutionalist, envisaged violence and bloodshed for attaining independence.

In the meantime, on 1 August 1920, Tilak, who disapproved Gandhi's methods in getting his Non-Cooperation Movement mixed up with the Khilafat issue, passed away, leaving Jinnah almost alone and the Congress fully in Gandhi's hands. Jinnah considered Tilak as 'a shrewd practical politician', unlike Gandhi. In fact, Jinnah left the Congress not because of any difference of opinion on the Hindu–Muslim question, but because he was not able to adapt himself to the new environment in the Congress under Gandhi, where he had to mingle with crowds dressed in Indian attire talking in Hindustani. He was used to the constitutional politics of the Legislative chambers and committee rooms, that is, elite politics and was totally unprepared for the Gandhian way of indulging in mass politics. Gandhi was only a few years elder to him. But in Indian politics, Jinnah was senior to Gandhi. He definitely could not countenance the fact that a late entrant into Indian politics could dominate the Congress in a few years, whereas he was being literally forced to play second fiddle to him. All these developments pushed him out of the Congress.

It is not right to claim that Gandhi wilfully pushed Jinnah out of the Congress. Gandhi simply followed his methods and pattern in politics. Jinnah did not want to fit into this pattern unlike many of his other colleagues in the League like Ansari. As a result, he had no alternative but to remove one of his legs from the Congress boat, so that he could have both his legs in the All-India Muslim League boat. By not coming out in support of the Khilafat and Non-Cooperation Movements, Jinnah proved to the whole world that the League was still a loyalist outfit, as during that time when the Aga Khan was President, not willing to engage in a show-down with the British.[13]

Jinnah was least worried about Indian-Muslim sentiments with regard to the safety of the *Kaaba* and the danger of it going into infidel hands. Very much like the Aga Khan, Jinnah did not support the Turkish Sultan when he called for *Jihad* or Holy War against the British. Another Muslim personality who stood aloof from the Khilafat Movement was the poet Muhammad Iqbal of the Punjab. He even accepted the knighthood awarded to him by the British during that period. Unlike Iqbal, Jinnah was more cautious when he refused to accept the knighthood conferred on him a couple of years later by Lord Reading.[14] The British would have, of course, taken note of all this.

Some scholars argue that the Khilafat was a purely religious movement, which had nothing to do with politics. They say that Gandhi by joining hands with the Khilafatists had mixed religion with politics. They give this as a reason for Jinnah not joining the movement.[15] They also argue that Jinnah being secular and westernized could not join or endorse a religious movement, forgetting that Jinnah was now having both the legs in a religion-based party, the All-India Muslim League. But what they seem to have forgotten is that the Turkish Sultan was actually fighting for the survival of his political empire, the last remaining Muslim empire in the world. Besides, the Turkish Sultan being the Caliph of the world Muslims and the protector of the Muslim holy places had a political dimension couched in religiosity. Maulana Abul Kalam Azad had held that the Caliphate was the political centre of the Muslim world. So the political weakening and the ultimate dismantling of the Ottoman Empire would endanger not just the existence of the Turkish Sultan, but also his Caliphate. Gandhi was aware of the political dimension and the consequences of the dismantling of the Ottoman Empire, which will be favourable to the reinforcement of British colonialism in the Middle-east and Asia. The Khilafat Movement was a political movement which had a religious pan-Islamist implication. Agitating for the maintenance of the Caliphate was the same as agitating for the maintenance of the Turkish Sultan and his empire.[16]

Gandhi could not agitate directly in support of the Turkish Sultan and his empire, especially when Turkey had allied with Germany during the First World War against the British. That would have been high treason. He chose the next best solution, that is, to agitate for the maintenance of the Turkish Caliphate, in support of the Indian Muslims, who, during that period in their great majority were more agitated and preoccupied by the fate of Turkey and Arabia than about the political problems of their native country. So the argument that Jinnah stood aloof from the Khilafat Movement because Gandhi was mixing religion with politics does not hold water. It was just a pretext for Jinnah to oppose Gandhi or may be, he simply did not understand the political implications of the Khilafat Movement, which involved the demise of the Turkish Empire, the last surviving Muslim Empire. Jinnah was never a convinced Khilafatist nor was he a pan-Islamist during that period; though later he changed his stripes.

Jinnah's stand was like that of Sir Sayyid Ahmad Khan during the last quarter of the nineteenth century, who maintained that Indian Muslims were obliged by law to be loyal, not to any Muslim potentate but to their British masters in India. Khan even contended that the true Caliphate had ceased to exist after the death of the fourth Caliph Ali in AD 661 and therefore, the Turkish Sultan not belonging to the Prophet's tribe was not entitled to be Caliph. Jinnah by staying aloof from the Khilafat Movement indirectly owed allegiance to the British, unlike Sir Sayyid who openly called the Muslims to be loyal to the British. Jinnah also disliked *ulama* participation in politics, especially those of the *Jamiyyat al-Ulama-i-Hind* (founded in 1919) and the Farangi Mahallis of Lucknow, who had come out openly in support of the Khilafat and Non-Cooperation Movements.[17]

In spite of leaving the Congress, Jinnah attended the second session of the All India Khilafat Conference at Amritsar on 31 December 1920. Gandhi, Annie Besant, Abdul Bari, M.A. Ansari, and Maulana Mohammad Ali were also present in the conference. In June 1921, Jinnah visited England and lobbied there for a constitutional response to Gandhi's activities. During the Ahmedabad Congress Session in December 1921, when the Khilafat leader Hasrat Mohani called for complete independence of India, Gandhi did not support it. Jinnah did meet Gandhi in Ahmedabad at that time and also later in a conference on 14 January 1922, when he moved a resolution in favour of convening a Round Table Conference. Gandhi, plunged in the Non-Cooperation Movement had nothing of it.[18] Hasrat Mohani, President of the League, made the plea for the declaration of an Indian Republic at the League Session of December 1921, in the presence of Jinnah. Jinnah did not take notice of it. Gandhi and Mohammad Ali became the undisputed leaders of Indians—both Hindus and Muslms, during that period. Jinnah was out of the picture. The British were in a quandary about how to deal with the agitators.

In the year 1921, Mappila Muslims of Kerala, inspired by the Khilafat Movement and the fiery speeches of leaders like Maulana Abul Kalam Azad and Hakim Ajmal Khan, revolted against the British and the Hindu landlords. The British reacted violently. By late 1921, 2,337 rebels were killed, 1,652 wounded, and about 45,000 arrested. Many Hindus were converted to Islam by force, in total disregard of the Hindu–Muslim unity that prevailed in other parts of India.[19] But Mahatma Gandhi did not think it necessary to suspend the Civil Disobedience Movement at this juncture because of the violence. An All Parties' Conference held at Bombay in mid-January 1922 in which Jinnah participated, condemned the repressive policy of the government and demanded a Round Table Conference. Jinnah, Malaviya, and other moderates met Gandhi at that time. It was of no avail.[20]

But on 5 February 1922 when at Chauri Chaura in Gorakhpur district of the UP, 22 policemen were killed by the peasant agitators,

Mahatma Gandhi suspended the agitation unilaterally. In March 1922, Gandhi was arrested on a charge of sedition. Many Congress leaders, the Ali brothers, and the Muslims in general were completely disillusioned by Gandhi's volte face. However, in the year 1923, Maulana Mohammad Ali presided the Kakinada Congress Session, only to leave the Congress party altogether in the course of time. But Maulana Abul Kalam Azad, Dr M.A. Ansari, and Hakim Ajmal Khan went along with the Congress party and Mahatma Gandhi.

Gandhi's volte face was followed by serious Hindu–Muslim riots in some parts of northern India.[21] This led to the foundation of *shuddhi* and *sangathan* movements to bring the Hindus back into the Hindu fold, who were earlier converted to Islam. Some Muslims, on their part, started the *tabligh* and *tanzim* movements to counter the Hindu revivalist movements. Gandhi remained aloof from these movements, which was purely religious in nature. Meanwhile, the Khilafatists were in for a greater shock when Kemal Pasha Ataturk abolished the Turkish Caliphate in March 1924. That put an end to the Khilafat Movement though the Khilafat Committee continued to function for some more years.

Men like Mohammad Ali never understood the secular nationalistic credentials of Kemal Ataturk. Neither did they understand the rise of Arab nationalism, which wanted to get rid of Turkish hegemony. The rise of nationalism in the Middle-east never fitted into the pan-Islamic vision of the Indian Khilafatists. They ran after the illusion of world Islamic solidarity, without ever realizing that the rise of nationalisms in Asia against colonial rule was militating against such solidarity.

Gandhi's Non-Cooperation Movement aimed at the British government had contributed to the rise of the feeling and idea of Indian nationalism among the masses of India, irrespective of caste and creed. But the same could not be said of the politico-religious Khilafat Movement which agitated for an extra-national and extraterritorial issue. It seemed to have awakened the religious identity of the Muslim masses to a great extent rather than their national identity. It was indeed a rude shock for them to know that in spite of their agitations, the Khilafat had been abolished by secular-minded Muslims in Turkey and the Ottoman Empire had been dismantled by none other than the British colonialists. They never really sought to understand the rise of nationalisms in the Middle-east, which overrode Islamic solidarity. All these events seemed to have destabilized them thoroughly and driven them inwards, and had prevented them from taking part in greater numbers in the rise of Indian nationalism of the Congress brand.

TOWARDS DELHI PROPOSALS

In March 1923, there was an internal split in the Congress party when Gandhi was in prison—between those who wanted to contest the elections in November 1923 and those who wanted to maintain the status quo. The former group known as Swarajists was led by Motilal Nehru, Hakim Ajmal Khan, C.R. Das, and Chaudhry Khaliquzzaman, while the latter group was headed by Rajagopalachari, Dr Ansari, Rajendra Prasad, and Vallabhbhai Patel. A compromise was struck at the Kakinada session of the Congress presided by Maulana Mohammad Ali, in which Congressmen were allowed to stand for elections even while faith in the constructive programme of Gandhi was reiterated. A generous inter-communal agreement in favour of the Bengal Muslims was negotiated by C.R. Das with Bengali Muslim leaders like Husayn Suhrawardy and Abdul Karim, known as the Bengal Pact. It was rejected by the Congress party due to opposition from Madan Mohan Malaviya and Lala Lajpat Rai, in spite of the efforts of Mohammad Ali to get it adopted.[22] Besides, Muslim Swarajists like Chaudhry Khaliquzzaman opposed the Khilafat Committee's pre-occupation with Pan-Islamic issues. But Mohammad Ali thought that the Congress was siding with communalist forces.[23] That situation was favourable to Jinnah who had always opposed the Khilafat Committee where the Ali brothers dominated. Actually the break in the Congress party brought Jinnah closer to the Swarajists.

Jinnah contested the 1923 elections to the Central Legislative Assembly as an independent candidate from Bombay Muslim constituency. The Swarajya party supported him. He was elected unopposed. He became leader of the Independent party consisting of 22 members in the Assembly. The Swarajists had 42 members. Motilal Nehru was their leader. Jinnah participated actively in the deliberations of the Assembly. He expressed his views off and on in favour of a measure of self-government. He supported the Swarajists' stand on many issues, which was a headache for the government. But he disliked Motilal Nehru's intention to destroy the legislatures from within, as it was anti-constitutional. Besides, at the Lucknow session of the League in 1923, Jinnah was at loggerheads with leaders like the Ali brothers and M.A. Ansari.[24]

It was during that period that Jinnah was thoroughly opposed to the rise of Gandhi in the Congress party and his non-violent programme for *Swaraj*. Gandhi grudgingly admitted that 'the result of the struggle of the last three years has this to our credit that there is an open movement for the achievement for *Swaraj* for India.' He made this statement in spite of the fact that Jinnah himself was not part of the struggle and openly opposed it. Jinnah expressed concern over Gandhi's health at Yerawada Jail where he was operated for appendicitis. He even tabled a resolution at the Indian Legislative Assembly demanding Gandhi's release. Gandhi was duly released on 5 February 1924. However, the split in the Congress drew Jinnah closer to the Swarajist faction of the Congress, but not Gandhi.[25]

In a debate in the Central Legislative Council on Motilal Nehru's proposal for a representative Round Table Conference in 1924, Jinnah while supporting the proposal had declared in his speech:

> India is not a nation, we are told. We were a people when the Great War was going on and an appeal was made to India for blood and money—We are a nation when we become a member of the League of Nations to which we had made a substantial contribution—We are not a people nor a nation when we ask you for...the establishment of responsible government and parliamentary institution in our own country.[26]

In the year 1924, Jinnah along with Motilal was invited to sit as non-official member of the Muddiman Reforms Committee. He was included in this Committee in his capacity as President of the Muslim League and leader of the Independent party in the Central Assembly. Sir Mian Muhammad Shafi, the Law Member of the Viceroy's council from the Punjab was also on the Committee. The Majority Report of the Committee consisting of 130 pages was signed by Muddiman, Sir Mian Muhammad Shafi, and others. Jinnah joined hands with liberals like Tej Bahadur Sapru and refused to sign the Majority Report. Instead, they prepared the Minority Report consisting of 74 pages where diarchy that gave some power and patronage to the provinces was criticized. They demanded provincial autonomy and responsibility in the Centre for Indians. The Minority Report was known as 'Jinnah Committee' Report due to Jinnah's involvement in it. Jinnah wanted the government to accept the Minority Report. He and the League also clamoured for the appointment of a Royal Commission. But the government was in no mood to give in to Jinnah. Later, Jinnah made it clear that he had not broached the Hindu–Muslim problem in his Minority Report as he thought that the communities could themselves settle this issue.[27]

At the Lahore session of the Muslim League in May 1924 presided by Jinnah and attended by Congress leaders like M.A. Ansari, Motilal Nehru, Annie Besant, and Vallabhbhai Patel, the League raised the demand for a weak federation with full provincial autonomy. Jinnah pleaded not only for Hindu–Muslim unity, but also for the retention of separate electorates for Muslims and demanded safeguards and reservations so that the Muslim-majority areas were protected from 'Hindu domination'. He considered the triple boycott of law courts, schools, and colleges and Councils led by Gandhi and the Ali brothers as a failure. He declared that the essential requisite condition to achieve *Swaraj* was political unity between Hindus and Muslims. He wanted a complete overhaul of the Government of India Act of 1919 and an improvement in the Lucknow Pact as a pre-condition for united action.[28] Under the influence of Jinnah a Committee had been appointed to formulate a constitution in consultation with other organizations.

This Lahore session was the beginning of Jinnah's unsuccessful foray into Punjab, which was under the control of the Unionist Party. At Lahore Jinnah had the greatest cooperation from the Punjabi Muslims including Malik Barkat Ali, the Punjab League representative. The following resolutions were adopted at the session:

1. The existing provinces of India shall be united under a common government on a federal basis so that each province shall have full and complete provincial autonomy, the functions of the Central Government being confined to matters only that are general and common concern.
2. Any territorial redistribution that might, at any time, become necessary shall not in any way affect the Muslim majority of the population in Punjab, Bengal, and NWFP.
3. No majority shall be reduced to a minority or even to an equality.
4. Full religious liberty, that is, liberty of belief, worship, observances, propaganda, association, and education shall be guaranteed to all communities.
5. The idea of joint electorates with a specified number of seats being unacceptable to Muslims, the representation of the latter shall continue to be by means of separate electorates as at present, provided that it shall be open to any community at any time to abandon its separate electorates in favour of joint electorates.
6. No Bill or Resolution or any part thereof affecting any community, which is to be determined by the members of that community in the elected body concerned, shall be passed in any legislature or in any other elected body, if three-fourth of the members of that community in that particular body oppose such a Bill or Resolution or part thereof.[29]

But Jinnah's stand was countered during the same period outside the Committee by none other than the Ali brothers of the UP. They, along with Gandhi, visited Lahore and offered the Muslims their proportional representation in the legislatures and services in exchange for the abolition of separate electorates. The Ali brothers were certainly more popular among the Muslim masses than Jinnah during that period. Sir Mian Muhammad Shafi of Punjab too opposed Jinnah's ideas vehemently. This once again proved the point that Jinnah was not the sole spokesman of the Muslims at that time. Jinnah's self-importance, his western clothes, and mannerisms had long been a subject for Maulana Mohammad Ali's satire. He disliked Jinnah's efforts to revive the League and renegotiate the Lucknow Pact with the Congress. Shaukat Ali always had a visceral grudge against Jinnah. But Jinnah was not the one who took things lying down. He retaliated ferociously against the Ali brothers off and on. Once he dismissed Shaukat Ali in the following terms: 'this little Maulana for the last three years has been making an annual attempt to destroy the Muslim League'.[30]

However, the underlying reason that seemed to have forced Jinnah to ask for a renegotiation of the Lucknow Pact was due to crucial demographic changes in the Northern provinces. The Lucknow Pact was devised on the basis of the 1911 census. But the 1921 census figures revealed rapid growth of the Muslim population in both Bengal (52.7 per cent) and the Punjab (54.8 per cent) respectively. The Muslims of these two provinces no longer wanted to rest content with the prospect of mere minority status as they then had a clear majority in these two provinces. Therefore, Jinnah had no other alternative but to demand revision of the Lucknow Pact.[31]

Jawaharlal Nehru, who was secretary to the Congress party in 1925, would not entertain Jinnah's new demands. Besides, during an All Party Conference, held in Delhi on 23 January 1925 in which Jinnah participated, the chances of a communal settlement in the form of a new

Lucknow Pact vanished. The Swarajist Motilal Nehru, the Hindu Maha Sabha, and even Gandhi were no more interested in it.[32]

Of course, Jinnah was neither a Khilafatist nor a pan-Islamist at this juncture. The abolition of the Caliphate paved the way for the revival of his fortunes in Indian politics, as Mohammad Ali and the Khilafatists had become irrelevant. The League which had gone out of action till then started regaining a certain vitality and relevance from 1924 onwards. However at the end of 1926, the League's total membership stood at a mere 1,184 and in 1927, it was just 1,330.[33]

On the other hand, the British as usual would not accept India as a single nation. On 7 July 1925, Lord Birkenhead, the Secretary of State for India reminded this in the course of a speech in the House of Lords. He held that to talk of India as an entity was as absurd as to talk of Europe as an entity. This simply echoed the views of Strachey and Seeley. Birkenhead challenged the Indian leadership to form a Constitution on the basis of a fair measure of general agreement among the people of India.[34] Jinnah and Congress leaders like Motilal Nehru seemed to have taken note of this challenge. But the idea that India was neither an entity nor a nation was being repeated quite often by high British officials. Indian leaders, especially Jinnah would not have failed to take note of it.

The year 1924 was a watershed in Jinnah's political career as thenceforth he was exclusively interested in the protection and promotion of Indian-Muslim interests within a united India through the revival of the Muslim League. Jinnah had emerged as a sectarian nationalist during that period. He did not want to participate in the rise of Indian nationalism in full swing, though off and on he would talk or pass resolutions in favour of self-government or talk about Hindu–Muslim unity. He was on the lookout for alternatives to Indian nationalism as promoted by the Congress party under Gandhi, where Muslim interests as he understood were fully safeguarded.

In the same year, Jinnah had struck a new-found friendship with Nawab Mohammad Liaquat Ali Khan of the Punjab and the United

Provinces. He was of Persian descent and had lands both in the Punjab and UP. He studied at Oxford and was called to the Bar at the Inner Temple in January 1921. Though he represented the UP in politics, he was 'very much a Punjabi'. In 1924, Liaquat Ali Khan hosted a dinner party at Shimla for Jinnah's wife, Rattanbai. Since then, whenever Jinnah visited Delhi, he would stay in Liaquat Ali Khan's magnificent house on Hardinge Avenue.[35] The relationship between Jinnah and Liaquat Ali Khan was going to have a lasting impact on the former.

Apart from the liberals, who counted for very little in Indian politics, Jinnah also tried to reach out to the Swarajists in order to come to a new communal settlement with a fresh set of demands which he could then present to the Government for acceptance, as it was the case with the Lucknow Pact. But the Swarajist Lala Lajpat Rai of the Punjab vehemently opposed communal electorates espoused by Jinnah at least since 1916. Between 26 November and 17 December 1924, Lala Lajpat Rai published thirteen articles in *The Tribune* condemning communal electorates and stigmatizing Jinnah as a communalist. Lajpat Rai wrote that communal electorates would divide India on the basis of religion. As the Punjabi Muslims were unwilling to grant weightage to Hindus and Sikhs, Lajpat Rai opined that it would be better to partition Punjab, and if necessary Bengal too, on religious lines and establish federations of autonomous Hindu and Muslim states. He even suggested transfer of population. Thus the ball was set rolling for the division of Punjab and Bengal for the first time in the form of an idea. Through this idea of partition, Lala Lajpat Rai aimed at consolidating the power of the Hindus in the Punjab and the Bengal. It is surprising to note that Lala Lajpat Rai called for the division of Bengal in 1924, while about two decades earlier he had opposed the partition of Bengal on religious lines as a Congress extremist leader. Jinnah would have taken note of Lala's new ideas and demands and its implications for the Muslims.[36]

Yet again in 1924, Maulana Mohammad Ali speaking at the League Session held in Bombay suggested that the Muslims of the NWFP be given the right of self-determination to choose between an affiliation with India or with Kabul. Even before these ideas of partition, a certain Muhammad Abdul Qadir Bigrami had advocated the division of the subcontinent between the Hindus and the Muslims in 1920. He even enumerated a list of districts fundamentally not too different from the present boundaries of Pakistan and Bangladesh. Three years later in 1923, in his evidence before the Frontier Enquiry Committee, Sardar Gul Muhammad Khan of Dera Ismail Khan had proposed a Partition of India by which Muslims would get the area from Peshawar to Agra and Hindus an area from Kanyakumari to Agra. In the same year, Bhai Paramanand of the Arya Samaj of Punjab published an Urdu book from Lahore setting forth the creation of a Muslim and Hindu zone in India, involving some exchange of population.[37] The preceding demands, especially that of Lala Lajpat Rai were undoubtedly communal demands.

Jinnah was most certainly aware of the existence of all such communal demands, which militated at various degrees against the concept of a united India. However, during that period, he seemed to have been anxious to draw himself closer to the Congress, which must not mean that he wanted to rejoin the Congress in order to find a solution to the Hindu–Muslim problem. In September 1924, Gandhi went on an indefinite fast to stem the tide of communal riots. He reached an agreement with Das and Motilal Nehru by which non-cooperation was to be formally suspended and the Swarajya party was to become an integral part of the Congress.

At the All Parties Conference meeting held at Bombay in November 1924, an All Parties Conference Committee was appointed for the purpose of bringing about Hindu–Muslim unity. Gandhi and Jinnah met again in Bombay on 20 November 1924 and agreed upon a resolution condemning preventive detention. On 23 January 1925, the All Parties Conference Committee met at Delhi. It was attended by Lala Lajpat Rai, Motilal Nehru, Ali brothers, Jawaharlal Nehru, Gandhi, Jinnah, and Maulana Abul Kalam Azad. Lala Lajpat Rai was not ready to grant the

Muslims representation that exceeded their population ratio, heeding to the demand of Jinnah. Many members—both of the Congress and other parties—favoured joint electorates with reservation of seats on the basis of the Lucknow Pact. Jinnah stressed during this meeting that reservation of seats for representatives of the Muslims in the Assemblies, local boards, and also the Universities should be made. After a week's discussion, there was no Hindu–Muslim agreement in sight and the conference ended in a failure. However, in spite of differences with Lajpat Rai, Jinnah seemed to have cultivated close personal relations with him and hailed him as 'one of the greatest sons of India'.[38]

On 16 June 1925 C.R. Das passed away. About two months later, Sir Surendra Nath Banerji also died. Condoling the death of these two on 22 August 1925 Jinnah declared:

> Sir, I might say that I learnt my first lessons in politics at the feet of Sir Surendra Nath Banerji. I was associated with him as one of his followers and I looked up to him as a leader.... As far as Mr Das is concerned, he was a personal friend of mine....

Motilal Nehru was left all alone to steer the Swarajya party. Jinnah saw eye-to-eye with Das on various issues like self-government, Dominion status, constitutional struggle, and inter-communal agreement. In the same year, Jinnah had been appointed by the Sandhurst Committee to study the feasibility of establishing a military college in India. Jinnah had to go to London for this purpose and Ruttie travelled with him for the last time to London. During that period their marriage had entered troubled waters.[39]

The elections to the Central Assembly in 1926 brought Jinnah back to politics. This time the Swarajya party did not support him. Instead he had the overwhelming support of the Memons. The Memons constituted the majority of the total Muslim votes of 2,730 of the Bombay Muslim constituency while the Bohras accounted only for 700 votes. Jinnah won the elections with the help of the Memon votes. Even before getting elected, he accused the Swarajists of indulging in anti-Muslim propaganda in the Assembly and made it clear that the Muslims of India would not accept any legislation that would attempt to override the Holy Quran, the highest authority which binds the Muslims. He also made sure in the Assembly that Muslims' interests and rights were safeguarded in any future constitution. Already during January to March 1926, Jinnah had carried through the North West Frontier Province Reform resolution in the Assembly against the wishes of orthodox Hindus like Madan Mohan Malaviya.[40]

In the newly elected Central Assembly in November 1926, Jinnah was isolated and alone. But he was not without a new set of his projects and ideas to protect Muslim interests. In February 1927, the head office of the League was transferred from the UP to Delhi. Jinnah convened a Muslim conference at Delhi on 20 March 1927. It was attended by Sir Muhammad Shafi, Mohammad Ali, Dr M.A. Ansari, the Raja of Mahmudabad, Nawab Mohammad Ismail, H.S. Suhrawardy, among others. Jinnah came out with a new set of proposals called the Delhi proposals, expecting the Congress to accept them. This was no doubt a departure from the Lucknow Pact of 1916 in certain crucial respects.

Jinnah had espoused the cause of separate electorates since his joining the League in 1913. But suddenly he was willing to give it up for joint electorates with reserved seats for minorities, fixed in proportion to the population of the different communities, in all provinces. Jinnah added that this giving up was possible if the Muslims were given one-third representation in the Central Assembly and representation in proportion to the population was conceded in the Punjab and Bengal. From a neutral and impartial point of view, the latter demand was reasonable, but the demand for one-third representation in the Centre was exaggerated, given that the total Muslim population of India amounted to only about 25 per cent.

More than these two conditions, there was a third demand to be met with for the giving up of separate electorates, that is, the creation of three new provinces—Sind, Baluchistan, and North-West Frontier Province in the northwest of India, where the Muslims will be in a majority. Sind was to be created by a division of Bombay province, while the latter two should be given equal status with other provinces through reforms. At the outset, this demand is reasonable as in the year 1912, the Hindu-majority province of Bihar and Orissa had been created by the British and there was a demand for the creation of Sind in 1915 itself by the Hindus. But the creation of these three provinces would create a consolidated bloc of Muslim states along with the contiguous Punjab province in the northwest frontiers of India.

The idea of the division of Sind from Bombay on religious lines seemed to have been inspired largely by the idea of the partition of the Punjab and Bengal on religious lines floated an year back by Lala Lajpat Rai. It must also be remembered that even before Lala Lajpat Rai, during the League Session of 1921, Maulana Hasrat Mohani of the UP, had envisaged, in the presence of Jinnah, self-determination for Muslims in the northwest and east where they had a political majority.[41] Besides on communal matters, no bill or resolution could be adopted if three-fourth of the members of the community concerned were opposed to it. So the Delhi proposals put forward by Jinnah, aimed at not only improving the position of the Muslims at the Centre, but also were paving the way for a consolidated Muslim bloc in the northwest. Jinnah made it clear that the offer of Delhi proposals were interdependent and can only be accepted or rejected in its entirety. He also maintained that even if Muslims were deprived of separate electorates, they will not 'completely' merge in the 'Indian nation'.[42] Jinnah forcefully affirmed the separate identity of the Muslims which cannot be completely subjected to the idea of the Indian nation or the ideology of Indian nationalism, as represented by the Congress.

In July 1927, a Hindu pundit published a pamphlet called *Rangila Rasul*, highly critical of Prophet Muhammad's marriages. This resulted in Hindu–Muslim riots. The author was stabbed to death by one Muslim called Ilm Din. Jinnah defended Ilm Din without charging any fee, although he lost the case. Ilm Din was finally hanged. This incident showed that Jinnah, contrary to popular and scholarly perceptions, was imbued with intense religious feelings and would not tolerate any insult to the Prophet. Three years later he ran to the defence of the Pir of Pagaro, an influential Muslim spiritual leader of Sind, who was accused of murdering a Muslim widow by the name of Mussamat Mariam. Jinnah argued that the entire case was cooked up.[43] Such sensational cases in some way popularized Jinnah among the Muslim masses.

At the same time, Jinnah convened a Unity Conference in Shimla on 24 August 1927. It was attended by the Ali brothers, Lala Lajpat Rai, M.A. Ansari, Madan Mohan Malaviya, and Motilal Nehru. Jinnah's intention in calling this meeting was to find a solution to the problems of cow killing, playing music before mosques, etc. But he was unsuccessful in his venture.[44] This shows that he was quite worried then about the cultural issues affecting the Muslims.

The Delhi proposals were reiterated at the December 1927 League Council session. However, a breakaway League group headed by Mian Muhammad Shafi of the Punjab, one of the founders of the Muslim League in 1906, consisting of prominent Punjab members like Firoz Khan Noon, Hasrat Mohani, and Sir Muhammad Iqbal, as well as Fazl-i Husain of the Unionist Party, did not accept Jinnah's proposal for giving up separate electorates, in order to improve the prospects of the Muslims of the minority provinces, especially at the Centre.[45] At the Calcutta session of the League held subsequently, there was only a lukewarm response to Jinnah's Delhi proposals. The Bengalis were not prepared to accept them totally, although a resolution during the session made it clear that the separate electorates would be dropped, once Sind province was created and reforms introduced in the NWFP. However, Tej Bahadur Sapru, the Liberal leader was willing to concede Jinnah's demands.[46]

In the light of the above, the theory that Jinnah and the Muslim League were only interested in the improvement and consolidation of Muslim power in the Centre is not completely right as Jinnah was, at the same time, creating the basis for a consolidated Muslim bloc of provinces in the northwest of India, whether the writ of the Muslim League ran in them or not. The irony is that Jinnah wanted the Congress to accept these proposals, whereas in reality it was for the British as rulers to decide. Whether the Congress accepted the Delhi proposals or not, a consolidated Muslim bloc in the northwest of India had not only become a political possibility due to Jinnah, but was also bound to become a political reality.

Jinnah's consent to give up separate electorates was a sop for the Congress to concede his demand for the creation of three more Muslim-majority provinces and for one-third representation of Muslims in the Centre, over and above their share in the total population. The creation of these three provinces had the potential to increase the bargaining power of the Muslims in any power sharing in future at the Centre. Having put forward such proposals, it is naïve to think that Jinnah was not aware of all the implications of his demands, especially the possibility for the creation of the Muslim bloc in the northwest. The argument and assertion by some scholars that Jinnah wanted to maintain the unity of India through these proposals is totally out of place at this juncture. Nobody can predict the future. Nobody can guess what was in Jinnah's mind regarding these proposals. He had never affirmed that it was the final set of proposals for a Hindu–Muslim settlement or that there would no more be any further demands in future.

In 1927, S. Srinivasa Iyengar was the President of the Congress party. He was willing to meet Jinnah's demands if joint electorates were accepted. He welcomed the Delhi proposals. It is believed that Jinnah wanted Motilal Nehru to preside the next Congress Session in Madras to be held in December 1927. But Gandhi opposed it. The Madras session, finally presided by M.A. Ansari, theoretically accepted Jinnah's Delhi proposals. However, later the Congress backtracked. There is no use arguing like Sumit Sarkar, that the Congress backtracked because of Hindu Maha Sabha pressure, insinuating that if the Congress had given in to the Delhi proposals, Jinnah would not have radicalized his stand and

Indian unity would have been maintained. It is not possible to predict such things. The contents of the Delhi proposals will remain unaltered, whether the Congress or the Hindu Maha Sabha accepted or rejected them.[47]

In November 1927, the British Government appointed a seven-member statutory commission, headed by Sir John Simon to enquire into the 1919 reforms and evolve reforms in the Constitution. A faction of the League under Jinnah decided to boycott the Simon Commission for there was no Indian member in it. The Congress also decided to boycott the Commission. Most other established parties like the Hindu Maha Sabha except the Unionist Party of Fazl-i Husain in the Punjab, the Justice Party of Madras, a faction of the League under Mian Mohammad Shafi, Sir Muhammad Iqbal, and the Aga Khan decided to boycott the Simon Commission.[48]

The Jinnah group met in Calcutta on 30–31 December 1927 and on 1 January 1928. A resolution was passed to boycott the Simon Commission. The session also adopted the Delhi proposals. It authorized the League Council to appoint a Committee to confer with the Congress and participate in the All Parties' Conference that the Congress had called for during the Madras session in order to form the Swaraj Constitution. Only 86 delegates attended the session. Nearly half of them were from Bengal. There were just 6 delegates from the Punjab, where Jinnah was not popular at all. At about the same time the Shafi group organized a grander meeting in Lahore, attended by 353 delegates. 300 came from the Punjab alone. Sir Muhammad Iqbal, general secretary of the Punjab League and Hasrat Mohani were among the delegates. A resolution was adopted in favour of the Simon Commission. Iqbal more than the others did not want the Muslims of the Punjab and Bengal to be deprived of their rights in the Provincial Councils as a majority in the population.[49]

The All Parties' Conference's recommendations for the Swaraj Constitution were to be placed before a special All Party Convention at Lucknow consisting of the Congress, the elected members of the Central and provincial legislatures and representatives of not less than

33 organizations including the Hindu Maha Sabha and the Muslim League. Gandhi did not attend the Convention, while Jinnah opposed it tooth and nail. The Ali brothers joined the Convention, but being vehemently opposed to Dominion status, instead of the previous demand for *Swaraj*, eventually they left the Congress. Jinnah, Gandhi, Motilal Nehru, and Tej Bahadur Sapru wanted Dominion status.[50]

Between February and March 1928, another All Parties Conference was convened by the Congress at Delhi, presided by M.A. Ansari. Very soon on 21 April 1928, the Congress came out with what is known as the *Nehru Report*, drafted mainly by Motilal Nehru and Tej Bahadur Sapru. The *Report* settled for Dominion status of India, instead of *Swaraj*. It agreed to the separation of Sind from Bombay province once Dominion status was acquired, subject to a weightage of the Hindu minority there. It did not object to reforms in the North-West Frontier Province. It went back on the separate electorates and proposed joint electorates everywhere, reserved seats being conceded only at the Centre and in provinces with Muslim minorities. It proposed a unitary political structure with the Centre keeping residual powers. It further proposed only one-fourth representation for Muslims at the Centre, instead of one-third as demanded by the League.[51] There was to be no reservation of seats for the Muslims in the Punjab and in Bengal. But as the franchise was restricted according to the 1919 Act, primarily on the basis of property and income tax, it was quite possible that the Muslims would be reduced to a minority in the legislatures even in these provinces as they would actually have less number of voters than the non-Muslims.

Jinnah did not react to the *Nehru Report* immediately, though the objective of the Dominion status of the *Report* suited him. The Report had the support of prominent Muslims like Maulana Abul Kalam Azad, Dr M.A. Ansari, Raja Sahib of Mahmudabad, T.A.K. Sherwani, Chaudhry Khaliquzzaman of the UP, and Dr Saifuddin Kitchlew of the Punjab. But the Khilafatists, Shaukat Ali, and Maulana Hasrat Mohani, president of *Jamiat-ul-ulema* and Sir Muhammad Iqbal repudiated the

Nehru Report forcefully. The Ali brothers opposed joint electorates, unlike M.A. Ansari and Maulana Abul Kalam Azad. Even Mohammad Karim Chagla, Jinnah's close associate in the League wanted to accept the *Report.*

Meanwhile Jinnah went away to London in May 1928 along with Srinivasa Iyengar, President of the Congress and Diwan Chamanlal in an attempt to include Indians as members of the Simon Commission. He came back in October, called a meeting of the League Council to decide about the *Nehru Report* and took part in the All Parties' Conference held on 22 December 1928 at Calcutta, dressed in his best Savile Row suit. He proposed three crucial amendments to the *Nehru Report.* He reiterated the Delhi proposals, demanding the immediate creation of Sind, residual power to be vested in the provinces, one-third Assembly seats in the Central Assembly, reserved seats in the Punjab and Bengal until adult suffrage was established. He also demanded Muslim representation in the Punjab and Bengal on population basis for 10 years subject to a re-examination after that period and no amendments or alterations in the Constitution without obtaining three-fourths majority in both the houses of Parliament, separately and jointly. He also condemned Shafi for his stand.[52]

The Hindu Maha Sabha opposed Jinnah's amendments. On the whole, as there was no positive result for Jinnah's proposals, he withdrew the Muslim League delegation from the Conference, which had a dampening effect on the subsequent proceedings of the Conference. He refused to participate in a Muslim All Parties' Conference held in Delhi, where it was made clear that no Constitution would be acceptable to the Muslims, which did not satisfy their demands. But it is wrong to insinuate like Mushirul Hasan that it was only due to the opposition of the Hindu Maha Sabha, an exclusively Hindu party and its allies in the Congress, that Jinnah's amendments were not accepted. Lala Lajpat Rai passed away in November 1928. Madan Mohan Malaviya and others opposed Jinnah's amendments. But Malaviya was also a close personal friend of Jinnah.

Jinnah as usual would never budge even an iota from the amendments he was proposing.[53]

Jinnah wanted everyone to accept what he was proposing. It was always under his own terms that he would accept to cooperate with the Congress and the Hindus. For example, he never thought for a moment why the Hindus had to accept one-third representation for Muslims in the Central Assembly when their population was hardly 25 per cent of the total population. He also never gave thought to the fact that his demand for the creation of three new Muslim-majority provinces enjoying equal status with the rest of the provinces was basically a communal demand, which resembled those of Lajpat Rai and others. This may be one of the reasons why Jinnah got along well with Lajpat Rai. Moreover, his rigid stand on such issues and the exaggerated nature of his demands could lead only to a deadlock. There is no point in arguing like Mushirul Hasan and A.G. Noorani that Jinnah was secular at this juncture and he was only acting as a mediator between the Muslims and Hindus. As a matter of fact, he was leading an exclusively Muslim party and fighting hard to obtain for the Muslims more than what was warranted by their numbers, always on a communal basis. But in reality, he never had any mandate from the Muslims and represented at the most a fraction of them, unless there were proofs to the contrary.[54] Besides, in all his speeches during that period, Jinnah had never told that his Delhi proposals will be the last set of his demands. This gives room to think that he might raise new demands always on a communal basis, once his current demands were met.

Thus the situation arose where the Congress would not accept Jinnah's proposals in toto, while Jinnah rejected the *Nehru Report*.[55] Jinnah made it clear that the Muslims would not join the freedom movement of the Congress if his proposals were not accepted. He and the Muslims would not be part of the Indian Nationalist Movement if his demands were not met with. So he applied pressure at a time when the Congress was getting ready to launch a major movement for complete independence.

One makes us wonder what sort of 'nationalist' or 'secularist' Jinnah was at this juncture. In fact, his Indian nationalism was subject to Muslim sectarian interests. He would never sacrifice these interests at the altar of Indian nationalism. But the Congress leaders probably thought at that time that Jinnah and his group was a minority among Muslims and therefore his demands could be ignored.

EXILE IN LONDON

FOURTEEN POINTS AND ITS AFTERMATH

There was no unanimity of opinion regarding Jinnah's proposals among the Congress leadership, the Liberals, the Hindu Maha Sabha, and even among the Muslims and the Sikhs. They would also not accept that Jinnah could speak for all the Muslims as he represented only a small minority of them. Jawaharlal Nehru, who was the president of the Congress then, ignored Jinnah's proposals. For Nehru, inspired by Marxian economy and class politics, indulging in politics in the name of religion like Jinnah was medieval and out of date; that did not bear any relation with modern problems which were economic and political. For him the realities of today were poverty, hunger, unemployment, class politics, and the conflict between Indian nationalists and British Imperialists.[1]

Jinnah, of course, would never succumb to Nehru's views. Instead, he held on to his view that the Muslims had a special destiny, unlike other Indians and therefore they needed special treatment.[2] This was the position that he has adopted since he joined the Muslim League in 1913. But he never mobilized the Muslim masses till then for pushing forward his agenda as he had no mass base, even in his own province of Bombay. He was rather an elite politician of a Muslim-minority province, who was interested in the elite interests of his community such as obtaining a maximum share of power in any institutional structure put up by the British. He restricted his political activities mainly to the legislative chambers, the drawing and committee rooms, the Muslim League annual and council sessions, and the all-party conferences. This was old-fashioned politics. He thought that he would oblige the Congress thus—which had become a mass-based party since Gandhi assumed its leadership; as well as the British, who were still the imperial power controlling the destiny of all Indians—to accept whatever he wanted.

Jinnah was never a charismatic figure till that period. He was neither a great orator nor a rabble-rouser. He hardly wrote anything. He was not a thinker or a philosopher like Sir Muhammad Iqbal; instead, he was a lawyer trained in London. He spoke impeccable English and hardly conversed in his mother tongue Gujarati. His Hindustani was very bad. But still he was respected by the Muslim politicians as a prominent and the seniormost Muslim leader. His western suits and mannerisms, language habits and way of conducting were not suited to Indian conditions, and hence largely prevented him from connecting with the non-westernized Indian-Muslim masses, who were mostly descendants of converts like himself.

Besides, Fazl-i Husain of the Unionist Party of the Punjab floated the All India Muslim All Parties' Conference in December 1928 in Delhi as a representative organization of the Muslims of India, apart from the Muslim League. It had the support of the Aga Khan, Mian Mohammad Shafi, Sir Muhammad Iqbal, and also Nawab Liaquat Ali Khan of the UP. Jinnah did not attend it, but many members of his Independent party in the Legislative Assembly attended it. This conference wanted provincial autonomy, retention of Muslim majorities in the Punjab and Bengal, retention of separate electorates until Muslims decide to give them up, weightage in the Muslim-minority provinces, retention of the existing one-third representation of Muslims in the Centre, and a true federal set-up with residuary powers vested in the constituent states. It also did not want the adoption of any bill if three-fourth of the affected community was against it. It is quite obvious that these demands were tailormade to serve the interests of the Punjabi, Bengali, and UP Muslims more than the others.[3]

Fazl-i Husain was the leader of a peripheral Muslim-majority state. He was never able to occupy centrestage in Indian politics. The Gangetic plains made up mainly of the United Provinces and Delhi remained the heart of Muslim India historically and traditionally, though the Muslims were in a minority there. Jinnah being a man of the minority province of Bombay was more acceptable to the Muslims of the minority provinces, especially the UP Muslims rather than anyone from the peripheral Muslim-majority provinces like the Punjab and Bengal. Jinnah enjoyed this advantage over the leaders of the Muslim-majority provinces. Both the Lucknow Pact and the Delhi proposals emanated from the heart of Muslim India. Besides, the British had a longstanding association with the Muslim League right from its start in 1906. They were still not prepared to abandon it during that period in favour of any other Muslim party as far as all-India politics was concerned.

Subsequently Jinnah took part in a series of informal discussions with the leaders of the above conference and agreed to accept the conference resolutions. In March 1929, in consultation with several Muslim leaders including those of the Shafi group, Jinnah put forward his famous Fourteen Points, on behalf of the All Parties Muslim Conference, which now contained delegates from a reunited Muslim League. Those are listed below:

1. The form of the future Constitution should be Federal with the residuary power vested in the provinces.
2. A uniform measure of autonomy shall be granted to all provinces.
3. All legislatures in the country and other elected bodies shall be constituted on the definite principle of adequate and effective representation of minorities in every province without reducing the majority in any province to a minority or even equality.
4. In the Central Legislature, Muslim representation shall not be less than one-third.
5. Representation of communal groups shall continue to be by separate electorates provided that it shall be open to any community at any time to abandon its separate electorate in favour of joint electorates.

6. Any territorial redistribution that might, at any time, be necessary shall not in any way affect the Muslim majority in the Punjab, Bengal, and the NWFP.
7. Full religious liberty, that is liberty of belief, worship, observance, propaganda, association, and education shall be guaranteed to all communities.
8. No Bill or Resolution or any part thereof shall be passed in any legislature or any other elected body if three-fourths of the members of any community in that particular body oppose it as being injurious to the interests of that community.
9. Sind should be separated from Bombay.
10. Reforms should be introduced in the NWFP and Baluchistan as in other provinces.
11. Provision should be made in the Constitution giving Muslims an adequate share along with the other Indians in all the services of the State and in local self-governing bodies having due regard to the requirements of efficiency.
12. The Constitution should embody adequate safeguards for the protection of Muslim culture, and for the protection and promotion of Muslim education, language, religion, personal laws, and Muslim charitable institutions, and for their due share in grants-in-aid.
13. No Cabinet, either Central or Provincial, should be formed without there being at least one-third of Muslim ministers.
14. No change shall be made in the Constitution by the central legislature except with the concurrence of the States constituting the Indian Federation.[4]

Jinnah further stressed that no scheme for the future constitution of the Government of India would be acceptable to Muslims unless the above points were conceded. It is quite obvious that the Fourteen Points was a further improvement upon the Delhi proposals. According to Jinnah, it was at this price that Indian unity or Hindu–Muslim unity could be maintained. It was a very high price indeed, even to a casual observer, that Jinnah was demanding. The Fourteen Points have been devised in such a manner that if adopted, no government measure was possible without the consent of the great majority of the Muslim members.

Apart from this, there were three other crucial points. Firstly, Jinnah wanted one-third representation for Muslims not just in the Central Legislature, but also in all Ministries of the provinces where they were in a minority. This was certainly a demand which was not at all warranted by their numbers. In the Madras Presidency for instance, Muslims constituted just 7 or 8 per cent of the population, but Jinnah wanted one-third of the Cabinet posts for Muslims. It was naturally excessive and extravagant. Secondly, separate electorates will not be given up. Thirdly and probably the most important point is that Jinnah—whether he was aware of it or not—following his Delhi proposals had stressed further the necessity to create the basis for a consolidated Muslim bloc of provinces in the northwest and the eastern frontiers of India, through the demand for the creation of Sind and reforms in NWFP and Baluchistan. Jinnah even ruled out accepting joint electorates if these demands were not met with.[5]

This point, however, was not lost upon at least one leading Muslim thinker, philosopher, and Leaguer, Sir Muhammad Iqbal. Drawing inspiration from Jinnah's Delhi proposals and its subsequent avatars, he dared to envisage the following in his presidential address to the All-India Muslim League Session in Allahabad on 29 December 1930 before an audience of less than 75 people:

> ...I lead no party; I follow no leader. I have given the best part of my life to a careful study of Islam...India is a continent of human groups belonging to different races, speaking different languages and professing different religions...The Muslim demand for the creation of a 'Muslim India' within India is perfectly justified... I would like to see the Punjab, North-West Frontier Province, Sind and Baluchistan amalgamated into a single state. Self-

> government within the British Empire or without the British Empire, the formation of a consolidated North-West Indian Muslim State appears to be the final destiny of the Muslims at least of North-West India.... The idea need not alarm the Hindus or the British. India is the greatest Muslim country in the world. The life of Islam as a cultural force in this living country very largely depends on its centralization in a specified territory....Thus, possessing full opportunity of development within the body-politic of India, the North West Indian Muslims will prove the best defenders of India against a foreign invasion.... The Punjab with 56 per cent Muslim population supplies 54 per cent of the total combatant troops in the Indian army.... The Right Hon'ble Mr Srinivasa Sastri thinks that the Muslim demand for the creation of autonomous Muslim States along the North-West border is actuated by a desire 'to acquire means of exerting pressure in emergencies on the Government of India'. I may frankly tell him that the Muslim demand is not actuated by the kind of motive he imputes to us; it is actuated by a genuine desire for free development which is practically impossible under the type of unitary government contemplated by the nationalist Hindu politicians with a view to secure permanent communal dominance in the whole of India... A redistribution of British India, calculated to secure a permanent solution of the communal problem is the main demand of the Muslims of India.... I see no reason why Sind should not be united with Baluchistan and turned into a separate province....[6]

Iqbal even claimed that a demand similar to the above was actually put forward before the Nehru Committee, but was summarily rejected on the ground that it would give a very unwieldy State. It seemed that Iqbal had even suggested the exclusion of Ambala division and those districts where non-Muslims were in a majority from his North-Western Muslim State. But Jinnah at that stage seemed to have dismissed Iqbal's idea as a poet's dream.[7]

It is quite obvious from the preceding that the genesis of Pakistan idea lies in the Delhi proposals and the Fourteen Points of Jinnah and not anywhere else. The Delhi proposals and the Fourteen Points had been put on paper by Jinnah. They were not some vague oral set of proposals made during a speech which can be altered during some other speech; although they might have been ignored by many top Hindu and Muslim leaders like Motilal Nehru, the Aga Khan, Sir Fazl-i Husain, Dr Ansari, and Maulana Mohammad Ali. Dr Ansari and Maulana Abul Kalam Azad, unable to put up with the communalist demands of Jinnah, started the All India Nationalist Muslim party at Allahabad on 29 July 1929, to promote nationalism among Muslims.[8]

Jinnah seemed to have always thought that the Congress leadership, fearing for Hindu–Muslim or Indian unity would give in to his demands. But then there was no leadership vacuum or a transition period in the Congress as it was during the signing of the Lucknow Pact. There were a string of other leaders like Jawaharlal Nehru, Rajagopalachari, Maulana Abul Kalam Azad, and Subhas Chandra Bose, but Gandhi was the undisputed leader of the Congress. Given the extravagant and excessive nature of Jinnah's demands, the Congress leadership preferred to ignore them. Jinnah could do nothing about it, except to wait and see if the British would accept at least some of its features.

The Delhi proposals came at a time when Jinnah's married life was in doldrums. Rattanbai had left Jinnah in 1927 and had gone to live separately in the posh Taj Mahal Hotel, belonging to the Parsi industrialist, Tata. Probably, being a Parsi, she did not appreciate the increasingly communal stands of Jinnah. In 1928, she was almost on her deathbed in Paris at the *Champs Elysées* Clinic. Jinnah who was in London then, rushed to her side, but they never patched up. She died two years later, leaving Dina under the care of Jinnah and his sister Fatima. It seemed that Jinnah sobbed for the first time at Ruttie's burial in the Muslim cemetery of Bombay. Her daughter, Dina was never brought up in a strict religious atmosphere, even of the Khoja variety. She seemed to have been more of a Parsi than a Muslim like her mother. She was educated in England and India and seemed to have grown up to be as westernized as Jinnah. Jinnah did not have much time for her as he was plunged in devising proposals and formulas to secure the future of the Muslims of India and himself. Besides, he was a chainsmoker which was to take a toll on his health later. However, since the estrangement of Rattanbai in 1927, Fatima had virtually become the caretaker of Jinnah.[9]

The Congress never paid attention to the Fourteen Points of Jinnah. Jawaharlal Nehru dismissed it as 'the most mitigated nonsense'. In December 1929 at the Lahore Session, the Congress revived its demand for complete independence, set aside the *Nehru Report*, and plunged the country headlong into the Civil Disobedience Movement under the leadership of Mahatma Gandhi. This time, Maulana Mohammad Ali opposed the Gandhian Movement. Both Shaukat Ali and he charged that the object of Gandhi's movement was to establish Hindu Raj.[10]

The Muslims, by and large, stood aloof from the Congress Movement that time, except in the NWFP. That did not mean that they were fully supportive of Jinnah's Fourteen Points or the Muslim League, as there were several Muslim organizations during that time who claimed to represent the Muslims like the Khilafatists, the Muslim Conference, the Ahrars, the nationalist Muslims, the ulema, and so on, each with their own agenda of reforms. In a subsequent All Parties Muslim Conference attended by Muslim members of the Central and provincial legislatures and representatives of various Muslim organizations, the stand of the All India Muslim Conference was criticized. Mohammad Karim Chagla, an associate of Jinnah from Bombay claimed that the League was the sole representative organization of the Muslims, which had looked after Muslim interests for more than two decades. But the Muslim League did not have a mass following at that time in any of the provinces; Chagla's claim was definitely hollow at that juncture. Jinnah never thought of mobilizing the Muslim masses. Instead, he approached Viceroy Irwin in a last-ditch attempt to arrive at a communal settlement by convening the different political groups. Nothing came of it. It seemed that he was in the good books of the Viceroy during that period. The Viceroy even gave letters of introduction to Jinnah to meet the British politicians during the Round Table Conference.[11]

ROUND TABLE CONFERENCES AND JINNAH'S VICTORIES

The *Simon Commission Report* of May 1930 promised to replace dyarchy with responsible government in the provinces. However, there was no reference to Dominion status in it. In fact, it suggested no change at all in the Central Government. It neither granted the separation of Sind, nor equal status to NWFP, nor was even unsympathetic to separate electorates. It suggested the creation of an all-India Federation and the abolition of dyarchy in the provinces and wanted the ministers to be made responsible to the provincial legislatures in all departments including law and order. It also suggested the separation of Burma from India.[12]

Nobody seemed to have been happy with the *Report*, including Fazl-i Husain and even the British. For Fazl-i Husain the interests of the Muslim majorities in the Punjab and Bengal could not be compromised by the principle of weightage for Muslims in the Muslim-minority provinces, based on the Lucknow Pact of which Jinnah was the main architect, acting under the influence of the UP Muslim elite interests. Jinnah was not happy with the *Simon Report*. Nevertheless, he got himself re-elected unopposed to the Central Assembly from Bombay.[13]

The British government called the Indian leaders to participate in a Round Table Conference in London in November 1930 in order to discuss constitutional reforms. The Congress under Gandhi refused to participate in the Round Table Conference, as, by then, the Congress wanted complete independence. No Congress leader attended it. Jinnah himself went to Sabarmati Ashram in Ahmedabad to persuade Gandhi to attend the Round Table Conference. He even exhorted Motilal Nehru to attend it, but to no avail. However, the Conference was attended by a strong contingent of Maharajahs and Nawabs of the Princely States, which constituted two-fifths of the area of British India and one-third of its population. It was also attended by the Aga Khan, some leaders of the Muslim League like Jinnah, Maulana Mohammad Ali, Mian Mohammad Shafi, and Fazlul Huq of Bengal, some liberal leaders like Tej Bahadur Sapru and the Hindu Maha Sabha leader Dr Moonje. Fazl-i Husain, who was then member of the Viceroy's Executive Council, was represented by Zafarullah Khan, an Ahmeddiya barrister of the Punjab and Shafat Ahmed Khan and the Nawab of Chattari of the UP. Sir Muhammad Iqbal also attended the conference. The Aga Khan was the leader of the Muslim delegation. He stayed in his luxurious suite at Ritz Hotel. They were altogether 57 delegates, handpicked by the Viceroy. The Aga Khan was subsequently elected as the Chairman of all British Indian representatives, except the princes. Due to the absence of the Congress delegates, no meaningful discussion took place on the constitutional reforms or the communal issues like separate electorates during the Round Table Conference. It seemed that the Liberals under Sapru accepted the Delhi proposals of Jinnah, but the Hindu Maha Sabha under Moonje would not accept reservation for Muslims in the Punjab and Bengal, while the Sikhs wanted 30 per cent of the seats for themselves.

The idea of an Indian Federation including princely India, where the British will still retain the ultimate control in finance, defence, and external affairs, while the provinces would enjoy autonomous rights and functions, was mooted for the first time. The Maharajah of Bikaner, the Nawab of Bhopal as well as Jinnah and Mian Mohammad Shafi, the leaders of the two factions of the Muslim League were also for it. Ramsay MacDonald himself spoke in favour of it, subject to certain safeguards and reservations. Jinnah spoke in favour of Dominion status to India within the British Commonwealth of Nations. He also stood by his Fourteen Points. Maulana Mohammad Ali claimed that as a Muslim, he was not a nationalist, but a supra-nationalist. But the Aga Khan stole the show. He first wanted the settlement of the communal question before any constitutional progress. No Muslim leader at this stage would accept

Jinnah's claim that he represented all the Muslims. Jinnah was just one of the leaders, but not the only leader.[14]

Maulana Mohammad Ali, who participated in the conference died on 4 January 1931. As per his wish, he was buried in Jerusalem near the Dome of the Rock. He was quite attached to the Muslim holy places, although he was born in Rampur in the United Provinces. His passing away cleared one of the major obstacles for Jinnah to stake his claim for the leadership of the Muslims. Maulana Mohammad Ali being from the United Provinces, the heart of Muslim India would have no doubt vied with Jinnah for this leadership and would have challenged him as he did all throughout the Khilafat Movement so successfully. With his death, the United Provinces lost a leader of all-India stature who was undoubtedly more popular with the Muslim masses of India than Jinnah due to his involvement in the Khilafat agitations. With Mohammad Ali out of the picture, Jinnah could now rely upon lesser and younger leaders of the UP like Liaquat Ali Khan, Chaudhry Khaliquzzaman (1889–1973), a lawyer and landowner of Avadh, and Nawab Ismail Khan (1884–1958), a barrister from Inner Temple, who had lesser experience in politics and did not command any following or influence outside their provinces. The latter two had earlier participated in the Khilafat agitations under Mohammad Ali. Of course, Syed Wazir Hasan, who, along with Maulana Mohammad Ali, had brought Jinnah into the Muslim League in 1913 was still around, but had retired from public life. Mian Mohammad Shafi was a leader of a peripheral state. The Aga Khan did not have a following, although he was boosted up by the British. Strangely, Jinnah was unaware of the situation in Indian-Muslim politics that had opened up for him. Having been spurned by most Muslim leaders during the Conference, Jinnah chose to settle down in London to pursue his legal practice at the Privy Council, when the Conference ended in January 1931. A few months later, he even bought a house on West Heath Road at Hampstead in London, furnished it tastefully, and acquired Chambers at King's Bench

Walk. His sister Fatima and his 13-year-old daughter Dina joined him in London.[15]

It is surprising to note that Jinnah who had been negotiating with the Congress leaders since his joining the Muslim League in 1913, in order to arrive at a communal settlement, had suddenly chosen to abandon politics, and settle down in London. This raises the question about his commitment to protect Muslim interests in a united India. But given the situation where he was isolated even among the Muslim elites, he seemed to have had no other choice. This does not mean that he was completely disconnected from India and its politics.

During that period, the influential and leading British newspaper, *Manchester Guardian* reported on 19 June 1931, certainly under the influence of the demands for new Muslim majority provinces raised especially by Jinnah in the northwest, that Muslims were drifting away from the Federation as it would mean permanent domination by Hindus. It added that they wanted to counteract this domination by creating a large northern block of Muslim provinces, in which the Hindus will be hostages for the good behaviour of the Hindus in the Centre and South. The paper further held that many Muslims did not believe in the permanence of Federal India, and they foresaw a Muslim State in the North stretching from Karachi to Northern Bengal. This was probably the first time a serious British newspaper floated the possibility for a separate Muslim State in northern India.

Jinnah, who was in London, would have been aware of the above report. The very next month, that is, in July 1931, Jinnah returned to India. He resigned from his membership of the Central Assembly, stayed for five weeks, before returning to London along with Sir Iqbal in early September 1931, with the intention of contesting elections to the British Parliament. Before he left India, a farewell party was held for him by the Muslim Students' Union of Bombay. During the party, he said that if 'the British gave India a constitution according to the Hindu demand, naturally the Muslims would oppose it and would resort to every possible means to destroy and break that constitution'. Jinnah had been using such strong words off and on since the Lucknow Pact.

After Jinnah reached London, in a letter to *The Times* dated 3 October 1931, Edward Thompson, who was later a Fellow at Oxford, expressed his alarm at the prospect of an Islamic State in northwest India. Jinnah, who was settled in London and other Muslim leaders like the Aga Khan, would have certainly taken note of the preceding.[16]

In the meantime, the Gandhi–Irwin Pact was signed by Gandhi with the then Viceroy of India, Lord Irwin on 5 March 1931. It promised Federation, release of political prisoners, and suspension of rule by Ordinance, thereby enabling Gandhi to suspend the Civil Disobedience Movement and attend the Second Round Table Conference in London, held in September 1931, as the sole representative of the Congress. It was believed that Gandhi had achieved a breakthrough as the Viceroy dealt with Gandhi on an equal footing. But what Gandhi seemed to have not realized was that the vengeful Raj had a long memory. They had not forgotten that Gandhi and his Congress had challenged British power in India during the Non-Cooperation and Khilafat Movements, and the Civil Disobedience Movement. Gandhi unwittingly walked into the Round Table Conference. He defied British chill and also their pomp and splendour by coming to London in his loin-cloth attire. He even had tea with King George at Buckingham Palace in the same attire. Gandhi and his dress became the talk of all British newspapers, while Jinnah was in his new home at Hampstead, unknown to the British public. He was included as one of the Muslim delegates by the Viceroy Lord Irwin, despite Fazl-i Husain's opposition.[17] The British were not ready to let him down completely, the man who had been so loyal to them during the Khilafat Movement.

The Labour Prime Minister Ramsay MacDonald, who headed a coalition government that time, began by addressing the delegates of the conference, not as Indians, but as 'My Hindu and Muslim Friends'. This subsequently demonstrated to the world that the British government visualized two nations in India: Hindu and Muslim. Gandhi objected by stating that there were only Indians in the conference, but to no avail. No Muslim leader present raised any objection to MacDonald's opening remarks. During the entire conference, the problem of minorities loomed larger than ever. This time it was not only the Muslim delegates who wanted separate electorates, but also the depressed castes, Indian Christians, and Anglo-Indians. Besides, the Muslim delegates claimed 33 and one-third per cent share in the representation at the Central Assembly. Jinnah's role during the conference was minimal due to opposition from other Muslim delegates, led by Mian Mohammad Shafi. He put forward his Fourteen Points before Gandhi. At one stage, Jinnah threatened that no Constitution in India would work for 24 hours without Muslim approval. He also claimed that there were four parties on the negotiating table: the British, the Princes, the Hindus, and the Muslims. Ramsay MacDonald would have agreed to this claim.[18]

The Round Table Conference seemed to have been deliberately designed in such a way that it highlighted the communal and sectarian problems in India rather than anything else. Ramsay MacDonald stressed on a solution to this problem before any constitutional progress could be made. Gandhi had gone to the extent of accepting all Muslim claims provided they supported the Congress demand for *Swaraj*. But the Muslim delegates led by the Aga Khan bluntly rejected Gandhi's offer. Gandhi was literally caught in a well-laid trap. He had never thought that the communal differences would further widen in his presence during the conference. But that was what had happened. All this could have been avoided if Gandhi had abstained from participating in the Round Table Conference and continued with the Civil Disobedience Movement, mobilizing the masses. Then he was not even in a situation to backtrack.

During the conference, the Aga Khan was used as a sort of a mediator by the British between Gandhi and the Muslim groups. While Gandhi stood for the unity of India and complete *Swaraj*, the Aga Khan maintained that there was no India before the British and stood for

Dominion status of India within the British Commonwealth. After the Great War, the Aga Khan urged the formation of a Commonwealth of Asian States in association with Britain adopted during the Paris Peace Conference. It is strange to note that the Aga Khan, a descendant of refugees who came to India from Persia during the nineteenth century, held such views. The Aga Khan, as we know, was always a close ally of the British. During the First World War, he was used by the British as a counterpoise to the Turkish Sultan. He owed his position completely to the British. He would not do anything against their imperial interests like dissociating Britain from India, which was Gandhi's demand. So it is not surprising that he not only took a stand against Gandhi's conciliatory gesture, but also led the Muslims against Gandhi's offer. Jawaharlal Nehru wrote that the Aga Khan represented Imperialist England at the Round Table Conference, although he was supposed to represent India and the Muslims. For Nehru, he was always a special agent of the British. The Aga Khan and his group like Fazl-i Husain had their own agendas during the conference. Shafat Ahmed Khan of the Fazl-i group wanted *Swaraj* through the provincialization of the Raj and demanded complete autonomy of the units of the Federation. Jinnah not only ignored them, but also was suspicious of Federation, to which the Aga Khan and the princes were inclined.[19]

Finally, as there was no agreement in sight, the conference was called off on 1 December. But before that MacDonald announced the creation of the new provinces of Sind and NWFP, which Jinnah had been demanding since the Delhi proposals. Ramsay MacDonald announced that due to the failure of the conference to reach an agreement, the British government would be compelled to apply a provisional scheme in the form of an Award. The Congress in its turn embarked on the second Civil Disobedience Movement in January 1932 which was much weaker than the previous one and lingered on till May 1933. Gandhi was imprisoned in Yerawada Jail in June 1932, while Jinnah had chosen to stay back in

London. Meanwhile on 7 February 1932, Sir Shafi had passed away in Lahore. This cleared another crucial political deck for Jinnah.

On 25 January 1932, a notification in the *Gazette of India* raised the status of the NWFP. It became thenceforth a governor's province. That was a first victory for Jinnah, although he had chosen to settle down in London during that period.

The British Government, keeping its word, unilaterally decided to make an award on 17 August 1932; the award came to be known as the Communal Award; it was more provincial and communal-oriented. Separate electorates with reservation of seats were to be retained. Besides, the Scheduled Castes or Untouchables and others like the Indian Christians, Europeans, and Anglo-Indians were given separate electorates. In Bengal, Muslims were given 119 out of 250 seats in the legislature and in the Punjab they were to have 86 seats in a house of 175. The Muslims got weightage in the minority provinces whereas the Hindus were given weightage in Sind and NWFP. The Hindus of Bengal stood to lose as the Award gave them only 80 seats out of 250, while under the existing constitution they had more number of elected seats in the Bengal Council, which was in accordance with the Lucknow Pact. The Muslims largely stood to gain by the Award in the provinces.[20]

The British went one step further in strengthening the foundations of the separate political existence of the Muslims in India. The Hindu Maha Sabha rejected the Award. The majority of the Muslim organizations and leaders accepted the Award while the Congress once again was caught unawares. The Congress was not in a position to oppose it, but it was indeed a setback for its nationalist ambitions. Madan Mohan Malaviya rejected the Award and formed the Congress Nationalist Party. The vengeful Raj had resorted once again to constitutional methods to cut Gandhi and the Congress to size, as it was the case in 1909. During that period, it was thought that all the Muslim demands have been met with by the British and that the Communal Award was the final settlement. But that was not going to be.

Besides, to conclude that the Communal Award was influenced by the standpoints of the Aga Khan or Fazl-i Husain alone, seemed to be an exaggeration, as some scholars tend to do.[21] It is on the contrary a purely British decision, having their interests in mind. The British, instead of arbitrating between the various sections of the Indians or making any pronouncement on self-rule, left the Indians to squabble between themselves on the basis of religion and caste, so that they could come out with their own solutions to the constitutional problem and postpone progress towards self-rule.

The Third Round Table Conference was held during November–December 1932 with just 46 delegates. Gandhi did not attend; The Aga Khan attended; Jinnah was ignored. But the Aga Khan seemed to have pursued more forcefully his own agenda during the conference and later. It must be remembered that the Aga Khan was a Prince without a territory. He contended that his grandfather the Aga Khan I should have been made the ruling Prince of Sind for the services that he rendered to the British in Sind, which had a population of 4 or 5 million in an area of 48,136 sq. miles. He initiated correspondence with the Viceroy Willingdon and Samuel Hoare, Secretary of State for India in order to become the ruling Prince of Sind so that his heirs and successors would enjoy a permanent influence in India, consistent with the prestige and dignity of his ancient Persian lineage and his family tradition of loyal and devoted service to the British Crown.[22] It should be noted that the Aga Khan had tried to obtain Sind for himself and his heirs, only a few years after Jinnah demanded Sind to be separated from Bombay and made it into a separate Muslim-dominated province. Whether Jinnah was aware of this or not is not known.

It was at this conference, that Samuel Hoare made the announcement about giving Muslims one-third representation in the Central Legislature, which was well above their one-quarter share of the total population. He also announced the creation of Sind province, which would be a Muslim-majority province. It was decided later to create the Hindu-majority province of Orissa as a sort of counterbalance. But the creation of Sind was an essential feature of Jinnah's demands since the Delhi proposals. This naturally opened a way for the creation of a Muslim bloc of provinces in the northwest of India. Jinnah secured his Sind province and one-third representation for Muslims in the Central Assembly, well above the Muslim share in the total population. That was indeed a victory for Jinnah. He was quite glad about it.[23] He never fought or agitated for it. But it was given to him on a platter through a British decision, within a short period of five years, at a time when his political fortunes was at its lowest and when he had taken to legal practice in London.

During the same period, at the Unity Conference held in Allahabad in November–December 1932 and attended by all the important Muslim leaders except Jinnah, Rajagopalachari, the southern lieutenant of Gandhi, proposed joint electorates, 32 per cent seats for Muslims in Central Legislature, reservation of seats for Muslims and Sikhs, and primary polling among Muslims and Sikhs to determine candidates for reserved seats. The All-India Muslim League, the *Jamiat-ulema-i Hind*, and some leaders like Madan Mohan Malaviya rejected Rajagopalachari's proposal.[24] Jinnah was settled in London during that period and probably never took note of it.

Officially the Congress neither accepted nor rejected the Communal Award. Gandhi was more worried by the conferment of separate electorates to the Scheduled Castes, which he thought would drive a wedge between the Hindus on a permanent basis. So he decided to go on a fast unto death on 20 September 1932, unless the factor of separate electorates was repealed. Fortunately for him, B.R. Ambedkar, the leader of the Untouchables, agreed to its suppression under the famous Poona Pact, which was accepted by the British Government. Then Gandhi undertook an all-India tour to uplift the Untouchables, whom he called *Harijan*s and to integrate them with other Hindus on an equal footing. In December 1933, during his tour of south India, Gandhi said that if the Harijan uplift failed, then 'Hinduism and Hindus will perish'. Thus Gandhi, the most important man in the Congress, catered overtly in his own way to reform Hinduism and strengthen it.[25]

This and other related activities of Gandhi like his talk of 'Ram Rajya' (Rule by Ram) went a long way in giving the Congress a communal colouring, though the Congress officially professed to be a secular party, open to all Indians, irrespective of caste or creed. Many Muslims thought that Gandhi's desire to reform his ancestral religion was motivated against the Muslims, the great majority of whom were descendants of Hindu converts. In fact, any strengthening of the Hindus or Hinduism by any means was considered as a menace to them by the Muslims.

During that time, Gandhi was very much engrossed by the British attempt to separate the Scheduled Castes from the main body of the Hindus. As a result, he did not give much attention to the added representation in the Central Assembly given to the Muslims by the British and other concessions at the provincial level. It came into force with some modifications under the Government of India Act of 1935. That was well above their share in the total population. That naturally vetted the appetite and ambitions of many Muslims including Jinnah. They were simply led to believe, to a great extent, through the Communal Award that the British will give whatever they asked for, whether the Congress was opposed to it or not. In 1909, they had given separate electorates and in 1932 the Communal Award.

The British were the chief architects who contributed through calculated moves to the construction and strengthening of a separate Muslim political edifice in the Indian body politic. Nobody can affirm reasonably with conviction that the British, during that time, gave importance to the necessity of unity between Indians. Every single move or measure in favour of the Muslims, on the pretext of their political and economic backwardness and vulnerability only strengthened the disunity of Indians, which was profitable to the British. The Communal Award was the eloquent symbol of this policy.

It was during the year 1933 that some enthusiastic but inexperienced Indian-Muslim students such as Choudhury Rahmat Ali, a Punjabi postgraduate student from Emmanuel College, Cambridge, published a four-page leaflet titled 'Now or Never: Are We to Live or Perish Forever?' through which they canvassed for the amalgamation of Punjab, Afghanistan, Kashmir, Sind, and Baluchistan into a new State called PAKSTAN, separate from India. 'Pakstan' literally meant 'Land of the Pure'. The other three who signed the pamphlet were Mohammad Aslam Khan, Sheikh Mohammad Sadiq, and Inayat Ullah Khan. The idea was dismissed by the Muslim delegates like Sir Muhammad Zafarullah Khan and Yusuf Ali of the Joint Parliamentary Committee as a 'student's scheme, ... chimerical and impracticable'. Jinnah himself hardly took any note of it. 'Pakstan' became 'Pakistan' in no time. It did not include the Muslim-majority province of Bengal. Rahmat Ali himself went on to found the Pakistan National Movement in 1934.[26]

The demand for 'Pakstan' by Rahmat Ali and others was the logical culmination of the demand for the creation of three new Muslim-majority provinces included in the Delhi proposals, drafted by Jinnah, which was reiterated in Jinnah's Fourteen Points and conceded by the Communal Award. Those three would constitute a Muslim bloc of provinces in the northwest along with the Punjab. The only innovation that Rahmat Ali made was the inclusion of the contiguous princely State of Kashmir in this bloc, ruled by a Hindu Maharajah, where the Muslims were in a majority. Sir Muhammad Iqbal had not included Kashmir in his conception of the northwestern Muslim State in 1930, though he was of Kashmiri origin.

BACK TO INDIAN POLITICS

From the time Jinnah attended the First Round Table Conference, he had chosen to reside and practise law in London. It however did not mean that he was completely disconnected from Indian politics and disinterested in it. In March 1933, the British government published a White Paper with proposals for an Indian Constitution. In April 1933, a Joint Parliamentary Committee under the chairmanship of Lord Linlithgow was set up to consider these proposals for constitutional reforms. The Congress rejected the White Paper proposals. Jinnah too criticized it. The White Paper wanted a Constituent Assembly to draw a constitution on the basis of adult suffrage as far as possible. Towards the end of 1934, Central Assembly Elections were held. The Congress won a majority of seats in the Assembly, while the Muslim League—in total disarray and with Jinnah still in exile—failed to contest the elections.[1]

Since 1930 Jinnah had talked several times with Muhammad Iqbal in London. In 1933, Jinnah's UP associate and landowner Nawab Liaquat Ali Khan, of Persian ancestry visited London with his new wife Raana and met Jinnah at a reception. Jinnah invited them for dinner at his home in Hampstead. It seemed that the couple convinced Jinnah to return to India and take up the leadership of the Muslims and the Muslim League, as there was an acute leadership vacuum among the Muslims. Jinnah seemed to have succumbed to this request, as he had succumbed about a couple of decades earlier, in the same city, to the request of Syed Wazir Hasan and Maulana Mohammad Ali to join the Muslim League. As a result, Jinnah paid a visit to India in January 1934. Speaking at a meeting held in his honour by the Bombay Muslim Students' Union, under the chairmanship of his associate Mohammad Karim Chagla, Jinnah stressed for a communal settlement.

During February–March 1934, on the initiative of the Aga Khan, the split in the Muslim League was patched up completely and a resolution was passed in a meeting on 4 March 1934 to elect Jinnah as President of the united body. Jinnah expressed his willingness to accept the office of the President of the League. He opened negotiations with Madan Mohan Malaviya for a communal settlement. It seemed that he was willing to give up separate electorates after a specified period for joint electorates under certain conditions. But Madan Mohan Malaviya was not the right person to talk to then, as the Congress was absolutely under the influence of Mahatma Gandhi and Jawaharlal Nehru during that period. At the All-India Muslim League meeting held on 1–2 April 1934, it was resolved to accept the Communal Award. Mr Asaf Ali expressed the hope that under the leadership of Jinnah, the doors of the League would be thrown open to all. Jinnah did not respond to it. Instead, he made a survey of the whole situation, appealed to the Muslims to do the best for the cause of the country, and asked them to financially help the League. This showed that Jinnah had decided to revive the League during that period. However, for Jinnah the only over-riding issue was how Muslim interests would be protected in a future constitution. Jinnah went back to London a few weeks later, where he remained until October.[2]

Meanwhile Fazl-i Husain of the Punjab who was opposed to Jinnah on the question of separate electorates and weightage wanted Jinnah to return to India. Even Sir Muhammad Iqbal wrote his famous letter to Jinnah requesting him to return to India.[3] Everyone who wanted Jinnah to return to Indian politics, from Liaquat Ali Khan and the Aga Khan to Fazl-i Husain and Iqbal, had their own agendas in their minds. Jinnah ran the risk of becoming an instrument in their hands, as it was the case during the Lucknow Pact, when he tilted in favour of the Muslims of the minority provinces, under pressure from some UP League leaders.

On 7 July 1934, the British conceded another one of Jinnah's Fourteen Points, with regard to Muslims' share in the public services, which was duly fixed at 25 per cent of all appointments—imperial and provincial. The *Report of the Joint Parliamentary Committee on Reforms* was published on 21 November 1934. Jinnah criticized this report. He returned to India in January 1935, after disposing off his property in London. During his absence, he had even been elected to the Central Assembly from the Bombay Muslim constituency, unopposed as an independent in November 1934. Meanwhile the *Joint Parliamentary Committee Report*, published in November 1934 was adopted by both the Houses of the Parliament and became law.[4]

In 1935, the British carved out another Hindu-majority province called Orissa from Bihar province. They also created another Muslim-majority province in northwest India by separating Sind from Bombay Presidency on 1 April 1936. Jinnah had reasons to be happy as it was he who demanded Sind since 1927. His demand for equal status to NWFP had also been conceded. But Jinnah would never give up separate electorates and accept joint electorates though he had promised this earlier if Sind and NWFP were created. There were altogether five Muslim-majority provinces including Baluchistan—which was a Chief Commissioner's province, against eight Hindu-majority provinces in British India. In 1937, Burma was separated from India as a colony, on the basis of ethnicity and religion. Indians, both Hindus and Muslims, hardly raised any objection to it.[5] This measure actually set the precedent that India can be divided on religious grounds.

The announcement of the devolution of power to the hands of the Indians through the Government of India Act of 1935 set in motion a general scramble for power throughout India. Under this Act, elections were to be held to the provincial Assemblies in the year 1937. Dyarchy was abolished. Provincial autonomy was given, subject to certain 'reservations and safeguards' and the governor's 'discretionary powers'. The number of voters was to increase from about six and half to about 30 million or from 3 to 14 per cent of the total population.

But the federal part of the 1935 Act envisaged the creation of a central legislature, with one-third of representation allotted to Muslims, and another one-third to nominated members from the princely States (104 out of 276 in the Council of State and 125 out of 375 in the Central Assembly). This would have virtually reduced Congress to a minority party in the legislature, whereas the Muslims would still be a minority, in spite of enhanced representation. It was none other than the Labour Party parliament member C.R. Attlee who claimed in the parliament that the Act has been 'deliberately framed so as to exclude, as far as possible, the Congress party from effective powers in the new constitution'.

Under the Act, the financial control was transferred from London to New Delhi, while the relations between the Crown and the princely States was transferred to the 'Crown representative', that is, the Viceroy through the official Political Department. No real power was transferred to Indian hands in the Centre. However, the Act gave the Muslims the best of both worlds—the Muslims in the Muslim-minority provinces retained weightage, while in Bengal, where the European community held 10 per cent of the seats, the Muslims acquired 48.6 per cent and in the Punjab a virtual statutory majority of 51.4 per cent. R.J. Moore had maintained that Muslim predominance in the northwest and northeast was emphasized, while in other provinces, they were given an importance disproportionate to their numbers. In short, the 1935 Act had enhanced the importance of the Muslims beyond their numbers.[6]

Jinnah could not but be happy about this. All this had been given to the Muslims by the British, even without the League or Jinnah or any Muslim organization agitating for it. Naturally the 1935 Act encouraged Jinnah further to pursue his politics on communal lines, as then he knew for sure that the British were favourably disposed towards the Muslims, which had the potential to turn them away from the aspirations of the Congress.

The Congress opposed the Federal part of the 1935 Act tooth and nail. Instead, they wanted the Indians to be allowed to frame their own constitution through a Constituent Assembly, elected by universal suffrage. The Hindu Maha Sabha was not opposed to Federation. Jinnah and the Muslim League were willing to give the Federation scheme of the 1935 Act a trial, though they feared Hindu domination at the largely unitary centre. They thought that the Hindus would, from that vantage ground, succeed in undermining the authority of the provincial governments in Punjab and Bengal where the Muslim majority held power. In the face of opposition, the implementation of the Federal part of the 1935 Act was postponed and the 1919 Act which provided for official control at the Centre continued to function. It is, however, not possible to predict as some British scholars like C.H. Philips tend to do that if the Federal part of the Act had been implemented, Indian unity would have been maintained. This is not only because the political situation in the country was volatile, but also because any unprecedented event or decision in the course of time had the potential to derail the whole process and oblige even the British to change course.[7]

But at this stage, Jinnah seemed to have desired to keep talking with the Congress party, which was extremely strong and well-organized, with a string of leaders like Mahatma Gandhi, Jawaharlal Nehru, C. Rajagopalachari, Vallabhbhai Patel, Subhas Chandra Bose, and Dr Rajendra Prasad. Nehru was increasingly socialist minded during that period which was disliked by conservatives like Vallabhbhai Patel, Rajagopalachari, Rajendra Prasad, and J.B. Kripalani.[8]

There was no League Annual Session in the year 1935. But Jinnah was not inactive. He was once again up to his old methods. He wanted to open negotiations with the Congress party yet again in order to arrive at a new communal settlement. Many of his earlier demands had been satisfied by the British through the 1919 Act, the Communal Award, and the 1935 Act. He had got his one-third representation for Muslims in the Centre, weightage for Muslims in the minority provinces, and the separate

Sind province. He wanted the Congress to once again recognize the Muslim League as the authoritative representative of Muslims. But Jinnah and the League were not in a position of strength during that period. In spite of that, since October 1934, Jinnah was able to open talks on the Communal Award with Rajendra Prasad, the Congress President and a close confidant of Gandhi. This showed that the Congress still believed that an agreement with him would settle the Hindu–Muslim problems. The Jinnah–Prasad Pact envisaged joint electorates and franchise qualification to reflect the proportion of population of the various communities in the electoral rolls. There was opposition to the Pact from the Sikhs, the Hindu Maha Sabha, and Madan Mohan Malaviya. Jinnah wanting the agreement of all the parties concerned for the Pact, refused to pursue it any further. On the other hand, Nehru belatedly contended that the happenings of the past few years had altered the position. He was not willing to take the demands of Jinnah and the Muslim League seriously in the changed political equations.[9]

With the failure of the Jinnah–Prasad Pact, Jinnah was all set to reorganize the League on a firmer footing. He tried to rope in provincial-minded Fazl-i Husain, without whom Jinnah had no chance of gaining a foothold in the Punjab, the most important Muslim-majority province. He wrote to him requesting him to preside the next League Session at Lahore. He was not successful in this attempt and left Punjab in disgust promising never to return to such a 'hopeless' place as the Punjab.[10] Having been rebuffed by the Punjabis and Fazl-i Husain, Jinnah had no other alternative but to count upon his followers in the Muslim-minority provinces, especially in the key province of the UP. On 10 May 1936, the League Annual Session was held at Bombay, where Jinnah resided. Jinnah, unable to rope in Fazl-i Husain to preside the session, finally settled for his old friend Sir Syed Wazir Hasan of the UP—who had brought him into the League in 1913—to preside over the session. The Chairman of the Reception Committee was the Bombay financial magnate Sir Currimbhoy Ebrahim. Another friend of Jinnah from the UP, who had actually enticed him back to India, Nawab Liaquat Ali Khan became the General Secretary of the League. This shows the importance that Jinnah attached to UP, the heart of Muslim India. The alliance between the UP Nawab Liaquat Ali Khan and Jinnah became a permanent feature of the League since then. It was to continue until the latter's death and spearhead Jinnah's movement thenceforth. During the session, in the presence of Jinnah, Sir Syed Wazir Hasan claimed that Hindus and Muslims were two nations in many respects. Jinnah's speech during the conference was designed to inflame the passions of the Muslims. He thundered: 'Are we content to lose our identity and to be relegated to the position of political pariahs?'[11]

The Raja of Mahmudabad (Junior) joined the League during that period. He even became member of Muslim League Working Committee. Later he was appointed as the Treasurer.

Having the minority UP Muslims behind him was far more important for Jinnah to stake his claim for all-India leadership, than the Muslims of the peripheral Muslim-majority states of the Punjab and Bengal. During the session, Jinnah was empowered to constitute an All India Parliamentary Board and the provincial parliamentary boards, to prepare the election manifesto and also to frame rules for contesting the elections on an all-India basis. One of the essential features of the manifesto was the protection of the zamindars against expropriation, contemplated by the Congress. This shows the elitist character of the League whose top leaders were mostly zamindars, talukdars, Nawabs, and other proprietors, who wanted to safeguard their privileges. The League Parliamentary Board Manifesto, 1936 included the protection of the religious rights of the Muslims, protection and promotion of Urdu, promotion of the general conditions of the Muslims, nationalization of the Indian Army, and the social and economic uplift of rural people. The Manifesto criticized the Federal Scheme of the Government of India Act of 1935 and wanted the British government to review it fully. It also called for free cooperation with any group or groups whose aims and ideals were approximately the same as the League.[12]

Jinnah became the permanent president of the League thenceforth. There was no one (anymore) in the League to stand up to Jinnah. His old rival in the Punjab, Mian Muhammad Shafi had passed away, while Fazl-i Husain of the Unionist Party refused to ally with Jinnah. Fazl-i Husain died in July 1936. This provided an opening for the League and Jinnah in the Punjab. Sikandar Hayat Khan, belonging to a landed family, had succeeded Fazl-i Husain as leader of the Unionist Party. He was the son of Nawab Muhammad Hayat Khan of Wah in the Attock district of the Punjab. Sikandar Hayat Khan seemed to have been interested to come to an alliance or agreement with the Muslim League, whose provincial branch in the Punjab was being led by men like Sir Muhammad Iqbal. The latter seemed to have had his own misgivings about this alliance.[13]

At that time, the All-India Muslim League Council consisted of 310 members. Punjab which had 13 million Muslims had 50 members on the Council while the UP which had 7 million also had 50 members; Delhi alone had 10 members. This showed that the Council was designed to project the power of the Muslims of the Muslim-minority provinces.[14]

In August 1936, Jinnah presided a meeting of the All India Students Conference. Nehru was invited by Jinnah to speak in the conference. Jinnah still thought that he could arrive at a new communal settlement with the younger Nehru as he had done with the older one; But Nehru was clueless about it. Instead, he talked of Marxism and considered Jinnah as a 'collaborator' with British imperialists and the communal problem 'a nuisance'. As for Jinnah, he had only contempt for Nehru. He once said of Nehru: 'He is a Peter Pan; he will never learn anything, or unlearn anything'.[15]

During the course of the year, Jinnah also visited Bengal and Lucknow. In Bengal he was greeted with black flags. The Krishak Praja Party, a party of affluent agrarian interests led by A.K. Fazlul Huq was fighting the elections independently of the Congress and the League. It seems that Fazlul Huq wanted the members of the Bengal League provincial parliamentary board to sign his party's pledge. When that was not possible,

Jinnah broke off with him and the League had to contest the elections in Bengal, led by Khawaja Nazimuddin of the Nawab of Dacca's family. In Lucknow, Jinnah's meeting did not draw much crowd. He appealed for funds but could get only Rs 23,000. The League was in an election fray on an all-India basis for the first time and so Jinnah went canvassing for the League to various parts of India. He made it clear that cooperation or coalition with the Congress has to be on an equal footing.[16] But he did not pursue the matter any further.

During that period Jinnah got his old bungalow at Mount Pleasant Road pulled down. In its place, he constructed a magnificent European-style palatial mansion with imported Italian marble and wood at a very high cost. He engaged a European architect for the purpose. Keeping with his British upbringing, he called the mansion 'South Court'; it was popularly known as 'Jinnah House'. Jinnah never chose a Muslim name for his house. He decided to reside like a Nawab in this mansion with his sister Fatima and his daughter Dina. With the construction of this huge mansion, it was understood that Jinnah had chosen permanent residence in Bombay; he had no intention or plan whatsoever to sever this relation with Bombay during that period. Jinnah had also acquired a splendid bungalow at 10, Aurangzeb Road, a posh area of Delhi, so that he could reside there whenever he visited Delhi. He was in the process of redecorating it. He purchased a new imported car at Rs 7,100. His seven rented flats assured him a handsome monthly income of more than Rs 2,000. All this clearly showed that Jinnah had amassed considerable wealth. He had not only earned good money through his legal practice, but also had invested prudently in shares and real estates, which brought him considerable profits. Naturally he had the capitalist bent of mind.[17]

At a time when Jinnah constructed his western-style mansion, he underwent a transformation in his way of dressing. He traded thenceforth his western costumes quite often for the traditional baggy trousers of the Punjabi Muslim, an *achkan*, and a Turkish cap. This transformation made him look more like a Muslim. He was in a position to connect himself with the Muslim masses more efficiently, which he had avoided earlier. He seemed to have realized quite lately that in order to protect the interests of the Muslim elite, he had no other alternative but to reach out to the Muslim masses who shared the same Islam religion with the elite. Though he was still not well-versed in Islam, never observed many of its rituals and ceremonies, never made any attempt to learn and speak Urdu, yet he started to convey a simple message to the Muslim masses of the impending dangers to Islam. He, however, never substantiated this assertion. Instead, he warned the Muslims of the impending Hindu Raj, in the name of the Congress party, implying that Islam was in danger in India.[18]

In a nutshell, he started using, to some extent, the Islamic card to mobilize the Muslim masses behind the Muslim League. His earlier demands and proposals on behalf of the Muslim League never attracted the masses towards the League, mainly because of its elitist character. Jinnah, who had accused Gandhi during the Khilafat Movement for mixing religion with politics and left the Congress, was himself mixing religion with politics in a greater intensity to mobilize the Muslims for the impending elections. It showed that Jinnah never had a steadfast line or policy in politics. In the beginning, he veered from joint electorates to separate electorates and then kept juggling between them to finally settle for separate electorates. Similarly, he veered from the Congress to the Muslim League, remained affiliated with both for seven years, and then parted ways with the Congress to remain in the League. Then he was veering gradually from elite politics to mass politics.

The Congress and the British had to deal with that new avatar of Jinnah in the forthcoming years. The man who was against the pan-Islamist Khilafat Movement launched by Maulana Mohammad Ali and Mahatma Gandhi, and had proved himself loyal to the British, was now talking in terms of pan-Islamism and raising his voice to protect the special destiny of the Indian Muslims, to which they were entitled by virtue of their belief in Arabian Islam. The British watched this transformation of Jinnah towards Islamism. But they did nothing about it as this Islamism was not directed against them, as during the days of the Khilafat agitations. Neither the Congress could do anything about it.

Jinnah was the unquestionable head of the Muslim League. His party had to contest the 1937 provincial elections. Early in January 1937, Jinnah renewed his harsh words. He warned the Congress to leave the Muslims alone. He had to contend with not only the Congress, which was the strongest and the most well-organized party of India, but also with some regional parties especially in the Punjab, Bengal, the UP, and NWFP led by the Muslims. In the Punjab, there was the Unionist Party; in Bengal Fazlul Huq, his former colleague in the League had founded the Krishak Praja Party; in the UP there was the landlord-oriented National Agriculturist Party of the Nawab of Chattari; while in the NWFP, there was the nationalist *Khudai Khidmatgar* (Servants of God party), founded in 1929 by Abdul Ghaffar Khan. There was no written agreement or pact between Jinnah or Liaquat Ali Khan and the top Congress leadership or the leaders of the Unionist Party, the National Agriculturist Party, and the Krishak Praja Party to contest the elections in alliance with one another or to form coalition ministries in the various provinces after the elections. Jinnah did try for alliance with Fazlul Huq and failed. In the UP, it appears that Liaquat Ali Khan cultivated the support of the Nawab of Chattari for contesting the elections.[19]

The relationship between the Congress and the League was never smooth since the Khilafat Movement and has been severed since 1920 due to Jinnah's various communal demands and proposals. Nehru thought only on economic lines and dismissed communalism as a 'nuisance' and a 'side issue'.[20] This, along with secularism, was his profound conviction and not a tactical move to counter or belittle the League or Jinnah. He held to this conviction even after Independence and until his death. Nor did Jinnah enjoy a good relationship with the Muslim leaders of the Muslim-majority provinces. Fazl-i Husain and his successor Sikandar Hayat Khan always looked upon Jinnah with suspicion. As a matter of fact, in spite of such drawbacks, Jinnah prepared the League for the elections with the help of his lieutenants of the Muslim-minority provinces like Liaquat Ali Khan and the Raja of Mahmudabad on an all-India basis. The elections were still held on a very restricted franchise composed of only about 14 per cent of the total population.

Out of 1,585 provincial seats, including the reserved constituencies, the Congress contested 1,161 and won 716. It gained absolute majority in five provinces out of eleven—Madras, Bihar, Orissa, Central Provinces, and the UP, while in Bombay it won 86 of 175 seats. That was indeed a spectacular victory. Strangely, the Congress contested only 58 out of the 482 Muslim seats in British India, where the elections took place on the basis of separate electorates. It won 26. But in spite of all the 'Islam in Danger' propaganda unleashed by the Leaguers and Jinnah, the League managed to win only 109 seats out of 482, that is, only 4.8 per cent of the Muslim votes. That was indeed a poor show for a party that was increasingly claiming to be the sole representative of the Indian Muslims. In the Muslim-majority provinces, it could not win a single seat in NWFP, it won just two out of the 84 seats reserved for Muslims in the Punjab, and 3 out of 33 in Sind. Raja Ghazanfar Ali Khan who won in the Punjab as a Leaguer defected to the Unionist Party. That left the League with just one member in the Punjab Assembly. In these three provinces, the total number of Muslim seats was 153, but the League won only four. In Bengal it fared a little better. It won 40 seats out of 119, but the League leader of Bengal, Khawaja Nazimuddin, descendant of Nawab Salimullah of Dacca, was defeated by the Krishak Praja Party leader, Fazlul Huq. In the Muslim-minority provinces, the League won 27 out of 60 Muslim seats in the UP, the heart of Muslim India, in Madras 11 out of 29, in Bombay 20 out of 30 seats. In Baluchistan, the organization called *Khadim-i-Watan*, which had Congress support, was the most influential.[21]

In the Punjab and Bengal, the League had not lost to the Congress, but to the Unionist Party and the Krishak Praja Party respectively. On the whole, it could be said that the League had won more number of seats in the Muslim-minority provinces than in the Muslim-majority provinces.

However, it became clear to the whole world that the League was not the sole representative of the Muslims and Jinnah was not the sole spokesman of the Muslims. The League and Jinnah had lost the race to power in the provinces. They were smarting under this terrible loss. At that time, Nehru claimed that there were only two parties in the country—the Congress and the British. Jinnah retaliated that there was a third party—the Muslims. He stressed that they would not be camp followers of any party.[22]

Although the Congress had won a thumping majority in the general constituencies, Nehru was still against office acceptance. But many other leaders, including the southern stalwart Rajagopalachari were for it. Nehru was obsessed with the economic problems of India, which prompted Sir Muhammad Iqbal to write to Jinnah that from the Muslim point of view, cultural problem was of much greater consequence to most Indian Muslims. He instructed Jinnah to summon a national convention and discuss that issue. But Jinnah never responded.[23]

Later, when the Congress decided to accept office, it became clear that the Muslim League would be in political wilderness for the coming five years when the next provincial elections will be held. The Congress was under no obligation to form a coalition ministry with the Muslim League in any of the provinces, as that was never agreed upon by the Congress High Command and Jinnah prior to the elections. In any case, the Congress ministries would include some Muslim ministers, elected on Congress ticket. So there was no reason for the Congress to open any sort of negotiations with the League.

But things were a bit different in the United Provinces, the heart of Muslim India. The League did not win even half of the Muslim seats there in the elections. But the Congress had won 134 out of 228 seats. It enjoyed the support of the Deoband ulama group, the Jamiat-ul-ulema-i-Hind, founded by Maulana Ahmad Sayeed and the ex-Khilafatist Ahrars led by Maulana Habibur Rahman of the Punjab. An Ahrar Conference in May 1937 denounced Jinnah as an 'out-of-date politician'—'making a fetish of constitutionalism', and the League as 'a coterie of a few knights, Khan Bahadurs and Nawabs'.

It was believed that there was a tacit understanding between some local Congress leaders and League leaders to form a coalition government there, so that the League could have a share in the power. Chaudhry Khaliquzzaman, the landowner, who was in the Congress until early 1937 and Nawab Ismail Khan, the President of the Muslim League of the UP wanted to become Ministers in the UP Ministry. As there was no settlement, there was no coalition ministry. Maulana Abul Kalam Azad, who was in charge of Muslim affairs in the Congress, made it plain to Chaudhry Khaliquzzaman on 15 July 1937 that the Muslim League group in the UP legislature must dissolve itself before one or two of them got a place in the Ministry.[24] Thus the Muslim League was out of the corridors of power in the Hindu-majority provinces. But it would be wrong to maintain that Muslims were systematically and deliberately kept out of power by the Congress, for many nationalist Muslims participated in the Congress-led governments.

It must be noted that the UP coalition problem was purely a local problem. If Maulana Abul Kalam Azad had asked the UP Muslim League legislature group to disband itself before one or two of them were taken into the League, it was for the League to accept or reject it. There was no constitutional obligation on the part of the Congress to form a coalition government with the Muslim League, just because the Muslims enjoyed separate electorates. Neither did Jinnah open any sort of negotiations with the Congress High Command in favour of a Congress-League coalition in the UP before the elections. There was no written agreement between UP League and Congress leaders for a coalition ministry after the elections. Contemporary evidence, especially by Donaldson, who was secretary to UP government in 1937, indicates that this supposed alliance was nothing more than casual cooperation between local Congressmen and Leaguers in a few constituencies where both saw the National Agriculturist Party of the Nawab of Chattari who had the support of many Muslim landlords in spite of Jinnah's appeal, as their main rival. The British scholar Tomlinson had further drawn our attention to an official of the Government of India Reforms Office who had recorded that these stories of coalition ministry had no currency (or very little) till a long time had passed and until the manufacture of Muslim League grievances had been organized.[25]

It is highly doubtful if Jinnah and the League leadership would have allowed Khaliquzzaman (who had disconnected himself from the Congress only lately) and Nawab Ismail Khan to chart an independent course in the formation of the UP ministry in cooperation with the Congress. There was opposition to them within the UP League itself. On 25 April 1937, Jinnah himself issued a public statement condemning Khaliquzzaman's move. During the months of April and May 1937, the League leadership including Jinnah cautioned Khaliquzzaman and his friends about their flirtations with the Congress. Jinnah himself visited Lucknow in May on a fact-finding mission. It is wrong to assert like Raza Khan, Mushirul Hasan, A.G. Noorani, and many others, following British scholars and legislators like Sir Percival Griffiths and Reginald Coupland, that Jinnah would not have radicalized his stand if a Congress–League coalition ministry had come about in the UP, especially when it did not have the public approval of Jinnah. Since the elections, Jinnah had been consistently demanding Muslims not to participate in any Congress demonstration or convention, whereas nationalist Muslims like Abul Kalam Azad and Sir Syed Wazir Hasan were asking the Muslims to join the Congress. Three Muslim Leaguers elected to the UP legislature had actually joined the Congress during that period.[26]

All this was happening at a time when the Congress had not yet formed the ministries and in the UP, the National Agriculturist Party of the Nawab of Chattari was running an interim ministry. Had the Congress accepted to form a coalition ministry in the UP, it would have set a bad precedent on which Jinnah could dwell upon in future and also would have vindicated the theory that there were indeed two nations in India, based on religion—one represented by the Congress and the other by the Muslim League.

There was hardly any problem in the other provinces in which the Congress had outrightly won with regard to the formation of ministries. More than anyone else, Jinnah must have known that separate electorates for Muslims, especially in the minority provinces do not qualify them to take part in the government automatically. Accusing Congress of 'totalitarianism' which led to the revival of the League is simply out of place at this juncture. The League had not fared well in the elections for which it had to bear the consequences. The Muslim Mass Contact Programme was launched under the influence of Nehru after the elections to bring more Muslims into the Congress. It was a programme on paper only. The Congress was exercising only its democratic right to represent all sections of Indians including the Muslims. Jinnah and the Muslim League saw in this a deliberate attempt of the Congress to poach in what they considered as their exclusive territory, which had the potential to endanger their very political survival.[27] In the general scramble for power in the provinces, the Muslim League and Jinnah were the greatest losers. They lost not just in the Muslim-minority provinces, but also in the Muslim-majority provinces. They were smarting under this loss and were on the lookout for alternatives to revive their fortunes.

In the NWFP, a Congress–Muslim nationalist coalition government came into existence on 6 September 1937, with Dr Khan Sahib as Chief Minister; in the Punjab, the Unionist Party under Sikandar Hayat Khan came to power; and in Bengal, Fazlul Huq of the Krishak Praja Party formed the government. For Jinnah, the sectarian nationalist that he was till then, it was a strong challenge and a personal setback in his long career in politics. Jinnah had entered politics even before Gandhi. Jawaharlal Nehru, Rajagopalachari, Vallabhbhai Patel, Subhas Chandra Bose, and Dr Rajendra Prasad were junior to him in the political front. But still he stood sidelined. He lacked the support of the Muslims too, though it was not the fault of the Congress. That was a strange situation which he had to face.

It was from that time onwards that Jinnah revised his strategy, in an attempt to revive his own fortunes and the fortunes of the Muslim Leaguers and its elite, in particular. It was a two-pronged strategy. In the first place, he laid a greater emphasis on 'Islam in danger' slogan to mobilize the Muslim masses in a larger scale. He used the Islamic cultural and religious card more and more to strengthen his position and that of the Muslim League among the Muslims. Viceroy Linlithgow had noted this change in Jinnah's strategy.[28]

From then onwards, Jinnah was sliding gradually from his position as a sectarian nationalist towards that of an outright separatist. With regard to mixing religion with politics, he did a monumental volte face to the surprise of everyone, including Congress leaders like the socialist-minded Jawaharlal Nehru. Thenceforth, he posed himself as a sort of messiah who had come to save the Muslims and Islam. In his quest for power and the protection and promotion of Muslim interests which principally included elite interests, he reached out to the Muslim masses more and more, using Islamic ideas and symbols, which cut across caste, class, and sectarian divisions among Muslims. Earlier, he had used the idea of separate electorates on the basis of Islam in his search for power for the Muslim elite. Then he started using the more fundamental and pervasive ideology of Islam itself in the same quest for power. That was a challenging development as pervasive ideologies like Islam had a great emotional dimension associated with them, apart from power.

Secondly he turned his attention to the Muslim-majority provinces of the Punjab and Bengal, where his party had fared very badly. The Congress was, in no way, responsible for the League debacle there. Instead, Jinnah had lost to the Unionist Party and the Krishak Praja Party. He knew that without the backing and help of the Muslims of these provinces, the Muslims of the minority provinces would never be a force to be reckoned with in Indian politics and they would always play a subordinate role to the Congress. So it was mainly in order to protect the interests of the Muslims in the Muslim minority provinces, especially of the UP that Jinnah opened negotiations with Sir Sikandar Hayat Khan and A.K. Fazlul Huq in order to bring them on the League platform and present a united Muslim front to the Congress and the British. This was done under the influence of the UP Muslim League leaders like Liaquat Ali Khan, virtually the number two of the party, Nawab Ismail Khan, the Raja of Mahmudabad and Chaudhry Khaliquzzaman. It was due to a similar influence of the UP League leaders in 1916 that he concluded the Lucknow Pact. Jinnah knew by past experience that without the support of the UP Leaguers, he would be nowhere. It is with their help that he could patch up with Sikandar Hayat Khan and Fazlul Huq. The question of sharing power at the Centre came handy to push forward Jinnah's claim for a unified Muslim front. From Jinnah's point of view, the assumption of power by the Congress in the Muslim-majority provinces as well as in NWFP made this union more than necessary and crucial. Jinnah succeeded in that attempt.

RADICALIZATION OF THE MIND

The Congress finally assumed office in various provinces around July 1937. It became increasingly clear what lay in store for the Muslim League, especially in the Muslim-minority provinces and at the Centre, where there was no possibility of coalition or cooperation with the Congress. The League also had doubts about the effectiveness of the Governor's safeguards for the minorities. That pushed Jinnah to radicalize his stand. He withdrew his former acceptance of the 1935 Act. By the time the All-India Muslim League Session was held in Lucknow in October 1937, Jinnah and the Muslim League were able to rope in the support of Sikandar Hayat Khan and Fazlul Huq. Sikandar Hayat Khan was not a Fazl-i Husain to hold Jinnah forever at a distance. A.K. Fazlul Huq was, after all, a former Leaguer. Jinnah had also acquired the support of the Chief Minister of Assam, Sir Syed Muhammad Saadulla Basha. Sir Abdullah Haroon of Sind also joined the Muslim League. For the first time in its history, the League undertook a policy of mass contact of Muslims. It reduced the annual subscription fee to two annas and turned towards the Muslim masses of the countryside.[1]

The Lucknow session was organized by the Raja of Mahmudabad. Jinnah was given a warm welcome. He was taken around in procession in a decorated open car. The Raja of Mahmudabad walked on foot, in front of Jinnah's car up to Kaiser Bagh, the venue of the session. Zafar Ali Khan of the Punjab hoisted the League flag. During the session Jinnah lambasted the Congress, took a strong position against the imposition of Hindi as the national language—against the singing of the *Vande Mataram* during the Assembly sessions and also against the hoisting of the Congress flag in government buildings. He declared that the League stood for full national democratic self-government of India, where Muslim interests were safeguarded. He rejected the Federal Scheme of the 1935 Act. He rose against the Congress appointing Muslim ministers who did not have public support. He considered the mass contact programme of the Congress as calculated to divide and weaken or break the Muslims and as an effort to detach them from their accredited leaders. He took a position against the socialist ideas of Congress leaders like Nehru. He opposed the idea of the Congress to call for a Constituent Assembly on the basis of adult franchise. He wanted Urdu to be the universal language of India, instead of Hindi, in spite of the fact that only a minority of about 28 million among the Indian Muslims spoke Urdu. He asked the Muslims to unite behind him without worrying about being branded as 'communalists, toadies or reactionaries'. Jinnah's hands as the undisputed all-India leader of the Muslims was strengthened during this conference. Gandhi himself considered Jinnah's defiant speech during the Lucknow session as a declaration of war.[2]

After the Lucknow session, Jinnah went on an all-India tour to mobilize the Muslim masses. Branches of the League were formed all over the country. Jinnah participated in several League meetings and conferences all over the country.[3] He, who was in the past an elite leader, was now donning the garb of a mass leader like Gandhi.

Jinnah entered into a pact with Sikandar Hayat Khan on 15 October 1937 named as the Sikandar–Jinnah Pact, which provided for the pre-eminence of the Muslim League in all-India affairs, while Sikandar retained his control over Punjab affairs through the Unionist Party. The pact was announced during the Lucknow session. That was an essential pre-requisite for Jinnah to legitimize his leadership in all-India Muslim affairs. Sikandar Hayat Khan had contributed to it through the pact and raised the status of Jinnah at the all-India level. He thought that this way he could keep the Muslim League in Punjab under control and also assure Muslim share in the power at the Centre. He was only partially right in this respect, as it became increasingly difficult for him to break away from the hold of Jinnah. In the process, he allowed Jinnah and the Muslim League to strike stronger roots in the Punjab.[4]

The Sikandar–Jinnah Pact was denounced privately by none other than Sir Muhammad Iqbal, the President of the Punjab Muslim League since May 1936 and also Malik Barkat Ali, League's representative in the Punjab Assembly. They were convinced that Sikandar and the Unionists wanted not only to slacken the activities of the Provincial Muslim League, but also to capture the Provincial Parliamentary Board, as they would not sign the League pledge or hold a League Session in the Punjab and wanted a complete change in the officeholders of the League and also control its finances. Iqbal wrote several letters to Jinnah, but Jinnah did not reply; instead, he wrote to Barkat Ali that the new members were as good as the old. However, due to ill-health Iqbal had to resign from the presidentship of the Punjab Muslim League in 1938, leaving the way for the wealthiest Pathan *jagirdar* and the former Unionist, the Nawab of Mamdot, Shah Nawaz Khan, to capture the party and become its president. The Nawab was close to Sikandar.

Even before this succession took place, Jinnah derecognized the existing Punjab Muslim League and appointed a new Punjab Muslim League Organizing Committee, dominated by the supporters of Sikandar and not the urban supporters of Iqbal. This clearly showed that Jinnah and Iqbal were at loggerheads as far as affairs concerning the Punjab were concerned. The brother of Liaquat Ali Khan, Sajjad Ali Khan was a Unionist member of the Punjab Legislative Assembly. Liaquat Ali Khan himself hailed from Karnal in the Punjab. These connections drew Sikandar towards the Muslim League and Jinnah. Sir Muhammad Iqbal suffering from ill-health was not in a position to undo the Sikandar–Jinnah alliance in the making, which he thought would be detrimental to the interests of the north-western Muslims and the Punjab Muslim League.[5]

Jinnah, on his part, with the help of Liaquat Ali Khan kept Sir Muhammad Iqbal and his supporters at a distance. He did not even send a congratulatory message for the 'Iqbal Day' celebrated by the students of Lahore on 26 December 1937.[6]

Earlier, just after the provincial assembly elections in which the League fared badly, Sir Muhammad Iqbal had written to Jinnah asking him to take up the cause of Muslim poverty and its eradication so that the League transforms itself into a mass-based party from an upper-class party. He made it known to Jinnah that the Congress was a Hindu organization like the Hindu Maha Sabha. He held that the Maha Sabha was the real representative of the Hindu masses. He further wrote that the new constitution with its idea of single federation was hopeless. He also claimed that the Muslims of North-West India (and Bengal) were 'nations', entitled to self-determination and asked Jinnah to concentrate on them and ignore Muslim-minority provinces. He wrote the following to Jinnah on 28 May 1937:

> ...the enforcement and development of the Shariat of Islam is impossible in this country without a free Muslim State or States ... in order to make it possible for Muslim India to solve their problems, it is necessary to redistribute the country and to provide one or more Muslim States with absolute majorities. Don't you think that the time for such a demand has already arrived? Perhaps this is the best reply you can give to the atheistic socialism of Jawaharlal Nehru.[7]

On 21 June 1937, Sir Muhammad Iqbal again wrote to Jinnah that Jinnah was the only person to whom the Muslim community had a right to look upon for safe guidance through the upcoming storm. He asked him to hold the next session of the League in Lahore. Reversing his earlier stand he advised Jinnah to favour the creation of a separate federation of Muslim provinces in the northwest (and Bengal), disregarding the Muslims in the Muslim-minority provinces. He had adopted this position since 1934.[8]

We do not know about the response of Jinnah to these claims and demands of Iqbal. Jinnah later acknowledged that many of his own ideas related to the constitutional problems of India, resembled those of Iqbal. But he never accepted that he was influenced by Iqbal's standpoints in any way.

Jinnah, belonging to the professional and propertied class, was never a socialist. In spite of Iqbal's advice, Jinnah never really took up the cause of Muslim poverty. Except for the 1936 manifesto, which mentioned some vague measures for the poor, Jinnah had never tackled Muslim economic problems in his political life till then. But he had never been against the Shariat, although westernized in his habits and manners. He had sought its protection and the protection of Muslim culture and religion through his Fourteen Points. It showed that Jinnah, though not a practising Muslim, was conscious of the importance of Shariat in Muslim lives. But what was new in Iqbal's advice to Jinnah was his desire to redistribute the country to provide Muslim States with absolute majorities. When Iqbal passed away, the very next year on 21 April, Jinnah simply claimed that Iqbal was his personal friend and the singer of the finest poetry. Later, he admitted that he was the sage, philosopher, and national poet of Islam. Strangely Jinnah failed to acknowledge Iqbal's signal contribution to the development of Muslim separatist political thought and the shaping of his own ideas.[9]

The reluctance of the Congress party under the influence of Nehru, Gandhi, Patel, and Abul Kalam Azad to form a coalition with Fazlul Huq's Krishak Praja Party in Bengal pushed Huq towards the Muslim League. However, Subhas Chandra Bose of the Congress wanted this coalition. Huq also had the support of the British mercantile community. He would not cooperate with the Congress if the Congress did not form coalition ministries with the League in other provinces and if they did not come to an agreement with the League in the matters of appointment to public services and in matters pertaining to the social and cultural life of Muslims. Jinnah himself arrived in Bengal on 17 August 1937 to firm up the alliance with Fazlul Huq. That came as a boon to Jinnah and the League. Fazlul Huq survived as Premier through thick and thin. The All-India Muslim League and Jinnah gained some form of legitimacy in the two main Muslim-majority provinces, which enhanced their prestige at the all-India level. However, Fazlul Huq was always suspicious of Jinnah's intentions.[10]

In Assam, Sir Syed Muhammad Saadulla Basha, an Ashrafi Muslim, was able to form an unstable ministry which was toppled in a few months. It was replaced by a Congress coalition ministry led by Gopinath Bardoloi in October 1938, which resigned in November 1939, following the decision of the Congress High Command. That allowed Sir Saadulla to become Premier again, with a narrow majority, with the help of the European members. That ministry lasted for two years, after which Assam was put under Section 93 of the Act of 1935. After some time Sir Andrew Clow, the Governor of Assam, allowed Sir Saadulla to form a new ministry.[11]

In Sind, the Muslim League was not present. Congress had won only 8 seats in a house of 60. The 1937 elections produced a ministry led by Sir Ghulam Hussain Hidayatullah, leader of the Sind Muslim party and zamindar from Shikarpur. It was soon replaced by a coalition ministry led by another zamindar of Shikarpur called Khan Bahadur Allah Baksh, leader of the Sind United or *Ittehad* party, with support from the Congress. Allah Baksh belonged to the Rajput Soomro dynasty who ruled Sind previously. He never believed in Jinnah's policies. On his part, Jinnah tried to enlist local Muslims and convert the Allah Baksh ministry into a League ministry. In early 1940, Baksh's ministry fell. In March 1940, it was replaced by a ministry led by Mir Bandeh Ali Khan Talpur of the 'Nationalist Party' and a strange combination of the Muslim League and Hindu independents, with support from the Congress. But within a few months, Allah Baksh was re-appointed as Premier. Allah Baksh was a Congress sympathizer. In September 1941, he renounced his 'Khan Bahadur' title and criticized British policy. That led to his dismissal by the British Governor, Hugh Dow. A new coalition ministry, led by Sir Ghulam Hussain Hidayatullah was sworn in, in his place. Thousands of Muslims congratulated the Governor on his action and affirmed their confidence on Jinnah. On 23 October, the new Premier formally joined the Muslim League.[12]

This closing in of the Muslim ranks and the increasing assertiveness of the Muslim League at the provincial and all-India level was a turning point in Muslim League history, which the Congress and its leaders failed to take adequate note of. There was no more stopping of the Muslim League from gaining popularity as a rival of the Congress in the institutionalized scramble for power in the provinces and in the Centre. Jinnah was fast emerging as the undisputed leader of the Muslims at the all-India level. But he still lacked a genuine electoral mandate.

Apart from the Muslims who were worried and even agitated about their place and position in future India, there were some south Indians, who too were worried in their own way about their future in a united India. Already in the Madras Presidency, the anti-Brahmin Dravidian Justice Party held provincial power since the institution of dyarchy in 1920. The party was routed by the Congress in the 1937 elections. C. Rajagopalachari, the southern lieutenant of Gandhi became the first prime minister of the new Congress ministry in Madras.[13]

Once Rajagopalachari became the Prime Minister, he decided to introduce compulsory Hindi in the secondary schools of the Presidency. As a result, he was accused of catering to Brahmin and north Indian Aryan needs by the atheist and Dravidian Self-Respect Movement, which was founded as a social reform movement in the year 1925 by a former Congressman, Periyar E.V. Ramasamy Naicker. It was Ramasamy and his Self-Respect Movement who launched the first anti-Hindi agitations in south India in 1938 which was quite popular and successful.[14]

But with the introduction of the Government of India Act of 1935, Dravidian leaders like Ramasamy began to fear the impending domination of the north Indians in any all-India set-up. In order to counter this eventuality, Ramasamy came out with the demand of a separate and sovereign Dravidian State in December 1938 when he assumed the presidentship of the Justice Party. The State was supposed to include all the Dravidian language-speaking areas of south India. That was the first major separatist demand in India.[15] Jinnah was aware of these developments in the south, when he chose to take a position against Hindi which was touted to become the national language by many Congress leaders.

Even after the elections and the assumption of office by the Congress and other parties in the various provinces, Jinnah did not always abandon his old methods of dialogue and negotiations with the Congress with the intention of thrashing out a new communal settlement, advantageous to the Muslims. The Congress leaders too did not refuse to talk to him. They probably thought that if they did not talk to him, he might use it as a pretext to heap the blame on the Congress for not settling the communal issue. So they kept talking to Jinnah.

Taking into account the electoral arithmetic, especially after the 1937 elections and the rallying of Sikandar Hayat Khan and Fazlul Huq under the League banner, Jinnah seems to have had no other alternative but to expand the League Council. This he did during the course of the year 1938. The Council was expanded to 465 members. Punjab and Bengal were each allotted just 40 more members, while the UP got 20. Punjab and Bengal alone had just over 40 per cent of the voters and even with Sind, NWFP, and Baluchistan, the Muslim-majority provinces had only a slender majority. This once again showed the weightage given to the Muslims in the Muslim-minority provinces. The Working Committee of the League was to be nominated by none other than the permanent president Jinnah, from among the members of the Council. This virtually established the unquestionable authority of Jinnah, who hailed from a Muslim-minority province. The dominance of the Muslims of the Muslim-minority provinces, especially those of the UP, the historical heart of Muslim India, continued in the League Working Committee.[16]

On 2 March 1938, the League Council appointed a five-member Committee under the chairmanship of Raja Syed Muhammad Mehdi of Pirpur, a descendant of the old Mughal aristocracy of the UP, to enquire into the grievances of the Muslims in the Congress-ruled provinces and make a detailed province-wise report of them. Such a sensational national move naturally created a renewed awareness among Muslims of their problems and grievances. By that time, Jinnah had lost the support of Sir Syed Wazir Hasan of the UP completely, who was instrumental in bringing Jinnah into the Muslim League in 1913, and who presided the revived League Session at Bombay in 1936. He did not believe in Jinnah's and League's propaganda that the Congress was a Hindu body, wanting to establish Hindu Raj. He neither believed that the League was the true representative of the Muslims. He wrote to Nehru about this on 11 February 1938, asking him to combat these falsities as it would affect the struggle for economic and political emancipation of India.[17]

On 17 March 1938, Jinnah wrote to Nehru 'to bring about a pact between the Musalmans and the Hindus and create a real united front'. Jinnah strongly expressed his desire to safeguard 'the rights and the interests of the Musalmans with regard to their religion, culture, language, personal laws, and political rights in the national life, the government, and the administration of the country.' But Nehru would not accept Jinnah's new claim that the Muslim League was the only representative organization of Indian Muslims, and made it clear that he could think of Indians only on economic lines and not on communal lines as wanted by Jinnah. He even asserted that there were only two forces in India—British Imperialism and Indian Nationalism. Nehru urged Jinnah to discuss his problems with Maulana Abul Kalam Azad. But Jinnah refused, considering Azad as a Congress 'stooge' and a 'show case Muslim'.[18]

In February 1938 Gandhi initiated correspondence with Jinnah. In April 1938, he met and conversed with Jinnah for three-and-half hours to find a settlement. In May he met him again for two-and-half hours, when Jinnah complained bitterly of Hindi (Sanskritized) being imposed in Madras. Gandhi affirmed quite frequently that there could be no *Swaraj* without Hindu–Muslim unity. Such statements by Gandhi seemed to have been exploited to the hilt by Jinnah. He would never commit himself to *Swaraj*. He would want Gandhi to come out with some new proposal to settle the communal problem. In the process, he would urge Gandhi to accept that the Muslim League was the only authoritative and representative organization of the Muslims; while, on the other hand, he stressed that Gandhi represented the Congress and the Hindus of India.[19] Jinnah's strategy was quite simple. If he made the Congress accept that the League was the only representative organization of the Muslims, then the Congress cannot represent them and will automatically become a Hindu body.

In spite of all the concessions that Jinnah had hitherto obtained from the British, Gandhi did not realize that Hindu–Muslim unity was never obtained. The Congress had accepted separate electorates for Muslims given by the 1909 Act. That had not brought about Hindu–Muslim unity. The Lucknow Pact as well as the Communal Award did not bring Hindu–Muslim unity either. But still Gandhi and even Nehru thought that Jinnah's appetite could be appeased through more talks and concessions and his consent obtained for *Swaraj*. Strangely, in all his talks with the Congress leaders Jinnah had never come out clearly with what he actually wanted further to protecting Muslim interests, given that the British had satisfied most of his old demands.[20]

Instead, Jinnah wanted the Congress to come with its proposals for a settlement, but would not disclose his own proposals. In the light of this, it was not right to hold that Congress spurned Jinnah's offer of cooperation. The claim that the Muslim League was the sole representative of the Indian Muslims and by implication that Jinnah was their sole spokesman, was indeed a totalitarian claim. It defied all accepted norms of democratic decency, not only with regard to the Congress and the Hindus, but also with regard to the Muslims who were offered no other alternative but to accept Jinnah's communal line. Jinnah had no electoral mandate from the Muslims to be their sole representative. However, the British hardly raised their voice against the claim of Jinnah; by their silence they seem to have been indirectly sympathetic to Jinnah's undemocratic and totalitarian claim.

In August 1938, Jinnah wanted the acting Viceroy Brabourne to recognize the Muslim League as the sole representative of the Muslims. But the Viceroy could not do it at that stage. During the year 1938, Jinnah also opened negotiations with Subhas Chandra Bose, the new President of the Congress party, in his supposed quest for a new Hindu–Muslim Pact. But Bose, like Nehru, refused to accept Jinnah's contention that the League was the sole authoritative representative of the Muslims, as there were Muslims not only in the Congress, but also in other parties like the Unionist Party. Besides, there was even a Congress coalition government in the Muslim-majority NWFP. It is noteworthy that the Congress—though it would not accept Jinnah as the sole spokesman of the Muslims—was still willing to appoint a Committee to discuss with the League representatives in view of a settlement. It became problematic when Jinnah insisted that the Congress should not appoint any Muslim to the Committee, as according to him, the Congress cannot represent the Musalmans of India.[21]

On 15 October 1938, Jinnah went one step further. He dismissed whatever assurances that the Congress gave to the Muslims at the Haripura Congress Session in February 1938 in order to protect their religion, culture, and language as mere 'paper resolutions'. He declared that the Congress was a Hindu body and demanded complete equality or parity with the Congress for the League.[22] That was a completely new development in Jinnah's strategy to acquire power.

On 15 November 1938, the *Pirpur Report* was published. It gave a unified picture of Indian-Muslim demands and grievances. But it was concerned mainly with the material needs of the Muslims. Jinnah made use of this report and also a similar report called the *Shareef Report* from Bihar to buttress his accusations against the Congress of trying to undermine Muslim interests in every field, economic as well as cultural.

In his turn Fazlul Huq published his 'Muslim Sufferings under Congress rule' in December 1939.

Maulana Abul Kalam Azad claimed that these reports and allegations were absolutely unfounded. But it was of no avail. The League even rejected a Congress offer of an enquiry into the charges by Chief Justice Maurice Gwyer. Instead Jinnah wanted a Royal Commission of Enquiry. At the League Session of December 1938, Jinnah criticized the character and skill-based Wardha scheme of education, as a 'Hindu scheme'. The scheme was evolved by the Zakir Husain Committee and adopted by Gandhi. Further Jinnah accused Gandhi of converting the Congress into a communal Hindu body, with the intention of reviving and propagating Hindu culture.[23]

Whatever might be the affirmations of Jinnah, history stands testimony to the fact that the Congress, which was from its inception a secular political party, open to all, had never a Hindu religious agenda. There were various shades of opinions and groups within the Congress, ranging from the left to the right. The Leftists within the Congress were quite influential. They included Jawaharlal Nehru and Subhas Chandra Bose, who only thought on economic lines. Individual leaders and members of the Congress like Gandhi might have talked of *Ram Rajya* or might have wanted to reform Hinduism and many others might have harboured Hindu communal feelings. But never did the Congress, in spite of the pressure and propaganda of Jinnah, ever think in terms of Hindu Raj or promoting Hinduism or protecting Hindu culture through the Congress. That was the job of the Hindu Maha Sabha. In 1938, the Congress even banned its members to be simultaneously members of the Hindu Maha Sabha and the Congress; and declared both the Muslim League and Hindu Maha Sabha as communal parties. At the Nagpur session of the Hindu Maha Sabha in December 1938, its President V.D. Savarkar even claimed that Hindus were a nation by themselves. The Congress never endorsed such assertions. In the light of the above, it would be misleading to qualify the Congress as a 'totalitarian' party or even as a 'Hindu' party like Reginald Coupland and some politician-turned-scholars like Jaswant Singh have done or seem to have done.[24]

In December 1938 at the Patna session of the League, as a retort to Nehru and Gandhi, Jinnah declared:

> I want to make it plain to all concerned that we Muslims want no gifts. …As I have said before, there are four forces at play in this country. Firstly, there is the British government. Secondly, there are the rulers and people of the Indian States. Thirdly, there are the Hindus. And fourthly there are the Muslims. … The Congress is nothing but a Hindu body. That is the truth and the Congress leaders know it. …Gandhi is the one man responsible for turning the Congress into an instrument for the revival of Hinduism. …If they get a majority they will accept the Federation with utmost glee, and then they will begin to pursue their nefarious scheme of destroying the Muslim culture and organization and to build up the Congress organization as the one and only totalitarian organization of the Fascist brand. And then they will be able to establish their ideal of Hindu Raj in Hindustan. …I say the Muslim League is not going to be an ally of anyone, but would be the ally of even the devil if need be in the interests of Muslims. It is not because we are in love with imperialism, but in politics we have to play one's game as on the chessboard.[25]

Inspired by the creation of Sind in 1936, two years later in October 1938, the first Muslim League Session of Sind, presided by Jinnah had passed a resolution for establishing 'independent States' in the north-western and eastern zones and devising a scheme of constitution under which the Muslims might attain full independence. Sir Abdulla Haroon, the leader of the League in Sind and a member of the Central Assembly recommended the division of India into two separate federations, each reflecting the strength of one of the two major communities or nations. The main body of the Muslim Federation would be the northwest area and Kashmir. The future of Bengal or Hyderabad was not discussed during the session. In his presidential address to the session, Jinnah accused the Congress of trying to destroy the Muslim League and divide and dominate the Muslims. He warned that this would result in India being divided. Fazlul Huq adopted a threatening posture by declaring in public that if Mohammad bin Qasim could conquer Sind with 18 soldiers, then nine crores of Muslims can conquer the whole of India. During the conference, Shaukat Ali, the former Khilafatist and ally of Gandhi, also used threatening language against the Congress.[26]

In July 1938, Sir Sikandar Hayat Khan of Punjab had asked the help of Penderel Moon—who was then secretary to the Governor of Punjab—to 'edit' a pamphlet written by him or under his direction entitled 'Outline of a Scheme of Indian Federation'. By this scheme he envisaged a loose federal Centre with a three-tiered constitution, with the objective of limiting the authority of the Centre to the lowest minimum and excluding the possibility of a 'Congress Raj' through certain provisions regarding the composition of the Federal Executive.[27]

In the year 1938, Jinnah who was mired neck-deep in politics, suffered a personal setback in his family affairs. Jinnah had no time for his only daughter, Dina, who grew up under the care of Fatima. Dina had enough time to fall in love with an Indian Christian Parsi, Neville Wadia, a flourishing Bombay businessman, whom she married in 1938. Jinnah is believed to have strongly opposed the marriage; but it was of no avail as Dina went ahead with the marriage and that too with a non-Muslim. Jinnah who claimed that he alone could protect the Muslims in India, could not prevent his own daughter from marrying a Christian. Dina and Neville Wadia continued to reside in Bombay. They had one son and a daughter. These two were Jinnah's only direct descendants who were not Muslims. Jinnah had never disowned her daughter, in spite of her marriage with a non-Muslim.[28] The marriage came at a time when Jinnah's health was deteriorating, but he never disclosed his failing health to anyone.

On 26 March 1939, the Working Committee of the Muslim League in its meeting in the UP, appointed a Committee to examine potential separatist schemes. Jinnah was the President of the Committee, while among other important members there were Sikandar Hayat Khan, Nawab Mohammad Ismail Khan, Sir Abdulla Haroon, Khawaja Nazimuddin, and Nawabzada Liaquat Ali Khan as the convener.

The Nawab of Mamdot, the President of the Punjab Muslim League, who was a Unionist at heart, financed the publication of a scheme devised by Mian Kifayat Ali for a confederacy of zones in India, which would be the first step towards a Muslim State embracing all-India. Under this scheme, the Muslim Zone in the northwest would be known as 'Indusstan'. There was also Dr Sayyid Abdul Latif's Federation Scheme which called for the creation of four Muslim and eleven Hindu cultural zones through exchange of population. Sir Sikandar Hayat Khan who was a member of the Committee, submitted a zonal scheme, according to which India was to be divided into seven zones which included the north-western Muslim zone, held by a loose all-India federal system. Professor Syed Zafarul Hasan and Dr Mohammad Afzal Husain Qadri of Aligarh Muslim University wanted British India to be divided mainly into three sovereign states—the predominantly Muslim States of northwest India and Bengal and the Hindu state of Hindustan in the rest of India. The Muslim State of northwest India was to be a separate Federation called Pakistan Federation, whereas Bengal was to constitute a separate Muslim State. Abdullah Haroon's Committee Scheme wanted one Muslim State in the northwest and another in the northeast, while the Nizam's dominion would be the third Muslim State. Then there was the scheme of Rahmat Ali. He wanted the creation of three independent Muslim States—Pakistan, Bangistan, and Usmanistan and seven other Muslim nations in the Hindu region, which put together would constitute the Pak Commonwealth or Pakasia.[29] Strangely none of the schemes envisaged a single Muslim State in India.

There was also the scheme envisaged by Muhammad Zafarullah Khan, the prominent Ahmeddiya from Punjab. He wanted the creation of a weak all-India Federation, composed of Muslim and non-Muslim Federations on the basis of provincial boundaries. Linlithgow was aware of this scheme. Jalal claimed that Jinnah saw the scheme, but we are not sure if the League's constitutional sub-committee really considered it. The President of the Punjab Muslim Students Federation, Abdul Sattar Khan Niazi, led a students' group called 'Khilafat-i-Pakistan', which submitted a proposal to Jinnah for the formation of a Pakistan Caliphate including much of northern India. Jinnah was aware of all the above schemes, but did not commit himself to any. In the League Working Committee meeting held on 4 February 1939, he seemed to have opposed the scheme of Sikandar Hayat Khan openly.[30] Besides, the word 'Pakistan' signifying a separate Muslim State was already doing the rounds in north-western India during the late 1930s.

It was not for fun that Jinnah had constituted a committee to examine the various potential separatist schemes. There is no indication that there was any hidden or secret strategy of Jinnah in constituting such a Committee. Why should he constitute such a Committee involving the entire party leadership and the Muslim stalwarts if his intention was to remain in a united India and not to split India on religious lines? In his long political career, there was no instance of Jinnah adopting a hidden strategy to achieve his objectives. He might not have kept his word regarding some of his declarations, statements, or proposals. But never did Jinnah resort to hidden, secret, or under-handed methods to achieve his objectives.

The constitution of this Committee had sent a strong message to the British regarding the intentions of Jinnah and the Muslim League. The British had reasons to be happy about the formation of this Committee which clarified Jinnah's intentions with regard to the future of India. They did not disapprove the formation of this Committee by outrightly ruling out the Partition of India; instead, the widening rift between the Congress and Jinnah suited them perfectly. They just had to watch and see how Jinnah and the League intended to split India.

The formation of the Committee had also forewarned the Congress and its leadership that Jinnah and the League were serious in their intentions to partition India. But the Congress leaders did not pay much heed to Jinnah's latest move which had the potential to cut down to size Congress power as well as their defiance of the British during the war.

Jinnah had made three consecutive moves, one after the other, within a couple of years, like on a chessboard. The first was the sole spokesman move; the second was the parity move; and the third was the examination of separatist schemes. At that juncture one can only wonder what could be Jinnah's next move.

Dr M.A. Ansari at the Jamiat-ul-ulema-i-Hind conference in Delhi, attended by 10,000 people lashed out at Jinnah and the Leaguers as agents of British imperialism who were fabricating fantastic schemes of 'Pakistan' and 'cultural ghettos'. The feudal elements in the League, under the guise of cultural safeguards, wanted to dominate Muslim politics and the masses. Apart from the Jamiat-ul-ulema, the Ahrars, the All India Shia Political Conference, and the All India Momin Conference declared that the Muslim League was not their representative and asked the Muslims to stand by the Congress.[31]

But Jinnah's health deteriorated during that time. So on 30 May 1939, Jinnah signed his last will appointing his sister Fatima, Liaquat Ali Khan, and his Bombay solicitor, Mahomed Alli Chiwalla as joint trustees of his huge estate. Fatima Jinnah stood to gain most of Jinnah's property and wealth by the will. To his three sisters and his brother Ahmed, he left a living of Rs 100 a month. Jinnah set apart Rs 200,000 to be invested in order to provide his estranged daughter Dina, who had married a Christian with a living. At 6 per cent, the amount would bring a regular income of Rs 1,000 for his daughter. In this respect Jinnah was very unorthodox and never stuck to the tenets of Islam regarding charging or accepting interest. It was mentioned in the will that after his daughter's death, the sum of Rs 200,000 must be divided equally between her children, male or female. If she has no issues, then the amount should be divided between Aligarh University, Peshawar's Islamic College, and the Sindh Madrasa of Karachi. Jinnah also left Rs 50,000 to the University of Bombay and

Rs 25,000 each to Bombay Anjuman-i-Islam school and the Arabic College of Delhi.[32]

If we take into account the above will, it becomes quite obvious that Jinnah had not, till then, made up his mind with regard to the future of Muslims in India. There were, of course, various separatist schemes. Jinnah at that point was not sure of the path he would take. What he was sure of was that his health was failing and time was pressing upon him. In such circumstances, it was natural for one to expect that Jinnah would be hard-pressed to take a radical stand for, after all, he had nothing more to lose except his life. Whether this radical stand was going to be advantageous to the Muslims or not is what we have to see.

When the personal situation of Jinnah was thus, the Second World War broke out on 1 September 1939. Lord Linlithgow proclaimed India at war without consulting the Indian leaders. Linlithgow then invited Gandhi and Jinnah to Shimla to apprise them of the war, on an equal footing. Even Jinnah was surprised by this new attitude of the Viceroy. He remarked later:

> After the war ... suddenly there came a change in the attitude towards me. I was treated on the same basis as Mr. Gandhi. I was wonderstruck why all of a sudden I was promoted and given a place side by side with Mr. Gandhi.[33]

This invitation came as a godsend to the Muslim League and Jinnah, who were now pitted more and more against the Congress, in the scramble for power. Jinnah and the Muslim League, unable to make an impression upon the Congress and its leaders, had to turn to the British who had given them almost everything they had asked for until then. Jinnah, taking advantage of the situation, asked the Viceroy to turn out all provincial Congress ministries. He even seemed to have hinted to the Viceroy at this juncture that the only ultimate political solution for India was in its partition. On 11 September 1939, Linlithgow announced the postponing of the Federation Scheme, thinking that through this he could get the support of Jinnah, the princes, and even the Congress for the war.[34]

In a resolution of the Muslim League passed on 16 September 1939, the League strongly condemned the Federal Scheme. Jinnah had, by then, built up alliances with Muslim Nawabs and princes against the Federation Scheme, particularly because the latter resented the arrangement by which the States' representatives were to be elected and not nominated, which would definitely reduce the Muslims in the Central Legislature to a minority. There was the risk and fear in the mind of Jinnah that the Congress might accept the Federal part of the Act in the new situation. Jinnah also condemned the working of provincial autonomy in the Congress-ruled provinces, where he held that Muslim religious rights, property, and life were being assailed by the Hindu majority. The resolution warned the British government that it cannot count on Muslim support for the war if the following two conditions were not met with: Muslims must be given 'justice and fair play' in the Congress provinces, and no assurances must be given as to the constitutional advance, nor any new constitution framed, without the consent and approval of the League, 'the only organisation that can speak on behalf of Muslim India'. Jinnah asked for the abandonment of the entire scheme and for a coalition government with the Congress not only at the Centre but in the provinces too.[35] The demand for coalition ministries by Jinnah is indeed surprising. If it was accepted then the problem would arise about the share of Muslims in the coalition ministries in the various provinces. But Jinnah kept quiet about this thorny problem. Earlier through the Fourteen Points, he had asked that one-third of the ministers should be Muslims in the provinces and the Centre. Then the situation had changed and he had asked for parity in the Centre with the Congress. Will he ask for parity in the provinces too? Jinnah never elaborated upon that.

In the same month, the Congress issued a long statement drafted by Jawaharlal Nehru declaring its inability to associate themselves or offer any cooperation in a war which is conducted on imperial lines and which is meant to consolidate imperialism in India and elsewhere. The Congress leaders demanded complete independence and the right to frame India's Constitution through a Constituent Assembly.[36] The defiance of the Congress was not appreciated by Lord Zetland, the Secretary of State for India.

The Congress declined to give unconditional support to British war efforts. When the war was raging, the British, probably in order to seek support of all the Indian parties for the prosecution of the war, suddenly felt that the time was ripe for a further constitutional advance. As a result Viceroy Linlithgow hurriedly met and interviewed 52 personalities including Jinnah and the Chancellor of the Princes. That drove home the message that the British government would not contemplate any change in their declared policy towards India except after full consultation with the several interests with whose help they shaped the Government of India Act of 1935. In other words, the British will thenceforth accept the League as the sole spokesman of the Muslims and will not accept the Congress' claim to speak for the whole of India. There could be no revised Act or plan without the approval and consent of the Muslim League.[37]

The above was embodied in the declaration of Linlithgow on 17 October 1939. He also emphasized that Dominion status was the goal of British policy in India. Further Lord Linlithgow decided to suspend the Federal scheme of the 1935 Act to which the Muslim League and Jinnah were always opposed. That went a long way to cater to the demand of Jinnah with the objective of securing the support of the Muslims in the war, who constituted the bulk of the Indian Army. Jinnah had won the first victory. The Viceroy further announced the constitution of a consultative committee consisting of members of the major political parties and the Princes, for the purpose of closer association of India with the prosecution of the war. Jinnah did not reject the Viceroy's declaration, unlike the Congress. The Hindu Maha Sabha and Sikandar Hayat Khan declared their support for the prosecution of the war.[38]

Lord Linlithgow was earlier involved intimately with the constitution-making process which ended up in the formulation of the Government of India Act of 1935. This Act, as we had seen, had deliberately sought to belittle the Congress in all-India politics, as noted by C.R. Attlee. Presently Lord Linlithgow sought to minimize the importance of the Congress by raising the prestige and strength of the Muslim League and Jinnah. Subsequently Zetland, the Secretary of State for India found it impossible to accept Congress claim that the rights of the minorities will be protected through the framing of a Constitution by a Constituent Assembly. Much like Jinnah, he even dismissed the Congress as a Hindu organization.[39] Such an approach and attitude at this particular time was definitely helpful to Jinnah and the Muslim League to press forward their claim forcefully to speak for the Muslims.

Lord Linlithgow explicitly accepted Muslim League's claim to speak for the Muslims of India, although the party lacked electoral mandate. Though Jinnah had mustered a lot of support for his party by then and his party had won some bye-elections, he was still an outsider, as he was out of the corridors of power, unlike the Congress which was in power. The British were aware of this.[40]

It was at this crucial time that Jinnah laid more emphasis on parity. He wanted parity between Muslims and Hindus in any pact or settlement, and also that thenceforth half the seats for Muslim India in any coalition in the Federal Legislature or the Centre, though the Muslims made up for only one-fourth of the total population of India. In the legislature of the princely State of Hyderabad, Hindus and Muslims were to have equal number of seats, although the Muslims formed only about 10 per cent of the population of the State. It seemed that this division of power had Jinnah's blessings. He wanted a similar division of power in British India at every level between the Congress and the League or the Hindus and Muslims, on the basis of half and half—half for the Muslims and half for the Hindus.[41] That way he felt that the Muslims would not be sidelined at the Centre. The parity demand came after Jinnah's claim that the League alone was the representative of the Muslims in India.

That was indeed an impossible demand from every point of view. With this new demand Jinnah was not only seeking to reduce the 75 per cent Hindu majority to a minority, but was also cutting into the political rights of other minorities like the Scheduled Castes and the Indian Christians. All that he was interested in was protecting what he thought were Muslim interests and rights. As Jinnah himself had admitted, in politics one has to play one's game like on a chessboard. Jinnah was doing exactly that. Parity demand was not the end; probably it was the means towards some undisclosed plan or strategy in Jinnah's mind at that time; or perhaps Jinnah raised the parity demand as a bargaining counter in order to get something more substantial for the Muslims in the future like Partition, for example.

Earlier on 8 October, in his speech at the Muslim League Conference at Karachi, Jinnah had compared the plight of the Indian Muslims to the Sudeten Germans in Czechoslovakia. He told that just as the Sudetens the Muslims were oppressed, persecuted, and ill-treated in India by the Hindus. He claimed that the Muslims were not defenceless and will not give up their national identity in this great continent.[42]

Thus Jinnah posed himself as the sole defender of Islam and the Muslim national identity in India. Only he knew what was good for them and Islam, while the other 'nationalist-minded' Muslims, though they might be deeply religious or knowledgeable people like Maulana Abul Kalam Azad, did not know anything about what was good for the Muslims or Islam or about his glorious mission. As a matter of fact, the statement of Jinnah at Karachi was exaggerated even to an impartial observer of the Indian situation. The Congress had already guaranteed the rights of the Muslims, especially cultural and religious rights within a united India. Maulana Abul Kalam Azad was a prominent voice in the Congress who stood for protecting Muslim rights. The Muslims had obtained various concessions from the British in politics and public services well above their share in the total population. The Congress had not resisted them. Jinnah however raised the slogan 'Islam is in danger', as there were some instances when Congressmen sang the *Vande Mataram* in the Assemblies and raised the Congress flag on government buildings in the five or six provinces ruled by them. Jinnah had never objected to *Vande Mataram* during his Congress days or during the Khilafat agitation or even later. So it becomes quite obvious that Jinnah's sudden opposition to *Vande Mataram* on the pretext that it was anti-Islamic was the product of his desire to use religious symbols, thenceforth to mobilize the Muslims in favour of the Muslims and himself.

However, in the four Muslim-majority provinces such petty problems never arose. The Muslim League and Jinnah were not yet powerful there. The problem for Jinnah was in the Muslim-minority provinces, where Muslims would be a minority in any case, as the Hindus will be a minority in the rest of the provinces. So the strategy of Jinnah was to use the problems of the Muslims in the minority provinces to assert his power not only in the minority provinces but also in the majority provinces. The only way to do this was to use the Islamic card as Muslims all over India shared the same religion. Jinnah did this to the best of his ability not only to undermine the Muslim regional parties, but also to mobilize the Muslims all over India behind his banner of Islam, although he was never known to have practised Islam and was highly westernized in his habits and mannerisms.

The anti-Jinnah and pro-Congress Muslims were well aware of this fact. The Jamiat-ul-ulema-i-Hind, the Shia Political Conference, the Momins, the Ahrars, and other nationalist Muslims, comprised even of prominent Maulanas, Maulvis, and Ulemas, trained their guns against this unIslamic side of Jinnah in their conferences, held especially at Delhi. The propaganda of Jinnah and the League was far more superior to these Muslims. Jinnah was winning the war against them in his attempt to project himself as the messiah or saviour of Islam in India. The League itself had become synonymous with Jinnah, the Quaid-e-Azam. No other

Muslim in the whole of India knew what was good for Muslims and Islam better than Jinnah, which was thenceforth the contention of the Leaguers including Jinnah himself.

In October 1939, Jinnah again met both Nehru and Gandhi in Delhi. He stressed that it was not possible to endorse the Congress demand of 10 October 1939 for Independence and for a Declaration from the British Government on its war aims. Thereafter, he did not want to carry on talks as long as the Congress did not accept the Muslim League as the authoritative and representative organization of the Muslims of India and the minority problem was not settled. He also made it clear that the Congress did not represent those who disagree with it, whether they were Hindus or Muslims.[43] At that juncture, one could venture to say that Jinnah had finally made up his mind about what direction the Muslim League should take and how the Muslim interests were to be protected in future. It would come to light in the next few months.

On 1 November 1939, Lord Linlithgow summoned Gandhi, Rajendra Prasad, and Jinnah to a joint meeting and urged them to settle their differences in the Provinces so as to make practicable their acceptance of a limited number of seats on the Governor-General's Executive Council. As the leaders failed to arrive at any agreement, the negotiations were suspended. Linlithgow actually wanted the Congress to agree to an interim settlement for the duration of the war by which the Congress and the Muslim League would form coalition ministries in the provinces and no legislation affecting Muslims would be adopted if two-third of Muslim members in a provincial Lower House opposed it. When the Congress had taken a strident position against the British government engaging India in an imperialist war and was asking for the Constitution of a Constituent Assembly, there was no more question for the Congress to form coalition ministries in the provinces, which would have created an irreversible precedent and validated the theory of two nations.[44]

The summoning of both Gandhi and Jinnah to a joint meeting by Linlithgow at that stage made it clear that the British considered

Jinnah and Gandhi on an equal footing, even though the former did not have any electoral mandate. It seemed that the British had deliberately decided to prop up Jinnah as the sole spokesman for the Muslims and as a countervailing force to the Congress and Gandhi, from that period onwards. That strengthened Jinnah's hands not only against the Congress but also against the Muslim regional parties like the Unionist Party of Punjab and the Krishak Praja Party of Bengal.

Every time when the British introduced reforms, since 1875 some Muslim stalwarts were always there to put forward new political demands on behalf of the Muslims. At any rate, past experiences showed that the British were quite sympathetic to many such Muslim demands and had fulfilled them in one way or the other, even without the Muslims agitating for them. Sometimes they even gave more than what the Muslims had asked for. Sir Mohammad Shafi of the Punjab had asked during the Round Table Conference for joint electorates if accompanied by statutory majority or if statutory majority was refused, then a minority of seats with separate electorates must be given. The British gave the Muslims statutory majority as well as separate electorates when he had not asked for either. They did this without undermining, in any way, the weightage given to Muslims in Muslim-minority provinces under the Lucknow Pact.[45]

Keeping with this tradition, the Britain had decided to bank upon Jinnah and Jinnah alone to offset Congress non-cooperation in the war effort. Lord Linlithgow himself wrote in February 1940 to the Secretary of State, Zetland that Britain should 'lie back for the present' without 'running after the Congress'. Linlithgow saw in Gandhi an 'implacable enemy of British rule in India, to the destruction of which he has dedicated every fibre of his mind'. Gandhi had cautioned earlier that vivisecting India would contribute to imperialistic growth and hoped that the League and Jinnah would not want to vivisect India.[46]

Unable to make any impression on the Viceroy, in November 1939 the Congress leadership decided to relinquish power in the provinces which were under their control on the pretext that the British had decided unilaterally to drag India into the Second World War. Thus, instead of carrying on with non-cooperation in British war efforts by staying in power, the Congress High Command committed the monumental blunder of relinquishing power, which put them at par with the Muslim League. Jinnah, to his surprise, was greatly relieved by this Congress move. This created a power vacuum in which the British could operate smoothly in order to safeguard their imperial and war interests. They no longer needed the Congress as they had relinquished power. The other parties which supported British war interests were the Hindu Maha Sabha, the Unionist Party of Punjab, and the Justice Party of Madras. Jinnah, taking full advantage of the Congress blunder, called on the Muslims to celebrate the resignation of the Congress ministries on 22 December 1939 as a 'Day of Deliverance' for the Muslims.[47]

On 13 December 1939, Jinnah defiantly wrote to Jawaharlal Nehru:

> ...So long as the Congress is not prepared to treat the Muslim League as the authoritative and representative organisation of the Mussalmans of India it was not possible to carry on talks regarding the Hindu–Muslim settlement. ...[48]

Nehru could not compromise with Jinnah's contention that the Congress cannot represent the Muslims, in any way, for the simple reason that Congress membership was open to everyone, unlike the Muslim League. In other words, it meant that for Jinnah, Congress was a Hindu organization and he wanted Nehru to accept it. Nehru refused to restart any talk or negotiations with Jinnah and challenged him to face election on the basis of adult franchise for the Constituent Assembly, if he thought that he alone represented Muslims.[49]

Thus once again Jinnah in his own way cashed in on Congress struggle for independence through the resignation of Congress ministries. It was the Congress which led all the agitations for the liberation of India until then. The Muslim League under Jinnah practically took no part in this struggle. But it was Jinnah who obtained concessions after concessions from the British as we had seen precedingly and then Jinnah was walking away towards his objectives without launching the least agitation for freedom.

On the other hand the resignation move of the Congress, engineered more as a counterblast to the British failure to consider their demands, had the chain effect of driving the British into the arms of the All-India Muslim League. Linlithgow became extremely conciliatory to Jinnah's demands. He conceded that the 1935 Act will not be reconsidered. He accepted that full weight will be given thenceforth to Muslim views. He even assured Jinnah that Britain was not at war with any Muslim power, implying that there was no chance of using Indian troops against them.

On 22 December 1939, the Muslim League celebrated the event of the resignation of the Congress ministries as 'Deliverance Day' for Muslims from Congress oppressive rule. Slogans like 'Islam in Danger' and pan-Islamism raised its head more than ever before.

In south India, the Justice Party under Ramasamy joined the Muslim League in the celebrations. Even Dr Ambedkar, the leader of the Untouchables extended his support for the celebrations. Gandhi welcomed Jinnah's move to rope in Ambedkar and Ramasamy, which according to him, gave the League a national character. He persisted in his opinion that as Muslims were descendants of converts, they cannot cut themselves off from India and change their nationality. Maulana Abul Kalam Azad, the President of the Congress stated with regard to the 'Deliverance Day' that 'no Muslim having an iota of the self-respecting consciousness of his political existence could ever give such a suggestion to his co-religionists'.

Jinnah, on his part, claimed that he had the backing of the Depressed Class Hindus as well as of others as opposed to the Congress all over India and dismissed Gandhi's policies as impractical. The British lost no time to cash in on this divisive situation and turn it to their advantage. Lord Linlithgow himself said that the return of the Congress to office was no more possible without a coalition with the Muslim League in the Centre and even in the provinces where the Congress had absolute majority. That was in accordance with Jinnah's earlier demand.[50]

The British were fighting the war that would determine their very existence and future as a world power and therefore they were likely at that stage to ally even with the devil or even prop up a devil, if it served their interests. The Muslim League was not a devil. It was a countervailing force to the Congress, which can be propped up still further with British connivance and made use of intelligently to bolster British war effort in India—the overriding imperial interest during that period. Nehru was aware of it when he wrote to Abul Kalam Azad, the Muslim face in the Congress on 22 February 1940 the following: 'You will have noticed the rebirth of the idea of pan-Islam. ...Pan-Islamism in 1914 and later was an anti-imperialist struggle. ...Today this very idea is being used in support of British imperialism.'[51]

The organization of the 'Deliverance Day' all throughout India proved to the British that the Muslim League and Jinnah had completely turned their back on the Congress and its objectives. The logical outcome was that they could bank upon the Muslim League, as the Muslims were the mainstay of the Indian Army. Indian troops consisting of Muslims were already deployed in France. The Unionist Party of Punjab which was the main recruiting ground of the Indian army had extended its support to the British war effort. In 1939, Muslim soldiers constituted more than one-third of the Indian army.[52] These numbers made it quite obvious that the British war effort had to depend more on the Muslims than on the Hindus, who on the whole were a minority in the Indian army.

It seemed that in March 1939, Jinnah was even glad to learn the following from Chaudhry Khaliquzzaman of the United Provinces. When the latter suggested to Zetland, the Secretary of State for India, that to solve the Hindu–Muslim problem the Muslim areas might be partitioned from the rest of India, in the form of two federations linked to a confederal centre, Zetland did not reject it. It is quite impossible to imagine that Khaliquzzaman would have dared to make such a crucial proposal to Zetland without Jinnah being aware of it. In his turn, in September 1939 Jinnah had conveyed to Lord Linlithgow that Partition was an alternative to federation in order to break the constitutional deadlock. Linlithgow apprised Zetland about Jinnah's views on Partition. Two months later, Khaliquzzaman met Rahmat Ali, the inventor of the word 'Pakistan' in London. That meeting would have occurred with the knowledge of Jinnah. In early January 1940, the Punjab Muslim Students Federation demanded the creation of 'Khilafat-i-Pakistan' which included much of northern India. The word 'Pakistan' was already doing its rounds among the Muslims to signify a separate Muslim State.[53] Much like Jinnah, Zetland continued to hold the view that the Congress was a Hindu organization.[54]

Jinnah must be aware of the launching of the demand for a separate Dravidanadu State by Ramasamy in December 1938 and his party's eventual participation in the 'Deliverance Day' along with the Muslim League. On 6 January 1940, Ramasamy along with his lieutenant, C.N. Annadurai met Jinnah in Bombay to enlist his support for a joint front with the Muslim League and the Scheduled Castes under B.R. Ambedkar, against the Congress. Ramasamy even spoke of the separatist Dravidanadu demand to Jinnah and had tried to enlist his support for it. We do not know how far Ramasamy was able to influence Jinnah's separatist thinking at that stage. During that month in an article in *Time and Tide*, Jinnah elaborated his 'two-nation theory'.[55]

When things were thus, Sir Stafford Cripps came to India in December 1939 with a scheme that C.R. Attlee and he had discussed with Nehru in June 1939. The scheme favoured abandonment of federation, a promise of self-government, a Constituent Assembly after the war, and the reconstruction of the Executive Council to include Indian members. He met several Indian leaders; but Jinnah never accepted a Constituent Assembly, unless parity was given to the Muslims at the Centre and veto power was given to the League. Cripps expected Jinnah to react positively to his scheme, but that was not to be.[56]

On 10 January 1940, in a last ditch effort to enlist Congress support for the war, the Viceroy reiterated his offer of Dominion status for India. He was even ready to reopen the Federal Scheme of the 1935 Act after the war and expand the Executive Council by including a small number of Indian political leaders. But the Congress would have nothing of it without its demands being met with.[57]

At the same time Linlithgow had been pressing Jinnah to come out with a 'constructive policy or plan' which can be used as a counterpoise to the Congress demands for independence and a Constituent Assembly. On 6 February 1940, Linlithgow firmly told Jinnah in the course of a meeting that the British could not help 'a party whose policy was one of sheer negation!' and that if 'the Muslim case should not go by default in the U.K. it was really crucial that they should formulate their plan in the near future.' That clearly showed that Linlithgow wanted Jinnah to come out with his plan regarding the future of India, as that was the declared intention of Jinnah since March 1939 when he formed the committee to examine all potential partition schemes. In the same month, most certainly under pressure from Linlithgow, Jinnah pressed forth the idea that India was not one nation but two. At about the same time, Aurangzeb Khan, League leader of NWFP told Governor Cunningham that the League would press for a Muslim homeland in the northwest and northeast of India.[58]

On 24 February 1940 Jinnah informed the Viceroy that he had not met the League Working Committee's request for a definite assurance that no declaration would be made, nor any constitution enforced by the British government or enacted by parliament, without the approval and consent of the Muslims of India. In the same month, he declared to the Press that the constitutional settlement must be governed by the fact that India was not one nation but two. On 13 March Jinnah met the Viceroy and told him that as the war was extending into Asia, cooperation between the Muslims and the British was necessary. Jinnah then evoked the possibility of the Partition of India as the Muslims were a nation, not a minority, if the British did not have a solution to the constitutional problem, other than installing a Hindu Raj. Jinnah even expressed his desire for a Muslim area run by Muslims in collaboration with Britain.[59]

It was during that crucial period that Maulana Abul Kalam Azad had been chosen to become the Congress President. At its annual session held at Ramgarh on 19–20 March 1940 the Maulana thundered that Hindus and Muslims were together bound by history and a common Indian nationality. At Ramgarh, the Congress demanded complete independence and a Constituent Assembly to frame a Constitution. It also held out the threat of Civil Disobedience. Linlithgow was naturally flabbergasted by the defiant attitude of the Congress during the war. Jinnah on his part did not accept neither the formation of a Constituent Assembly nor a common nationality and demanded the termination of the Federal part of the 1935 Act.[60]

Some British scholars like R.J. Moore think that the devolution of power to the Muslim provinces through the 1935 Act encouraged separatism in those provinces and that the process of devolution generated the crisis of Indian unity.[61] This is not completety true. Provincial autonomy was accorded to all the British Indian provinces in equal measure. There was no distinction made between the provinces where Muslims were in a majority vis-à-vis the provinces where Muslims were in a minority. Separatism did not strike root in the Muslim-majority provinces. The Unionist Party of the Punjab, the Ittehad Party of Sind as well as the Khudai Khidmatgar of the NWFP were not separatists, in the light of what we have seen. They stood at varying degrees for a united India. Provincial autonomy had not really contributed to separatism among them. Islam was in no danger of being submerged by the Hindus in those provinces.

But that was not the case with the Muslim-minority provinces where the Muslims were a minority. Jinnah, the Gujarati belonged to the Muslim-minority province of Bombay. The All-India Muslim League of which he was the unchallengeable chief was dominated mostly by Muslim stalwarts from the UP, the heart of Muslim India. Liaquat Ali Khan from the UP was the General Secretary of the League. Muslim League leaders from the Muslim-majority provinces never played a predominant role in the all-India structure of the Muslim League. They were mainly provincial leaders.

Jinnah was under pressure to protect the interests of the Muslims in the Muslim-minority provinces against the Hindu majority more than the interests of the Muslims in the Muslim-majority provinces, where the Hindus were a minority. In order to achieve that, Jinnah adopted a two-pronged strategy, especially after the defeat of the Muslim League in the Muslim-majority provinces in the 1937 elections. In the first place, he started using the Islamic card and raised the cry that 'Islam is in danger'. Divided as the Indian Muslims were on linguistic, ethnic, caste, and class lines, the only common factor that united all Indian Muslims—both the elite and non-elite masses—was Islam. Through incessant propaganda, the Muslims of all the provinces were made to understand that the Muslim League alone stood to protect Islam and Muslim culture and traditions in India. Jinnah and the League called upon all Muslims including the Muslims of the Muslim-majority provinces to unite in this endeavour of protecting Islam and Muslim culture. The leaders of the provincial Muslim parties were increasingly unable to counter that religious propaganda, in spite of the fact that there was no danger for Islam in the Muslim-majority provinces due to their numerical preponderance. As a result, eventually the Muslim League made serious inroads into the Muslim-majority provinces, to the detriment of Muslim-dominated provincial parties.

The second strategy adopted by Jinnah was more ambitious and pervasive. There was no more talk of giving up separate electorates or wanting one-third representation for Muslims in the Central Assembly. Those had been given to Jinnah on a platter by the British, along with Sind province and equal status to NWFP. Jinnah realized that in spite of all the concessions, the Muslims would still be a minority in the Muslim-minority provinces, unlike the Muslims in the Muslim-majority provinces. The Muslims on the whole would be in a minority in any Central Government. In order to get over these obstacles and assert Muslim power, he struck upon an ingenious idea of demanding equal share of power for Muslims in the Centre—fifty for Muslims and fifty for Hindus. This, despite the fact, that the Muslims constituted only about 25 per cent of the Indian population. He also demanded the Congress to recognize that the Muslim League was the only authoritative representative of Muslims in India.

The demand for 50 per cent share for Muslims at the Centre would naturally mean that the Muslims of the Muslim-majority provinces would have a greater share than the Muslims of the Muslim-minority provinces in the overall Muslim share. That demand was benefitting the Muslims of the Muslim-majority provinces. Jinnah never elaborated upon how he was going to share the 50 per cent share that he was demanding for Muslims, between the Muslims of the Muslim-majority provinces vis-à-vis the Muslims of the Muslim-minority provinces. In my opinion, he would have definitely defended the interests of the Muslims of the Muslim-minority provinces adequately as he did when he devised the Lucknow Pact through weightage for Muslims in the Muslim-minority provinces, which was resented by provincial leaders like Fazl-i Husain; or when he constituted the League Council and Working Committee.

But as Jinnah had not elaborated upon the preceding, it seemed quite obvious that he was having other options in his mind at that time. Both the battle cry that 'Islam is in danger' and the demand for a 50 per cent share in the Centre for the Muslims were raised in order to mobilize the Muslims of the Muslim-majority and Muslim-minority provinces, behind the banner of the League and Jinnah, in their quest for power. Earlier Jinnah toyed with the idea of giving up separate electorates if Sind was created and NWFP was given equal status with other provinces. He got both. But he never gave up separate electorates. Then he asked 50 per cent share for Muslims in the Centre and the status of sole spokesmanship for the League. He was in the process of examining the various partition proposals and had even suggested Partition as a solution to the Viceroy. At that juncture, the real intention of Jinnah was questioned which would come to light shortly.

FINAL CALL FOR PAKISTAN

Almost a year had passed since the constitution of the Partition Committee by Jinnah. Various schemes were submitted to the Committee and examined. Jinnah had rejected almost all of them. Sikandar Hayat Khan's zonal scheme was also rejected. But Sikandar persisted. Later he submitted another scheme paving the way for the constitution of two Muslim States in the northwest and eastern areas where the Muslims were in a majority. These areas were to be parts of a federated India.[1] Through this scheme Sikandar Hayat Khan once again affirmed his ultimate desire for a united India. This scheme seemed to have drawn the attention of Jinnah. He did not reject it, although he did not disclose his intentions immediately.

In March 1940, Jinnah gave a number of interviews to the foreign press including the *Manchester Guardian*, wherein he stressed upon the freedom of Muslim India to 'develop its own political, economic, social, and cultural institutions according to its own genius, and not to be dominated and crushed, while wishing Hindu India well and giving it the fullest scope to do likewise'. Like Sayyid Ahmad Khan in the nineteenth century, he stressed that the democratic parliamentary government and democracy in India was impossible as it could only mean Hindu Raj all over India. He further added that the Muslims were not a minority and that they were 'in a majority in the Northwest and in Bengal, all along the corridor stretching from Karachi to Calcutta'. This naturally implied that Jinnah had decided upon the creation of separate Muslim state or states in the preceding areas.

Strangely, the area specified by Jinnah was exactly the same that was advanced by the *Manchester Guardian* in 1932 when Jinnah was in London. It is quite possible that the idea of Partition that had appeared in this reputed British journal had been working on in Jinnah's mind since 1932 or probably even earlier, when he demanded the creation of Sind and reforms in NWFP, which would result in the emergence of a solid north-western Muslim-dominated bloc. Then Jinnah must have felt that the appropriate time had finally come for him to give shape to it. He had decided to spell it out in more concrete terms during the next session of the Muslim League to be held at Lahore. But he did not disclose this decision to the world. However, there is evidence to show that Jinnah took the Viceroy into his confidence and mentioned the Pakistan resolution to him several weeks before the League held its Lahore session.[2]

In the same month on 9 March 1940, Jinnah wrote the following in *Time and Tide*:

> Democratic systems based on the concept of a homogeneous nation such as England are very definitely not applicable to heterogeneous countries such as India.... India is inhabited by many races...as distinct from one another in origin, tradition and manners of life as are nations in Europe. Two-thirds of its inhabitants profess Hinduism in one form or another as their religion, over 77 million are followers of Islam, and the difference between the two is not only of religion in the stricter sense, but also of law and culture. ...Hinduism is distinguished by... caste, which is the basis of its religious and social system...; the religion of Islam on the other hand, is based upon the concept of the equality of man.... A constitution must be evolved that recognises there are in India two nations, who must both share the governance of their common motherland.[3]

Two months after Ramasamy's meeting with Jinnah and hardly a few weeks after Linlithgow's meeting with Jinnah, the All-India Muslim League organized its annual conference in Lahore on 22 March 1940. By the 20th of March most delegates to the Conference, Council members, legislators, State and all-India leaders assembled in Delhi on their way to Lahore. A special train was arranged to take Jinnah and other League leaders to Lahore. But at that moment, there was a clash between the Khaksars and the police at Lahore and many Muslim youth had lost their lives. There were rumours that the League conference will be postponed due to this. In spite of pressure from the government, particularly Muslim members of the Viceroy's Executive Council, Jinnah decided to go ahead with the conference, giving up only the presidential procession. Jinnah left for Lahore in great pomp on the 20th as decided. The train sped through East Punjab to Amritsar and then to Lahore. Wherever the train stopped or even in places where it did not stop Muslims rushed in great numbers to meet him. Every time he was forced to make a short speech or at least gratify them with his appearance. Such was the mighty welcome that Jinnah received in the Punjab, which was generally thought to be behind the Unionist Party of Sikandar Hayat Khan. The first thing that Jinnah did on his arrival at Lahore was to visit the wounded Khaksars in various hospitals.[4]

Muslims gathered in large numbers at the conference venue. Jinnah made his entry triumphantly. But Sikandar Hayat Khan, the premier and son of the soil of the Punjab was not able to come through the main gate as the crowds were hostile to him. He had to be brought in from behind the dais. Sikandar Hayat Khan was not in favour of Jinnah's impending move to break away from India. His misunderstanding with Jinnah on this issue somehow seemed to have reached the crowds assembled. They showed their fury by shouting 'Death to Sikandar'. Unable to bear the hostility of the crowd, Sikandar had no other alternative but to leave the conference. Jinnah did not intervene to calm the crowds. Neither did he ask Sikandar to stay back. At that stage, it seemed that Jinnah wanted to prove his strength to Sikandar even in the Punjab.

When Jinnah got up to speak and waved his hand to the crowd, there was instantly a pin-drop silence. First he assured the crowd (which consisted of a good number of Khaksars) that he would do everything in his power to see that justice was done to the Khaksars. Then he went on to speak about the necessity to reconsider the whole constitution. He wanted the British government to recognize the League as the only representative of the Muslims. He said that the Congress was exploiting the war situation to obtain complete independence for India, in which the Muslims will be subjugated.[5]

Jinnah proudly asserted that after the outbreak of the war he had suddenly become very important to the Viceroy to the point of him being invited by the Viceroy on an equal footing with Gandhi. He considered this recognition of his importance as a terrible shock to the Congress High Command, because it challenged their sole authority to speak on behalf of India.

He continued further:

> … Mr Rajagopalachari, the ex-prime minister of Madras says the only panacea for Hindu–Muslim unity is the joint electorate. That is his prescription, as one of the great doctors of the Congress organisation … Why does not Mr Gandhi honestly now acknowledge that the Congress is a Hindu Congress, that he does not represent anybody except the solid body of a Hindu people? … I may point out to Mr Gandhi and the Congress that they are fighting for a Constituent Assembly which the Muslims say they cannot accept. … Future constitution of India should be examined de novo…if any declaration is made, if any interim settlement is made without our approval and without our consent, the Muslims in India will resist it. And no mistake should be made on that score.
>
> … We want the British government should in fact and actually meet the demands of the Arabs in Palestine… What we wanted the British government to give us assurance of was that Indian troops should not be sent against any Muslim country or any Muslim power… But surely Musalmans are not a minority… we occupy large parts of this country, where the Muslims are in a majority—such as Bengal, Punjab, NWFP, Sind, and Baluchistan.
>
> The problem in India is not of an inter-communal but manifestly of an international character, and it must be treated as such. …

> the only course open to us all is to allow the major nations separate motherlands by dividing India into autonomous national States. There is no reason why these States should be antagonistic to each other. … it is a dream that Hindus and Muslims can ever evolve a common nationality…. The Hindus and Muslims belong to two different religions, philosophies, social customs, and literatures. They neither intermarry nor interdine; indeed, they belong to two different civilizations, which are based mainly on conflicting ideas and conceptions…. It is quite clear that Hindus and Musalmans derive their inspiration from different sources of history. They have different epics; their heroes are different with different episodes…. To yoke together two such nations under a single State, one as a numerical minority and the other as a majority, must lead to growing discontent and final destruction of any fabric that may be so built up for the Government of such a State. … The present artificial unity of India dates back only to the British conquest and is maintained by the British bayonet…
>
> I have devoted most of my time during the last six months to the study of Muslim history and Muslim law and I am inclined to think it (Hindu–Muslim unity) is neither possible nor practicable. … I am not afraid of the seven crores of Mussalmans. But I think the seven crores in Hindustan plus the armed hosts of Afghanistan, Central Asia, Arabia, Mesopotamia, and Turkey will be irresistible….
>
> I do honestly and sincerely believe in the necessity and desirability of Hindu–Muslim unity. … But what about the injunctions of the Quran and the Hadis? The leaders cannot override them. …
>
> Musalmans are a nation … and they must have their homelands, their territory and their State. We wish to live in peace and harmony with our neighbour as a free and independent people.[6]

Thus Jinnah exposed to all those assembled his theory of two nations in India, one Muslim and the other Hindu. Never did he dwell upon the fact that the great majority of the Muslims including himself belonged to the same racial and linguistic stock as their Hindu counterparts. Nor did he talk of the fact that most Muslims were actually descendants of converts from Hinduism. He also did not want to evoke the truth that both Hindus and Muslims shared the same common history, however good or bad, since more than two thousand years. Instead, he dwelt upon the differences in religion to buttress his assertion that Hindus and Muslims constituted two different nations and therefore they needed two different motherlands. He even used strong language against the British as well as the Congress when he said that the Muslims would resist any settlement or constitution adopted without their consent; or when he claimed that seven crores of Muslims plus the armed hosts of Afghanistan, Central Asia, Arabia, Mesopotamia, and Turkey will be irresistible. It appears that threat of violence had become part of Jinnah's strategy increasingly in order to achieve his objectives.

Another significant feature of the Lahore speech was the candid admission by Jinnah that he had studied Muslim history and law only for the past six months, that is, from about September 1939. This is not surprising because as we have seen Jinnah was a highly westernized person, who was even used to some unIslamic habits. He had been run down earlier by stalwarts like Maulana Hasrat Mohani and Maulana Mohammad Ali for his lack of knowledge and grounding in Islam, when he chose to speak for Muslims. Jinnah seemed to have made up for this lacuna during the last six months in order to be in a position to claim at Lahore that the injunctions in the Quran and the Hadiths did not allow for Hindu–Muslim unity. That showed that Jinnah was frank and straightforward even in the most unexpected circumstances. It also reflected that he had realized emphatically the importance of religion in the lives of Muslims, without which it was impossible for him to connect with the Muslim masses in his quest to safeguard Muslim interests at every level.

The Lahore Resolution was the latest of Jinnah's demands after the 1937 elections, the previous two being his demands for parity and sole spokesmanship for the League. Did Jinnah get the cue from Ramasamy's demand for a separate Dravidanadu State to launch his own separatist demand? Nobody can affirm this with certainty. Ramasamy had met Jinnah on 6 January 1940 and had spoken about the Dravidanadu demand, on the basis of the Dravidians being a separate nation, racially and linguistically. Strangely it was only later that Jinnah, for the first time, elaborated the two-nation theory in *Time and Tide*.[7]

Besides, Jinnah was already 65 when he decided upon the two-nation theory. He was old and tired and his health was failing. Coincidentally, he had also drafted a will just a few months before. Only his doctor and Fatima knew of his precarious health.[8] It is quite possible that knowing very well that his days were numbered, Jinnah decided to radicalize his stand, in spite of the fact that most of the schemes submitted to the League never envisaged separation from India including that of Sikandar Hayat Khan. Thus it was Jinnah's decision and his decision alone to Partition India.

The Subjects Committee of the League which met during the night agreed upon the principle of Partition. Some council members of the Muslim-minority provinces expressed their doubts and apprehension about the partition plan. That was natural because the Muslims of the Hindu-dominated provinces were not going to be part of the proposed Muslim State or States. It was clear to them that Jinnah's demand for Partition would liberate the Muslim-dominated areas from Hindu rule, but would not liberate the Muslims in Hindu-dominated areas. Many of them wondered what was going to be their future in such an India. Some were worried about the various Islamic institutions situated in India, while others spoke about the Jamia Masjid in Delhi, Taj Mahal, and other historic monuments built by Muslim emperors. The discussions went on till 3 am. Jinnah himself stepped in to allay their fears. The Muslims in the minority provinces were assured that they had nothing to fear as the treatment of Hindus in the new Muslim State and of Muslims in Hindu-dominated India would be on a reciprocal basis. It was argued that there would always be an earnest desire on the part of Hindus in India to treat the minority well in order that they might demand the same treatment for Hindus in the Muslim State. Some Council Members even declared that they would treat the Hindus in the new State in such a magnanimous way, in keeping with Islamic traditions and history that it would be an object lesson for India. Hence, it was believed that the Muslims left in India had nothing to fear as they would enjoy a better position and status for themselves in India as a result of Partition. It was also said that they will be in a minority whether India was divided or not and although their position may be a little difficult, they should not stand in the way of Muslims in the majority provinces who would be having full and complete power free from the Hindu-dominated Centre. They were even asked to make some sacrifice for the sake of the Muslims in Muslim-dominated areas. The League Council Members from the Muslim-minority provinces were persuaded to endorse the separatist course adopted by Jinnah.[9]

Jinnah who belonged to the Muslim-minority province of Bombay played a significant role during the session in persuading them to toe his line. Theoretically in the event of Partition, Jinnah being based in Bombay had to remain in Hindu-dominated India, if we follow the wordings of the Lahore Resolution. He, however, never disclosed during the conference that in the event of separation, he would stay in India to lead the remaining Indian Muslims in Hindu-dominated India. He never made his intention obvious to migrate to the north-western Muslim state as the leader of the Muslims there, although that might have been in his mind, when he chose to belittle Sikandar Hayat Khan in the Punjab and affirm his own leadership there.

Though Jinnah was a Gujarati by birth, he was born in Karachi and had spent some time of his life there. Therefore, Jinnah can be deemed to be a Karachiite belonging to the north-western Muslim-majority bloc or state. But that was not the case with the large majority of his co-religionists who were bound to live in Hindu-majority areas, in case of Partition. Jinnah seemed to have never cared about that. He was hell-bent in his pursuit of power for Muslims and himself, that he would never countenance anything else. The latest idea of Pakistan came in handy to him in this pursuit, for power and idea or ideals go hand-in-hand. One cannot be without the other. The Cambridge school of scholars who hold the view that in politics what really counts is power and profit and not ideas and ideals have, no doubt, erred in this respect.

One of the League members Mohamed Raza Khan from Madras who was present during the fateful night discussions at Lahore and with whom I had the privilege to speak with several times at length in Madras in 1986, apprised me that even if the Council Members from the Muslim-minority provinces were not happy with the partition decision of Jinnah, none of them were in a position to fight back with Jinnah on that issue. He even told me that the partition decision was not a decision taken in panic or in thoughtlessness; instead, it was a well-thought out decision and everybody expected that the Congress would come to a peaceful settlement with the League on the issue of Partition as wished by Jinnah.[10]

At a time when Neville Chamberlain was the Prime Minister of Great Britain and Zetland was still the Secretary of State for India, the revised resolution demanding Partition (originally drafted by Sikandar Hayat Khan), was moved by Fazlul Huq, the Bengal Premier and seconded by Chaudhry Khaliquzzaman of the UP. It was adopted by the Muslim League at Lahore in the presence of Jinnah and Nawab Sir Shah Nawaz Khan Mamdot, the feudal landlord of Pashtoon descent and President of the Punjab Muslim League, by the midnight of 23 March 1940. It read as follows:

> Resolved that it is the considered view of this session of the All-India Muslim League that no constitutional plan would be workable in this country or acceptable to the Muslims unless it is designed on the following basic principles, viz., that geographically contiguous units are demarcated into regions which should be so constituted, with such territorial readjustments as may be necessary, that the areas in which the

> Muslims are numerically in a majority as in the northwestern and Eastern zones of India should be grouped to constitute 'Independent States' in which the constituent units shall be autonomous and sovereign.
>
> Adequate, effective, and mandatory safeguards should be specifically provided in the Constitution for minorities in the units and in the regions for the protection of their religious, cultural, economic, political, administrative, and other rights and interests in consultation with them; and in other parts of India where the Musalmans are in a minority, similar safeguards shall be provided in the Constitution for them and other minorities for the protection of their religious, cultural, economic, political, administrative, and other rights and interests in consultation with them.[11]

This session further authorizes the Working Committee to frame a scheme of the Constitution in accordance with these basic principles, providing for the assumption finally by the respective regions of all powers such as defence, external affairs, communications, customs, and similar matter as may be necessary.

There were appendices to this resolution according to which the question of whether all the Muslim-majority provinces including Assam would be made part of the new Muslim States without any adjustment of their frontiers or not was to be settled by a referendum. Pakistan was contemplated only for the provinces of British India and not for the Princely States, who, according to Jinnah himself, were free to join India or the Muslim States or remain outside both and could maintain whatever relationship they pleased with Britain.[12]

During the session Jinnah had categorically stated that Muslim India cannot accept any Constitution which must necessarily result in a Hindu-majority government or Hindu Raj. Jinnah wanted the British to create separate homelands for the major nations—Hindu and Muslim, by dividing India into autonomous national States.[13] By claiming that there were two nations in India, Jinnah shed once and for all his garb as a sectarian Indian nationalist and donned the garb of a Muslim nationalist, on the basis of which the Muslims of India formed a distinct nation. He asked the British and the Congress—which for him was just a Hindu body for quite some time—to recognize the existence of a Muslim nation and Muslim homelands in India. He avoided being branded as a separatist or a secessionist especially by the British, for according to him, Muslims constituted a nation and they had the right to have their own sovereign homelands.

One week later Jinnah made a statement clarifying certain points in the Lahore Resolution. He insisted that the 60 million Muslims residing in areas where they form a majority should have their own homeland. He assured the Sikh community of the Punjab that they will be better off in:

> ...the Muslim homelands constituted of the western zone of the federated autonomous states, including the autonomous sovereign state of the Punjab.... As regards other zone or zones that may be constituted in the rest of India, our relationship will be of an international character. An example already exists in the relationship of India with Burma and Ceylon.

Jinnah even stressed that the princely States like Kashmir, Bahawalpur, Patiala, and others can willingly agree to come into the federation of the Muslim homeland, but the League would not force them or coerce them in any way to do so.[14] It is clear that Jinnah wanted complete independence for the Muslim States.

Although the Lahore Resolution was framed within a very short period, it cannot be said that the leaders involved in the framing of the resolution were not fully aware of its various implications. They were experienced men in politics and constitutional reforms. First of all we have Jinnah who was the most experienced of them all, not only in politics but also in constitutional legalities and reforms. Jinnah was the main architect of the Lucknow Pact of 1916. Since then off and on, he had come out with various constitutional proposals to safeguard Muslim interests. Sir Sikandar Hayat Khan and A.K. Fazlul Huq were no less experienced, as we have seen. Fazlul Huq had a hand in the drafting of the Lucknow Pact. So it is not possible to believe that these men could make mistakes in the elaboration of the Lahore Resolution, a resolution which was going to determine the very future of Muslims in India. Nevertheless, the demand for Pakistan was largely a product of the cream of the Muslim urban society who did not have any mandate from the largely backward Muslim masses, who were the great majority among Muslims, but were subject to manipulation by the former due to shared religious values.[15]

At the very outset, it is quite obvious that the framers of the Lahore Resolution did not follow the examples set by Sir Muhammad Iqbal and Rahmat Ali and asked for the entire Muslim-majority provinces to form their Muslim States. They did not even ask for the entire stretch of land from the northwest to Bengal, as suggested by the *Manchester Guardian* in 1932. Instead they were quite modest in their claim. They just wanted contiguous Muslim-majority areas to be included in their demand for separate Muslim States, given that non-Muslims were predominant in other areas. This might be due to the influence of Sir Sikandar Hayat Khan who was the original draftsman of the Lahore Resolution. It is simply preposterous and misleading to read 'provinces' instead of 'areas' in the resolution and then spin theories around it.

Of course they did not demarcate the contiguous Muslim-majority areas or produce any map of the separate Muslim States. That was not necessary. That would have been an arduous task, which would have raised a lot of unnecessary controversies within the Muslim communities as well as with the Hindus and Sikhs, especially in the Punjab and Bengal provinces. The framers including Jinnah seem to have been quite conscious of it. So they had thought it fit to leave it to the British to take up the task of demarcating the Muslim areas, instead of getting embroiled in it at that stage. That was a judicious decision.

But Sir Sikandar Hayat Khan's original draft which did not envisage complete separation from India was amended later by Jinnah himself, most certainly with the help of Malik Barkat Ali, an opponent of Sikander in the Punjab, to provide for such a separation, on the basis of two nations. This was admitted by Sikandar in the Punjab Assembly itself on 11 March 1941. Thus it is clear that Jinnah and the Muslim League wanted complete separation from Hindu India, if we strictly go by the wordings of the Lahore Resolution. The plain fact was that Jinnah did not make any room for a common centre in the resolution. No amount of juggling with one or two words here and there in the resolution like the Cambridge scholar, Ayesha Jalal seems to have done and trying to read things in it that did not exist really, can hide this fundamental fact.[16]

For instance the usage of the word 'constitution' in the resolution with regard to minority safeguards implies two separate constitutions, one for the Muslim States and the other for the Hindu-dominated State, and not just one single constitution as assumed or mis-read by Jalal. Further, according to the resolution, it was the Muslim-majority areas and not Muslim-majority provinces that should be 'grouped to constitute Independent States in which the constituent units shall be autonomous and sovereign'. There is a world of difference between the Muslim-majority areas and Muslim-majority provinces. It is not right to gloss over this difference and pretend that 'areas' signified 'provinces'. Further, the grouping of northwest and northeast into Independent States meant the creation of two Muslim States and not one. Therefore the usage of the terms 'constituent units' must signify the two Muslim units or two independent federated States which were to be sovereign and autonomous. There is no contradiction or vagueness in this respect. As for the usage of the term 'finally' in the third para of the resolution, there is nothing abnormal about it. The demand for Muslim States was a new demand. The Muslim States cannot be created overnight. Naturally, the Muslim League had to work for it and it was going to involve some time, which will 'finally' (meaning in the end) usher in the creation of the Muslim States according to the resolution.

In the light of the above, it is simply out of place to attribute secret motives and vagueness to the wordings in the resolution, as if they had been deliberately coined as a colossal but hidden strategy of Jinnah in the shape of a bargaining counter to secure Muslim position in the Centre. The so-called 'inwardness of Jinnah's strategy' according to which the Lahore Resolution was acceptable to the Muslims of the majority provinces and 'totally unacceptable to the Congress and in the last resort to the British also', definitely seems to be far-fetched and groundless, if we stick more closely to the wordings of the resolution as we have done and in the light of what we are going to see in the following pages.[17]

The Lahore Resolution was actually moved by none other than Fazlul Huq, who was the Premier of Bengal. That was no accident. Punjab and Bengal were the main Muslim-majority provinces in India. Jinnah and the All-India Muslim League leadership which consisted mostly of leaders from Muslim-minority provinces were conscious of it. They cannot demand for separate autonomous Muslim States in the northwest and northeast, when they did not actually belong to that area. Besides, the Muslim League was not still very strong in the Punjab to challenge the leadership of Sir Sikandar Hayat Khan. So Jinnah and the All-India Muslim League had to somehow rope in Sir Sikandar Hayat Khan, the most prominent Punjab Muslim leader at that time to contribute his bit to the drafting of the resolution in order to give added credibility to the demand. Of course Sikandar did not agree to Jinnah's insistence for a total separation of Muslim areas from the rest of India. They also needed the support of Fazlul Huq who was the strongman in Bengal at that time.

Sikandar Hayat Khan accepted to cooperate with Jinnah in formulating the Lahore Resolution, according to his own understanding of the Muslim situation in India and Punjab. It should not be forgotten that earlier he had proposed a plan to divide India into seven zones, including a northwestern zone where Muslims were the majority. This naturally found place to some extent in the Lahore Resolution. He could not demand the whole of the Muslim-majority provinces because that was never his line of thinking. That is why he made use of the words 'contiguous Muslim-majority areas in the northwest and east' instead of provinces. That is why he also demanded protection for the minorities in the new states.

He or Jinnah did not even dare to demand a single sovereign Muslim State, combining the northwest and east, for the simple reason that there was no precedent to such a demand. Even the Committee appointed by Jinnah on 26 March 1939 and the various schemes put forward at that time never envisaged a single Muslim state in India. They were also aware of the impracticality of such a demand because the northwestern and the eastern Muslim states would be divided by more than thousand kilometres of Indian Territory. The demand of Sir Muhammad Iqbal was for the creation of a separate Muslim province consisting of Punjab, Sind, Baluchistan, and the NWFP, united with India. The demand of Rahmat Ali was somewhat the same in area, but he wanted complete separation from India. None of them had considered to include the Muslim-majority province of Bengal in this new Muslim State. That is why, Sir Sikandar Hayat Khan, with the consent of Fazlul Huq and Jinnah, proposed the creation of separate and sovereign autonomous States and not a single Muslim State, and that too only in contiguous Muslim-majority areas. It seems that many Muslims in Bengal and Assam sincerely believed that the Lahore Resolution intended to give them a separate State, free from the domination of north Indian Muslims, who, as Sikandar Hayat Khan privately remarked thought that the Bengalis were as different from them as the Chinese.[18]

Jinnah and the rest of the Muslim leadership, mainly from the minority provinces had no other go but to accept the wordings of the Lahore Resolution because nothing would have been possible without Sikandar Hayat Khan and Fazlul Huq, who wielded great influence in their respective provinces. Both Sikandar Hayat Khan and Fazlul Huq along with Jinnah and the Muslim League leadership were aware that the creation of the Muslim states on the basis of the Lahore Resolution would endanger the unity of the Punjab and Bengal. It would be political naivety to claim the contrary. But they don't seem to have been worried about it at that juncture, for they knew that they cannot claim contiguous non-Muslim areas to be included in their states. Otherwise they would have claimed for the whole of Punjab and Bengal provinces straightaway through the Lahore Resolution, which they never did. Besides, Sikandar at least had never envisaged in his original draft the splitting of the Muslim States from India.

The demand for the creation of sovereign Muslim States in the northwest and northeast did not mean that those who were involved in the drafting of the Lahore Resolution were unmindful of the Muslims who would still remain to be part of a Hindu-dominated State. They sincerely believed that the clause for minority safeguards in the constitutions of the respective States in the event of partition would be more than sufficient to cater to the interests of those Muslims remaining in India and also the Hindus who would be part of the Muslim States. There is nothing vague, illogical or irrational in it. If the Lahore Resolution had been accepted by the British as well as the Congress as it was, Jinnah and the Muslim League leadership were sure that it would vindicate their two-nation theory and at the same time solve the problems of the Muslims and safeguard their interests in every field, not only in the contiguous Muslim-majority areas of the northwest and northeast, but also in the contiguous non-Muslim-majority areas in the rest of India. That is what they believed.

However, they seemed to have overlooked the fact that partition on the lines of the Lahore Resolution will not solve the minority problem as it was supposed to. Instead, it had the potential to recreate minority problems in both India and the new Muslim States. It is also bit naïve on the part of Jinnah to assume that Hindus and Sikhs in the Punjab and Bengal will agree to live in Muslim-dominated independent States. Besides, it is significant to note that the Lahore Resolution did not foresee any necessity for the exchange of populations. However, if we stick strictly to the wordings of the Lahore Resolution, it becomes obvious that there were no contradictions or vagueness in the strategy of Jinnah and the Muslim League at this juncture.

Another significant feature of the Lahore Resolution was that it never demanded the establishment of Islamic States in India, but only separate Muslim states. It was by implication a secular demand. It was in conformity with Jinnah's line of thought and policy. In this he was not in line with the policy of Sir Muhammad Iqbal or even the Raja of Mahmudabad. Besides, Jinnah's demand for Muslim states would be more palatable and acceptable to the British than the demand for the creation of Islamic states.

Jinnah and the All-India Muslim League leadership seemed to have been in a hurry to get across their master plan to protect Muslim interests in the Indian subcontinent in the form of the Lahore Resolution. As a result within a space of few weeks, the demand was launched in Lahore, the capital of Punjab with the initial cooperation of Sikandar Hayat Khan, who was allowed to play a prominent role in the drafting of the resolution, instead of other stalwarts from Muslim-minority provinces. Besides, Fazlul Huq of Bengal was allowed to move it. That only added credibility to the demand not only in the eyes of the Muslims of the Muslim-majority provinces, but also among other Muslims and also the British.

Of course, Sikandar Hayat Khan did not consider it necessary at that stage to coin new names for the autonomous Muslim States. The word 'Pakstan' or 'Pakistan' was not used in the resolution at all, for the demand was for two autonomous Muslim States and not just one. Besides the word 'Pakistan' was the invention of Choudhury Rahmat Ali, who did not belong to the Muslim League or the Unionist Party of Sikandar Hayat Khan. Neither Sikandar Hayat Khan nor Jinnah would have wanted to borrow the name from Rahmat Ali who was then running his own little show, for the credit for the name at least would go to Rahmat Ali. Pakistan was used by Rahmat Ali to refer to only the northwestern Muslim State. Besides, during that period, Rahmat Ali made some extravagant demands to protect Muslims all over India. First he wanted three Muslim States—

Pakistan, Bangistan, and Osmanistan and then in 1942, he extended it to another seven Muslim States in India, which he called Siddiquistan, Faruqistan, Haideristan, Muinistan, Maplistan, Safristan, and Nazaristan. He wanted all these ten States to be united under a Pak Commonwealth of Nations or the *Pakasia Union*.[19] Neither Jinnah nor the Muslim League leadership took any note of these demands.

It is true that the Indian and the British press in a hurry without really giving thought to the demand for the two autonomous Muslim States put forward by the Lahore Resolution, made use of the only available term 'Pakistan', invented by Rahmat Ali to refer to the new demand. It was from that time onwards that the word 'Pakistan' was also supposed to include Bengal and later even Assam. The Muslim League leadership including Jinnah, who were then talking in terms of the existence of two nations in India—Hindu and Muslim—did not think that it was necessary to clarify at that juncture that the demand was actually for two Muslim States and not just one, because that would have raised intra-Muslim problems between the two wings of Pakistan and weakened the Lahore Resolution.

But Sikandar Hayat Khan was always opposed to the usage of the word 'Pakistan', unlike Jinnah, who did not mind adopting the name coined by Rahmat Ali, on the pretext that it was foisted and fathered by the 'Hindu press' and also the British press on them. This 'fathering' had been reported by Mohamed Raza Khan in his book and conveniently repeated by other more recent scholars like Ayesha Jalal, who have the goodwill of British scholars like Francis Robinson and also Indian-Muslim scholars like A.G. Noorani.[20]

There are four distinct words used in the Lahore Resolution to designate what we may call the Muslim homelands. They are: units, region, areas, and zones. Administratively speaking, British India was composed of provinces and the provinces were composed of districts and *tehsils*. But the framers of the resolution had not chosen either the provinces or districts or *tehsils*, as a basis at this stage to designate the Muslim States. Instead the resolution wanted the demarcation of contiguous areas in the northwest and east in which Muslims were in a majority, with such territorial readjustments as might be necessary, and group them to constitute 'Independent States'. Though the region where these independent States were to be created had been identified clearly in the resolution, yet the responsibility for the demarcation of contiguous areas was left to the British authorities, subject to territorial readjustments. We do not think that it could have been otherwise, for neither Jinnah nor the Muslim League had the constitutional right to decide upon such matters. They could at the most raise demands, but it was for the British to satisfy or not satisfy them.

In the light of the above, it is wrong to contend or insinuate that the Lahore Resolution was vague, imprecise, and undefined, so that everyone could make whatever they wanted of it. It is regrettable that the thesis of Ayesha Jalal on Jinnah is principally based on the supposed vagueness of the Lahore Resolution, vagueness which she claims Jinnah maintained from the beginning till the end. Nothing is farther from truth than this supposition, which was actually put forward in the beginning by some prominent Indians like Dr Ambedkar and Sikandar Hayat Khan. It is clear that Jalal and more recently Jaswant Singh had borrowed their vagueness theory from either Ambedkar or Sikandar Hayat Khan or both.[21]

Although considerable discussions had taken place in the Subjects Committee before the adoption of the Lahore Resolution, there was one glaring omission all throughout the discussions. This omission was international and geopolitical in character. Jinnah had talked of the Hindu–Muslim problem as an international problem, but never did the discussions centre upon the international and geopolitical implications of the Partition of India. So engrossed were Jinnah and the top brass of the League on protecting the Muslims from Hindus that never in their wildest dreams they weighed the international and geopolitical dimension of a united or divided India.

Congress was a purely Indian power, while Britain was a world power with interests all over the world and particularly in the Indian Ocean region. They were not going to retreat from India because the Congress or Jinnah had asked for it, without protecting in whatever manner they can their geopolitical interests in the region. But never did Jinnah talk about it all throughout the discussions leading to the Lahore Resolution. He behaved as if he was ignorant of the problem or that such a problem did not exist. It is quite surprising that Jinnah failed to take note of the geopolitical implications of Partition when the World War was raging.

Whatever it be, the partition demand would not have seen the light had Linlithgow not raised the standing of Jinnah by giving him virtually a veto right regarding constitutional reforms. Linlithgow, by his words and actions, had definitely contributed to the strengthening of the separatist idea and solution in Jinnah's mind, though he could not be accused of openly proposing the idea to Jinnah. Besides, the acceptance of 'territorial readjustments' as mentioned in the Lahore Resolution, opened the possibility of redrawing the boundaries of the provinces.

On 18 April 1940, Zetland actually stated in the Lords that Indian unity depended upon the agreement between the Indian communities. He even proclaimed that the British would not force a constitution on the Muslims.[22]

Viceroy Linlithgow reacted to the Lahore Resolution without the slightest thought of rejecting it when he wrote:

> This plan has been adopted by the leaders of the League because it offered the sole means of escape from the dilemma in which the Muslim minority finds itself in the face of the introduction of democratic institutions.... They refuse to contemplate a future in which they would be in constant subordination to the Hindu majority. They are therefore constrained to suggest the constitutional severance of the country in such a manner as to secure to them political control in those areas in which the Muslim population exceeds the Hindus.... It is alleged that Mr Jinnah and certain of his friends regard it as no more

> than a bargaining counter against the Congress. If this is indeed the case I am inclined to doubt whether they will find it an altogether easy matter at some future date to persuade their followers to abandon this objective.[23]

It is quite clear that Linlithgow took a sympathetic attitude towards Jinnah's demand. He harped upon the old argument that Hindus and Muslims must settle their differences for them to work together, as if it was not the responsibility of the British to settle those differences and unite the Indians. Following the Lahore Resolution, he too used the word 'areas' to designate the Muslim state. He never used the terms 'vague' and 'imprecise' or 'indefinite' to describe the Lahore Resolution, for he knew where Pakistan could come about, if at all it came about. But he outrightly dismissed the 'bargaining counter theory' which was doing the rounds then among certain high British officials. Linlithgow thought that this theory was fraught with danger for the Muslim League and Jinnah at some future date and therefore impossible.

Besides, there is no direct evidence that the British establishment invented the idea of Partition and asked Jinnah to accept it as his own, though they pushed and expected Jinnah to raise his stakes even more to defy the Congress. The statements and attitudes of both Zetland and Linlithgow during that period went a long way to comfort Jinnah's defiant postures to the detriment of the ideals of the Congress and its leaders. British created the conditions necessary for the demand for partition to flourish. In other words, they laid the groundwork for it. As Linlithgow and Zetland were representatives of the British government in India, they cannot but reflect British policy in their dealings with Indians, whether Hindus or Muslims. The British government was responsible for what was happening to India and in India since the outbreak of the World War.

Nobody can deny the fact that the British were catering to the particular interests of the Muslims for some time after the Revolt of 1857. They used the All-India Muslim League as a counterpoise to the nationalist aspirations of the Congress on several occasions. The outbreak of the Second World War had drastically altered their geopolitical and political calculations, both short-term and long-term with regard to India. From catering to the particular interests of the Muslims, they seemed to have switched over to lay the groundwork for Partition since the outbreak of the Second World War. Jinnah and the Muslim League proved very useful to them at this juncture and they did everything possible to prop them up as a countervailing force against the Congress. They were so much engrossed in their own quest for power to protect Muslim interests in India that they hardly gave thought to the fact that the British were using them as a bulwark against the increasing defiance of the Congress towards the British Empire, with the objective of furthering their own imperial interests and needs.[24] Jinnah unwittingly played into the hands of the British. He even provided a timely and precious handle to the British to determine the final contours of Indian independence. In the process, the British set aside the Federal part of the Government of India Act 1935, which in spite of all its drawbacks, stood for a united India.

Besides, the talk of Jinnah that Muslims and Hindus constituted two different nations and the Lahore demand itself, would not have come about if the Muslims were uniformly distributed all over India. It was because of the historical fact that the Muslims were in a majority in the top two corners of India that the idea of Pakistan itself took root. Jinnah had, on his part, laid the ground for the creation of the northwestern corner through his Delhi proposals of 1927, which was conceded by the British in due course of time, with a view to increasing his bargaining position at the all-India level. But then with the Lahore demand Jinnah's position had evolved towards separation. That was not possible without the support of the Muslim-majority provinces and its regional Muslim leaders. Jinnah sought, by all means, to acquire their support by using the Islamic card and by driving home the point that though the Muslims were a majority in the northwest and in the northeast, they were a minority at the all-India level and therefore, they had no choice but to accept his leadership at the all-India level. While the Muslims in the Muslim-minority provinces with Jinnah in the lead needed the solidarity of the Muslim-majority provinces in order to protect and safeguard their interests in the provinces and in the Centre. The Lahore Resolution was the outcome of such thought process. It was framed to weaken the resistance to Jinnah in the Muslim-majority provinces.

Another aspect is that theoretically it was for the British as rulers to take a decision on this demand. The Congress leaders may have their opinions about it, but it was still the British who had to concede it or not concede Pakistan. The British had conceded many demands of Jinnah in the past though the Congress was against many of them. The situation was the same then and Jinnah more than anyone else knew it. But Viceroy Linlithgow would not commit on the question of separation at that juncture. Some senior British officials seemed to have welcomed the Pakistan plan as a means to checkmate the Congress' quest for Independence. Jinnah had no other alternative but to work so that his demand finds full favour with the British. That would naturally involve time. The British had already conceded the veto power to Jinnah, but they had not deprived the Congress from representing a section of the Muslims, however small or big that section may be. Otherwise Abul Kalam Azad would not have been its President and four out of fifteen members of the Congress Working Committee would not have been Muslims.[25] They had not also conceded parity for the League with the Congress in the Executive Council. Jinnah still had to fight hard on two fronts—the parity front and the partition front.

Parity was necessary for him to legitimize the claim that the League was veritably the sole spokesman of the Indian Muslims as long as India was not partitioned. Will Jinnah stop with demanding parity in the Executive Council or will he extend the demand to cover the Central Legislature as well as the provincial legislatures? As the British and the Congress would not accept parity in the Executive Council at that juncture, there was no question or chance of them accepting it in the Central and provincial legislatures and ministries as well as in the army and the services. That was because it will be against all norms of democratic decency and therefore impossible to implement, except if the Hindus were willing to sacrifice their interests. Jinnah most certainly knew this. But he kept on harping on parity as he had no other better demand to formulate. Earlier, he had used separate electorates in order to acquire Sind, NWFP, and one-third representation in the Central Assembly. By then he had developed the demand for parity as a sort of weapon in his hand in order to acquire Pakistan, the latest of his demands. Many of his earlier demands have been met with by the British government without the least agitation on the part of Jinnah or much opposition from the Congress. Then there were just two main demands—parity and partition. Those demands could not be reasonably fulfilled by the Congress as it was not in power. The British were still in the saddle and it was for them to decide (once again) about Jinnah's latest demands. If the Congress would accept parity with the League and between the Hindus and Muslims everywhere and in everything, thinking that it can save Indian unity by sacrificing majority interests, then that would be another concession in the long line of concessions awarded to the Muslims and Jinnah. Jinnah by raising the demand for Pakistan had given the Congress a chance of settlement of the Hindu–Muslim problem once and for all. It was a wonderful opportunity to get rid off Jinnah and a sizeable section of his followers. Will the Congress seize this opportunity offered by Jinnah?

REACTIONS TO JINNAH'S PAKISTAN DEMAND

The Pakistan demand had serious implications for India's future. Strangely some top leaders of the Congress did not reject the Pakistan demand outrightly. Instead, they adopted an ambiguous attitude. The Lahore Resolution for separate 'autonomous Muslim States' had been squarely condemned and rejected by some leaders of the Congress High Command.

But Gandhi, the topmost leader of the Congress wrote as early as 23 March 1940 in *Harijan* that he hoped that the Muslims would not want Pakistan, but if they did:

> ...the Congress cannot forcibly resist (it)....the Congress can never seek the assistance of British forces to resist the vivisection...If I can carry the Congress with me, I would not put the Muslims to the trouble of using force. I would be ruled by them for it would still be Indian rule.[26]

The same Gandhi also wrote in *Harijan* on 6 April 1940: 'The two-nation theory is an untruth. The vast majority of the Muslims are converts to Islam or descendants of converts. They did not become a separate nation as soon as they became converts.' He even said, 'Vivisect me, before you vivisect India. You should not do what even the Mughals who ruled over India for over two centuries did not do.' In short, Gandhi was against the whole idea of a nation on the basis of religion.[27]

In another statement of 13 April 1940, Gandhi expressed his desire to persuade the Muslims not to insist on Partition, but in case they did, he would not forcibly resist it.[28] In the same month, he also wrote:

> Unless the rest of India wishes to engage in internal fratricide, the others will have to submit to the Moslem dictation, if the Muslim will resort to it. I know of no non-violent method of compelling the obedience of eight crores of Muslims to the will of the rest of India, however powerful a majority the rest may represent. The Moslems must have the same right of self-determination that the rest of India has. We are at present a joint family. Any member may claim a division.[29]

On 4 May 1940, he wrote again in *Harijan*, '...if the eight crores of Muslims desire it (Pakistan), no power on earth can prevent it, notwithstanding opposition, violent or non-violent.' It seemed that Gandhi had even confided to Liaquat Ali Khan, Jinnah's close confidant, that as a man of non-violence, he would not resist the proposed partition if the Muslims of India really insist upon it.[30]

On his part, Jawaharlal Nehru dismissed the Lahore Resolution as 'a mad scheme'. He maintained the following in the same breath:

> If people wanted such things as suggested by the Muslim League at Lahore then one thing was clear. They and people like him (Jinnah) could not live together in India. He would be prepared to face all the consequences of it, but he would not be prepared to live with such people.[31]

Of course Maulana Abul Kalam Azad, the new President of the Congress party had rejected the Lahore Resolution and never adopted an ambivalent attitude like Gandhi or Nehru. The selection of Maulana Azad, a long-time associate of Gandhi and a devout Muslim, to head the Congress party just before the adoption of the Lahore Resolution, must have been an embarrassment for Jinnah at a time when he was claiming that Hindus and Muslims were two different nations and the Congress was a Hindu body. Nationalist Muslim groups like the Ahrars, Jamiat-ul-ulema, and the All India Shia Political Conference organized the 'Azad Muslim Conference' in Delhi in April 1940 under the Presidentship of Allah Baksh, the premier of Sind. They supported the Congress plan for a Constituent Assembly and condemned Jinnah's plan of partition.[32] During that period the nationalist Muslims were losing ground to Jinnah.

The Hindu Scheduled Caste leader, B.R. Ambedkar was among the first to realize the gravity of the demand and wrote a book on Pakistan and published it in 1940. That added some credibility to the demand. Two years later, he founded the All India Scheduled Caste Federation, which was recognized as the legitimate representative of the Hindu Scheduled Castes by the British. The Hindu Maha Sabha on its part condemned Pakistan.[33]

The demand found some Hindu supporters in south India. Ramasamy, the leader of the Justice Party came out openly in support of it.[34] He never bothered about the unity of India. But his political foe, Rajagopalachari, the southern lieutenant of Gandhi, had always wanted the south Indians to learn Hindi in order to participate more effectively in the national life of a united India. Jinnah's demand had introduced a new dimension into Indian politics. It had the potential to drastically alter Rajagopalachari's calculations and his future political postures. The Lahore Resolution was a turning point in Rajagopalachari's understanding of the events to come. He knew that Jinnah had taken the first crucial step towards the Partition of India, however unsure that step might be.

Rajagopalachari rejected the Lahore Resolution. He said: '...Surely, he can ask for many things, other than cutting up of India into two parts based on a medieval conception to attain this laudable desire.'

In a statement dated 31 March 1940, Jinnah held the following:

> ...Exchange of population...as far as practicable, need to be considered.
>
> ...Whatever happens they would remain a minority (in a united India)...It was because of the realization of this fact that Musalman minorities in the Hindu India readily supported the Lahore Resolution.
>
> ...The division of India will throw a great responsibility upon the majority in its respective zones to create a real sense of security amongst the minorities and win their complete trust and confidence.
>
> ...I am sure that they (Sikhs) would be much better off in the North-West Muslim zone than they can ever possibly be in a united India or under one Central Government, for under one Central Government, their voice would be negligible. The Punjab in any case would be an autonomous sovereign unit. And, after all they have to live in the Punjab. It is obvious that whereas in a united India they would be mere nobodies, in the Muslim homeland constituted of the western zone of the Federated Autonomous States, including the autonomous sovereign state of the Punjab, the Sikhs would always occupy an honoured place....
>
> ...The only important states (princely states) which matter, are not in the Eastern, but in the northwestern zone. They are Kashmir, Bahawalpur, Patiala, etc. If these States willingly agree to come into the Federation of Muslim homeland, we shall be

> glad to come to a reasonable and honourable settlement with them. We have, however, no desire to force them or coerce them in any way.
>
> ...As regards other zone or zones that may be constituted in the rest of India our relationship will be of an international character. An example already exists in the relationship of India with Burma and Ceylon.
>
> ...One set of criticism has come from some Congressite Musalmans. Obviously they are speaking in their master's voice and I do not think anyone would need to worry about it.
>
> As for the criticism of some of the Congress leaders, it is like a parrot-like cry and thoughtless. The only person who had made any serious attempt to criticize the Lahore Resolution is Mr Rajagopalachari...
>
> Mr Rajagopalachari's arguments of dividing the baby as was the case in the parable of King Solomon have gone beyond the zenith of his intellectual powers. He wants to apply this analogy to our proposals.
>
> Surely India is not the sole property of the Congress and if the real mother was to be discovered, she would be Dravidian or still further aborigines. She would be neither Aryan nor Muslim. The Aryan claim to India is no better than that of the Muslim, except that the Aryans were earlier arrivals in point of time.

What is most astounding is Mr Rajagopalachari's talk when he says:

> Indeed, not even Tipu Sultan or Hyder Ali or Aurangzeb or Akbar, all of whom lived during the days when differences seemed more deep-rooted than now, imagined that India was anything but one and indivisible. These great men might have differed from one another in many respects, but they agreed in looking upon this precious land and this great nation as one and essentially indivisible.
>
> Yes, naturally they did so as conquerors and parental rulers. Is this the kind of government Mr Rajagopalachari still envisages? And

> did the Hindus of those days willingly accept the rule of the 'great men'? I may or may not be suffering from a diseased mentality, but the statement of Mr Rajagopalachari and his criticism of the Lahore Resolution indicate that in him there is no mind left at all. I hope Mr Rajagopalachari does not represent true Hindu opinion and I doubt very much whether he represents the opinion of the Congress or its High Command as far as his statement on the Lahore Resolution is concerned.[35]

The preceding attack of Jinnah on Rajagopalachari was so pointed, uncouthed, and severe that the latter must have been stung by it. Rajagopalachari did not retort to it at once; rather, he preferred to bide his time.

Rajagopalachari seemed to have realized unlike many other Congress leaders including Gandhi, that Congress non-cooperation in the war effort was driving the British against the Congress and closer to the Muslim League. He boldly put forward the proposal that Congress should abandon civil disobedience and pledge full support to the British war effort if Britain was prepared to accept India's right to Independence and agreed to set up a national government. That proposal was embodied in the famous Poona Offer of 27 July 1940, much against the wishes of Gandhi. He persisted with that proposal later in Bardoli, to which Jinnah vehemently opposed. At that time, Rajagopalachari even made a 'sporting offer' to Jinnah to become the prime minister and form his own cabinet, if the British accepted his proposals.[36]

But neither Linlithgow nor Jinnah were tempted by Rajagopalachari's attractive offer. Linlithgow had been forewarned by Lord Erskine, the Governor of Madras, that Rajagopalachari was 'a very cunning Madrasee Brahmin' and 'a slippery customer' who 'alters his views periodically to suit his party's advantage'.[37] Rajagopalachari somehow wanted the Congress to be in the good books of the British.

In the Muslim-majority provinces, Sikandar Hayat Khan, premier of Punjab, Sir Ghulam Husain Hidayatullah, premier of Sind, and Khan

Bahadur Allah Baksh had outrightly rejected the Pakistan demand of Jinnah. Allah Baksh characterized the Lahore Resolution as 'grotesque' and unreasonable. It was then that the Muslims of Sind raised the cry of 'Sind for Sindhis'. Khan Abdul Qaiyum of the NWFP declared that his province will resist Partition with its blood. Even Fazlul Huq who moved the resolution at Lahore, was talking only a month later, of working for a united India.[38]

Given that the top leaders of the Congress like Gandhi and Nehru had stated in clear terms that they would not resist Partition, although they were against it, all that remained for Jinnah was to bring around the provincial Muslim leaders to his point of view and make them accept separation. Once that would be done, Jinnah knew that he could present his case for Partition in a more forceful manner to the British for their acceptance. He set about this task in right earnest from that period onwards.

In May 1940, Sir Winston Churchill of the Conservative Party took over as Prime Minister of a national coalition ministry and L.S. Amery succeeded Zetland as Secretary of State, at a time when the German army had swept across France and had isolated Britain. Labour leaders Attlee and Sir Stafford Cripps were part of Churchill's Cabinet. Thenceforth, India's future largely depended on what may be called the Churchill–Linlithgow–Amery trio. Amery was particularly interested in the formation of a British Commonwealth in which all Member States were free and equal. He fixed Dominion status as his objective for India.[39]

But in his interview with Linlithgow, Jinnah made it clear that it was out of question to go straight to Dominion status or anything approaching it in the existing conditions. He was neither in for Congress returning to office, in which case he threatened Civil War in India. He apprised Linlithgow of his efforts to form a League ministry in the NWFP where the Congress had resigned and asked the support of Sir George Cunningham in this venture. He seemed to have been convinced by that time that complete weight should be given to the Muslims as they were the ones who worked the Constitution in the provinces and they constituted the bulk of the Indian army so essential for the war.[40] On 27 May 1940, Jinnah issued the following statement to the Press:

> Up to the present moment, we have not created any difficulty nor have we embarrassed the British Government in the prosecution of the war. The Provinces where the Muslim League has a dominant voice have been left free to cooperate with the British Government, pending their consideration with regard to the assurances that we have asked for, and in particular that the British should make no declaration regarding the future constitutional problem of India and the vital issues that have been raised in that connection without our approval or concern.[41]

Further, in a message to the Bombay Presidency Muslim League Conference at Hubli, Jinnah held:

> ...India is held by the British power and that...gives the impression of United India and the unitary government. Indian nation and central government do not exist. ...Autonomous provinces are in existence even under the present constitution where the Musalmans and Hindus dominate respectively. ... Our proposal is more practical than 'ahimsa', 'chakra' or for the matter of that the ideal of Ram Raj and complete independence of Mr Gandhi's conception.[42]

Jinnah met the Viceroy once again on 27 June 1940 and told him that he was prepared to work on the basis of his November 1939 offer. He insisted that the British government take into consideration his proposal for two Indias, in the event of any declaration pertaining to the constitution.[43]

After the interview, Jinnah sent a memorandum to the Viceroy on 1 July 1940 in which he held:

> In view of the rapid developments in Europe and the grave danger that is facing India, it is fully realized that everything should be done that is possible to intensify war efforts and mobilize all the resources of India for her defence, for

> the purpose of maintaining internal security, peace, and tranquillity, and to ward off external aggression. But this can only be achieved provided the British government is ready and willing to associate the Muslim leadership as equal partners in the Government, both at the Centre and in all the provinces. In other words, Muslim India leadership must be fully trusted as equals, and have an equal share in the authority and control of the Governments, Central and Provincial.

In the memorandum, he also asked the British government to give definite and categorical assurance to the Muslims of India that no interim or final scheme of constitution would be adopted by the British Government without the previous approval and consent of Muslim India. No pronouncement or statement would be made by the British government which will, in any way, militate against the basic and fundamental principles laid down by the Lahore Resolution for the division of India and for the creation of Muslim states in the northwest and eastern zones. He demanded the enlargement of the Executive Council under the existing constitution where Muslims will have equal representation with Hindus if the Congress came in. Otherwise they should have a majority and in the provinces ruled by the Governors he wanted non-official advisors with Muslims in a majority. He also wanted the creation of a War Council where there must be a similar arrangement as in the Executive Council. Of course, the Viceroy did not fulfil all demands of Jinnah. But the preceding proves clearly that Jinnah was pursuing his strategy of parity for partition or parity until partition with great tenacity.[44]

On 9 July 1940, Maulana Abul Kalam Azad as President of the Congress apprised Jinnah that the Congress intended to constitute a national government with a composite Cabinet not limited to any single party. He asked Jinnah if the League would agree to a provisional government only if it was based on the two-nation scheme. But Jinnah refused to initiate any correspondence with him. Instead he castigated him as a tool of the Congress party and a Muslim show-boy who was Congress

President to deceive the world that the Congress was national, while in reality it was Hindu. He asked the Maulana to resign from his post and give up his actions against the League.[45]

Such was the hatred Jinnah had for the Maulana that he, as President of the Congress was effectively blocking and rendering Jinnah's meaningless demands for League parity with the Congress, on the basis that the League alone represented the Muslims. Maulana was a reputed divine Sunni Islamic scholar and a Muslim to the core right from his young days, unlike Jinnah who was a highly westernized Gujarati Khoja since his youth and whose knowledge of Islam was never established. Jinnah claimed that he alone knew how to protect the Muslims and Islam by breaking away from India, while the Maulana stood for achieving the same by remaining united in India with their Hindu blood brothers.

Linlithgow came out with an offer on 8 August 1940, inspired by none other than Winston Churchill himself, in order to comfort Jinnah's position and counter the Congress moves. There was no further question of formation of any national government. There was also no question of transfer of responsibilities 'to any system of government whose authority is directly denied by large and powerful elements in India's national life. Nor could they be parties to the coercion of such elements into submission to such a government.' Instead, he simply declared that he would invite a number of representative Indians to join the existing Executive Council and would also set up a War Advisory Council. He repeated the old offer of Dominion status. He also said that after the war a body which will be entrusted with the task of framing a new Constitution, comprising the principal elements of India's national life, including the princes, communal organizations, and Europeans.[46] In other words, it meant that the British did not and will not accept the Congress as the sole representative of the whole of India. Instead, it gave a virtual veto to Jinnah to block any constitutional advancement without his consent. The demand for a national government by the Congress was disregarded. Naturally the Congress rejected the August Offer.

Jinnah had reasons to be happy about the August Offer. He personally met the Viceroy on 11 and 13 August 1940. The League felt that the August Offer was a considerable advance towards its stand. Jinnah had also asked parity with the Congress and offered to shoulder full responsibility to run the government, either singly or with the assistance of other parties in case the Congress declined to join the Executive Council. He had also asked a right to veto over Congress entry into the Executive Council. Linlithgow would not concede these demands. He would not also allow Muslim non-official advisors in provinces under the Governor's rule. As a result, Jinnah too turned down the August Offer.[47]

On 14 August 1940, Amery held the following in the House of Commons: 'India cannot be unitary in the sense that we are in this island, but she can still be a unity. India's future house of freedom has room for many mansions.'[48] This statement in itself was ambiguous. It conceded Jinnah's demand that there will be no unitary government in India. At the same breath he asserted that there was place for several mansions in it, which could be interpreted to mean that Jinnah could get his Pakistan mansion.

All this pushed the Congress to revert to individual civil disobedience on 17 October 1940 with Gandhi once again in the lead. The Congress Working Committee decided to withdraw their 'Offer' of support to British war effort. But the British never took the new round of civil disobedience seriously. Jinnah refused to come into the Executive Council unless he got a 50 per cent share in the council. Sir Sikandar Hayat Khan, the Punjab Premier and Khawaja Nazimuddin, Minister in the Bengal government were in favour of British war effort.[49]

While the Government came down heavily on the new Gandhian Movement and arrested its leaders, it did not adopt a harsh attitude towards the Muslim League. Instead, the British government was particularly careful to respect the rights and claims of the Muslim minority, both by reason of the position of that community in the army and because of the importance to the British during the war of being in the good books of Muslims throughout the world. On the contrary, Linlithgow was particularly severe with Gandhi (whom he qualified as an uncompromising dictator), whose aim was to engineer the political supremacy of the Hindus in India by destroying British power in India.[50]

Linlithgow himself admitted in a letter to His Majesty that 'the Muslim League was a valuable counterweight to Congress and its existence in effective form during the period following the war, when the major question of constitutional reform will have to be considered, will be of advantage in securing an inadequate hearing for the Muslim point of view'. He also admitted that he would avoid doing anything which would damage the prestige of Jinnah, in view of the latter's attitude towards the government. It is surprising that it was the same Linlithgow who considered Jinnah as 'a vain and difficult creature', unpredictable to the core. But he would never let Jinnah down because Jinnah was the only counterweight to the Congress, on whom he could rely upon in times of need to further imperial interests. The Secretary of State, Amery asserted on his part that parliamentary democracy was not suitable to India and even talked in favour of a mild form of Pakistan.[51]

The British high authorities at that juncture were highly favourable to the Muslim League and Jinnah, for they were convinced that the League and Jinnah were a countervailing force to the Congress under Gandhi. They envisaged propping them up still further and using them even after the war at the time of constitutional reforms and settlement. The Viceroy Linlithgow himself had admitted this fact in his letter to the King. Neither the top Congress leaders like Gandhi, Nehru, or Rajagopalachari nor the League leaders like Jinnah or Liaquat Ali Khan were aware of the designs of Lord Linlithgow.

SOME OBSERVATIONS AND CONCLUSION

It could be safely concluded that M.A. Jinnah entered politics as a Congressman and as a nationalist. That was his ***first avatar*** in politics. He did not participate in the foundation of the All-India Muslim League in 1906 by the Muslim upper class Ashrafs who thought they were the 'natural leaders' of India by virtue of their past history as rulers and conquerors and by political importance. In the evolving democratic set-up, there was no question of the Hindus accepting their 'natural leadership'. So they were left with no other alternative but to safeguard their elite interests by staking their claim as the 'natural leaders' of the Muslims of India, by founding the All-India Muslim League on the basis of religion. The British were sympathetic to this claim.

The large majority of the Muslims of India were not of Ashraf or foreign descent. They were descendants of local Indian converts to Islams, collectively known as Ajlafs. M.A. Jinnah was one of them. No wonder he was neither part of the Muslim deputation of 1906, nor was he one among the founder-members of the Muslim League. He opposed their demands for separate electorates for Muslims and even dismissed them as unrepresentative of the Muslims. He militated against the very idea of separate electorates as he claimed that it would set apart the Muslims from the Hindus politically.

When Jinnah joined the Congress party, there was a string of top Congress leaders in every province of India, mostly Hindus and some Muslims like Badruddin Tyabji. Jinnah stood no chance of emerging as a top Congress leader of the front rank. But the 1909 Act accorded separate electorates for Muslims. Jinnah was in two minds then. Sometimes he spoke in favour of it, sometimes against it. By 1912–13, the leadership of the Muslim League was going into the hands of lesser and younger leaders who did not belong to the upper class of Muslims, led by the Aga Khan. Jinnah was finally persuaded by Mohammad Ali and Syed Wazir Hasan to join the Muslim League in 1913, which espoused the cause of separate electorates. But Jinnah did not resign from the Congress. He had one leg in the Congress boat and the other in the League boat. It was in that new political avatar that he brought about the Lucknow Pact as a communal settlement between Hindus and Muslims in 1916, which served the interests of the Muslims of the Muslim-minority provinces more than the Muslims of the Muslim-majority provinces. He was hailed as the ambassador of Hindu–Muslim unity for that achievement. He claimed that the League was the 'chief' representative of the Indian Muslims. He never claimed that it was the only representative. He always worked for a measure of self-government within the British Empire all throughout that period until the Round Table Conferences, where Indian–Muslim interests would be adequately protected. Jinnah's Indian nationalism was always subject to Muslim sectarian interests. As a result, he can be rightly described as a 'sectarian nationalist' during that period and not as a full-fledged unconditional nationalist. That was the ***second avatar*** of Jinnah.

The period during the First World War and its aftermath brought about a wave of changes in the Indian political situation. That was not to the advantage or taste of Jinnah. Exasperated by the rise of Gandhi in Indian politics and the Gandhian style of non-violent mass agitational politics, Jinnah, though senior to Gandhi in politics, felt that he was unwanted in the course of time even by his Muslim colleagues like the Ali brothers. That pushed him out of the Congress. He dissociated himself from the Non-Cooperation and Khilafat Movements, on the pretext that Gandhi was mixing religion and politics. He continued to be a leader of the Muslim League, an exclusively Muslim and religion-based political party. That was his ***third avatar***. By not coming out in favour of the Gandhian and Khilafat Movements, he proved to be loyal to the British indirectly.

The abolition of the Khilafat by the Turks themselves in 1924 rendered the Khilafatists irrelevant in Indian politics. It provided an opportunity for Jinnah to reassert himself in Indian–Muslim politics. He resumed his demands for a measure of self-government and a communal settlement. He came out with a series of proposals, first in the form of the Delhi proposals and then the Fourteen Points in 1929. He was willing to give up separate electorates under certain conditions. But he demanded the creation of a new Muslim-majority province, Sind from Bombay, and the introduction of reforms in NWFP and Baluchistan so that they become full-fledged provinces. He also demanded one-third representation for Muslims in the Central Assembly. Those two demands had far-reaching implications for Muslims, whether he intended it or not.

Firstly, the creation of Sind and reforms in the NWFP and Baluchistan had the potential to create a northwestern bloc of Muslim-majority provinces. That bloc along with Bengal, where the Muslims were in a majority, could play a major role in the evolving political situation of the country. I think Jinnah was conscious of this when he put forward such demands. There was no indication that he ever thought of demanding Independence for the Muslim bloc during that period, although there was potential for it. But the point was not lost upon his colleague Sir Muhammad Iqbal, who put forward such a separatist demand for the northwestern Muslims in the year 1930. Three years later in 1933, Rahmat Ali, a Cambridge student from the Punjab put forward a similar proposal and called the new State first as 'Pakstan'. 'Pakstan' became 'Pakistan' very quickly. It would be naïve to think that Jinnah was not conscious of those implications of his Delhi proposals and the Fourteen Points. The genesis of Pakistan was actually found in those proposals. That was Jinnah's invention. However, Jinnah never demanded a separate Muslim State or States at that juncture and even dismissed them as unrealistic.

Secondly, Jinnah asked for one-third representation for Muslims in the Central Assembly. That was at least 8 per cent above the share of the Muslims in the total population of India. One cannot claim at that juncture that he was demanding parity for Muslims with the Hindus in the Central Assembly, which proves that he was still envisaging the future of Muslims in a united India, with a strong Muslim presence in the Centre, and the creation of a northwestern bloc of Muslim-majority provinces. In a democracy, numbers count. It is obvious that Jinnah was demanding more than what was warranted by the Muslim numbers. The *Nehru Report* would not accept Jinnah's demand. It proposed only one-fourth representation for Muslims in the Central Assembly, keeping in mind the number of Muslims, although it conceded the creation of Sind. At that stage Jinnah did not ask one-third representation in the Central Assembly for the Muslim Leaguers alone, but for all Muslims to whichever party they might belong.

During the Round Table Conferences, Jinnah played a subdued role, although he was in touch with top British politicians including Ramsay MacDonald. Not surprisingly the Conference got deadlocked on communal and sectarian issues. The British would not mediate. Instead, they watched the Hindu and Muslim delegates squabble. When there was no way forward, the Labour Prime Minister Ramsay MacDonald, announced unilaterally, what came to be known as the Communal Award. It must be remembered here that Ramsay MacDonald had at the beginning of the Second Round Table Conference chosen to welcome the Indian delegates as 'My Hindu and Muslim Friends', obviously implying that there were two categories of people in India. Quite surprisingly the Communal Award gave Jinnah what he wanted—the creation of Sind which would pave the way for the formation of a northwestern bloc of Muslim-majority provinces and also one-third representation in the Central Assembly. Separate electorates were re-confirmed. The Muslim groups including Jinnah, on the whole were happy with the Award, while the Congress and Gandhi were caught unawares. Jinnah had never agitated for the creation of Sind or for one-third representation in the Central Assembly. It was nevertheless given to him on a platter, as separate electorates were given to the Muslims through the 1909 Act, defying all norms of democracy. The Congress watched only with bewilderment and silence the unfolding political scenario. Jinnah realized that there was not much use in discussing with Congressmen to arrive at a communal settlement, as long as the British were there to satisfy his needs along with the needs and demands of the Muslim League. The Communal Award came as a shot in his arm to re-affirm the separate political existence of the Muslims and their special destiny.

The Communal Award, the Government of India Act of 1935, and the subsequent provincial elections of 1937 gradually pushed Jinnah to radicalize his stand related to the separate political existence of Muslims in India, which ended up in the demand for a separate Pakistan in 1940, affirming that the Muslims were a nation by themselves. Thenceforth he was the Quaid-e-Azam, who would lead the Muslims to the promised land of Pakistan. That was the ***fourth*** and ***final avatar*** of Jinnah where he posed himself as a Muslim and Islamic nationalist, while his opponents accused him of being a separatist.

It has been demonstrated in the preceding pages that Jinnah was not a charismatic person until the elections of 1937. He was highly westernized, belonging to the elite group of wealthy Muslims, unable to connect himself with the Muslim masses, which were culturally Islamic and largely poor. All that changed after 1937, when Jinnah deliberately chose to espouse Islam and raised the cry 'Islam in danger'. Jinnah, who during his youth had even tried to hide his Muslim name and origin by shortening it to M.A. Jinnah, had undergone a radical transformation in 1937. He was then increasingly donning the mantle of messiah or the saviour of the Muslims. Thus by playing the Islamic card, Jinnah connected himself with the Muslim masses to counter his opponents, in order to protect what he perceived as the interests of the Muslims which included elite interests. Therefore, Jinnah was not a charismatic figure by himself; after 1937 his charisma was intimately related with his closer and deliberate association with the ideas and beliefs of Islam.

Democracy is an abstract political idea associated with power. But in the democratic political structures contemplated by the British and introduced into India in its elite representative form, many Muslim stalwarts felt that Hindus would dominate by virtue of their numbers. In order to counteract this eventuality, some Muslim stalwarts like the Aga Khan came out with the idea of separate electorates for Muslims in their quest for power. Jinnah, who started as a Congressman, later adopted this idea. The idea of separate electorates was also associated with power, but it is itself a by-product of another pervasive abstract idea or ideology which is Islam. There could be no separate electorates for Muslims if there was no Islam in India. Historically speaking, Islam has always been associated with power since its inception primarily because it was associated with an idea or a series of ideas. Without a certain power or identification with power, Islam would not have spread in India. So the point that needs to be understood is that abstract ideas, ideals, and principles are most of the time, if not always, associated with power. It is simply illogical and irrational to divide idea and power as two separate things, as some Cambridge scholars like Anil Seal, Gordon Johnson, and David Washbrook tend to do. Men who quarrel and fight over power, prestige, and social standing always fight with an idea, ideal, or ideology in mind. The two processes are inseparable. Power cannot stand alone nor can an abstract idea. Jinnah was not an exception to this phenomenon.

Besides, Indian nationalism is an idea and a feeling of belonging to a particular group above everything. It was pitted against British imperialism which is another idea. Both ideas are naturally associated with power. Like any other idea, the idea of Indian nationalism had to be developed, promoted, and propagated. But many Muslims could not participate in this idea of Indian nationalism, where the Hindu element predominated. Therefore the search for other ideas was associated with power. When the idea of separate electorates for Muslims could not guarantee this power, some Muslims like Rahmat Ali and later even Jinnah veered towards the idea of Muslim nation or Muslim nationalism or Pakistan, which was an assertion of power. The theory of the Cambridge scholars like Anil Seal and C.J. Baker that men in politics are motivated by power, status, and prestige alone and that ideas, principles, and ideologies do not really count in the scramble for power needs to be set aside in the light of the above.

EPILOGUE

It is worth noting at this juncture that the total population of British India according to the 1941 census was 386,666,623 of which the Muslims made up for 24 per cent.[1] There were in addition some 660 Indian States with a total population of 90,857,901 of which 13.3 per cent were Muslims. There were nearly 220 million Caste Hindus in the whole of India of whom about 160 million were in British India.[2] There were about 100 million Muslims in the whole of India of which 84 million were in British India, while the Scheduled Castes formed 52 million in the whole of India and 42 million in British India.[3]

Pressurized and prodded by Viceroy Linlithgow, Jinnah and the Muslim League ended up asking for two separate Muslim states, one in the northwest and the other in the northeast which would comprise only contiguous areas (and not the whole provinces), where the Muslims were in a majority. This demand adopted in Lahore came to be known as the Pakistan demand. That was a straightforward move. There was nothing mysterious about it.

While reaching at that decision, neither Jinnah nor the other front-ranking League leaders had given adequate thought to the geopolitical and strategic interests of an eventual Pakistan and India or the Hindus and Muslims in a divided India. In the beginning, Jinnah thought somewhat naively of uniting the Muslims of India and the Middle-east and confronting the British.[4] Muslim League leaders like Khaliquzzaman thought on similar lines.[5] Others like the Nawab of Bhopal, Liaquat Ali Khan, and the Aga Khan wanted a close understanding between the Muslim world and the Anglo-Saxon world.[6]

Pressurized by Japanese advance towards India, Sir Winston Churchill sent Sir Stafford Cripps to India in March 1942 with some proposals in order to break the constitutional deadlock. The most important feature of these proposals was the right given to the provinces to secede from the Indian Union.

Stafford Cripps did not concede Pakistan on the basis of contiguous areas as demanded by the League and Jinnah. Instead, it conceded the right to whole provinces to secede. Jinnah was caught unawares by this measure. He had doubts about the proposals. He was not sure if, in the case of secession of Punjab, Bengal will join. There were doubts about the Pathans of North-West Frontier Province or Sind joining Punjab to form Pakistan. So he along with the Congress rejected Cripps Offer. Gradually Jinnah altered his position, most certainly under the influence of Cripps' Plan. With the death of Sikandar Hayat Khan in December 1942, Jinnah started equating 'the contiguous Muslim-majority areas of the Lahore Resolution' with the 'Muslim-majority provinces'. Thenceforth, he claimed the whole of the five Muslim-majority provinces for Pakistan, which was definitely not envisaged in the Lahore Resolution.[7]

On the other hand, the Congress party and its leaders maintained an ambiguous position with regard to the demand for Pakistan. They asserted that the Muslims could go their own way if they wanted. They even adopted a resolution that unwilling parts need not remain with the Indian Union. At the same time, they also stood vehemently for a united India.

Of all the Congress leaders, only Rajagopalachari struck a conciliatory note. He wanted to concede the Pakistan that Jinnah was asking for on the basis of contiguous Muslim-majority areas, under certain conditions. He was not averse to the creation of a Hindu-dominated India and a Muslim-dominated Pakistan, provided areas like trade, commerce, and culture between 'Hindu India' and Pakistan would continue to be the same as it was then. That comforted and justified Jinnah's position to a great extent and created a rift in the Congress with regard to Pakistan. Though Rajagopalachari quit the Congress in favour of cooperation with the British in the war, he was successful in the course of the years 1943–44 in converting Gandhi to his point of view with regard to Pakistan, and even arranged for direct negotiations between Gandhi and Jinnah in September 1944. The negotiations failed. Even Jawaharlal Nehru had admitted that there was no disagreement between his colleagues of the Congress High Command and him on the fundamentals of the Rajaji Formula put forward in 1942 when they were imprisoned in the Ahmednagar Fort, on the basis of which Gandhi had opened discussions with Jinnah.

However, Jinnah beat a hasty retreat from his talks with Gandhi affirming more than ever before that his Pakistan would consist of all the Muslim-majority provinces. He knew then what he could get from the Congress: a truncated Pakistan. So he turned towards the British in order to achieve his 'big' Pakistan. Rajagopalachari was instrumental in taking Gandhi towards a 'restricted' or 'truncated' Pakistan, under certain conditions.[8] But Rajagopalachari's and Gandhi's moves were fraught with danger for the unity of India as they had both taken the crucial step to concede Pakistan in some form or the other. It was just a question of time before other Congress leaders followed suit.

Jinnah tried hard for five long years to get his 'big' Pakistan. In the year 1943, the British constitutional expert Sir Reginald Coupland put forward a plan to break the constitutional deadlock. Coupland wanted the British to recognize the existence of two nations in India—Hindu and Muslim. Those two nations must rule at the Centre on the basis of parity. That plan which appeared in the *Manchester Guardian* was adopted by the Cabinet delegation, despatched to India in 1946. The British Cabinet Mission Plan gave Jinnah his 'big' Pakistan on the basis of provincial boundaries, in the form of two groups, which included Assam. Jinnah considered it as a stepping stone to Pakistan. V.P. Menon, the Reforms Commissioner, K.M. Pannikar, another constitutional expert, Sir Penderel Moon, and Rajagopalachari have all affirmed that if Congress accepted the Plan, Jinnah would have ultimately got his province-wise Pakistan. In the light of that, it was not judicious to think or assume that Jinnah stood for the unity of India, or that he was using the Pakistan demand only as a bargaining counter to get more concessions for Muslims in a united India. It was also wrong to think like Ayesha Jalal and Jaswant Singh that the British too were for the unity of India. The British were creating the necessary basis for a 'big' Pakistan in future, under the cover of the Cabinet Mission Plan.

But Congress' refusal to accept the Plan put Jinnah in a quandary. As a last resort to get his 'full' Pakistan, he launched the 'Direct Action', which caused murders and bloodshed, and unsettled the minds of the top Congress leaders as to the feasibility of a peaceful united India. Jinnah did not succeed in getting his full Pakistan. Finally, he ended up getting a truncated one from the British, which strangely corresponded with what was demanded in the Lahore Resolution. He got it after all top Congress leaders, coaxed relentlessly by Lord Mountbatten and his team which included his wife and his trusted Reforms Commissioner V.P. Menon, gave their assent to a 'truncated Pakistan'.[9] In its turn, the Hindu Maha Sabha too accepted Partition, after opposing it for sometime when the demand was raised by Jinnah.

The Congress leaders as well as Jinnah and the Muslim League leaders never really gave adequate thought to the geopolitical and strategic implications of a united or divided India at that juncture. Jinnah, like other Muslim League leaders, thought that Pakistan could always ally with brotherly Muslim countries against Hindustan. In 1946, Nehru waxed eloquently in the most undiplomatic manner that there were only four big powers in the world—America, Russia, China, and India. He said that at a time when India was still under the British. He even declared that small countries could only be 'hangers on' of big powers.[10] Patel was never known for his knowledge of international politics. Gandhi relied on Nehru as far as foreign relations or politics were concerned. Rajagopalachari thought that India could still play a positive role in the reconstruction of a new world order after Independence even if it was divided. But he was never enthusiastic about India becoming a member of the British Commonwealth.[11] In spite of all the legendary dexterity attributed to Rajagopalachari, even he failed to appreciate the dangers, and the geopolitical and strategic implications of a divided India. Of all the Congress leaders, only Maulana Abul Kalam Azad opined that Partition was dangerous to the Muslims and also to India because through it British or western powers would gain a foothold in south Asia.[12] He seemed to have somehow understood that the division of India was a grand plan of the British to reduce the power of united India and the Muslims by laying the foundation for a permanent enmity between Hindus and Muslims, in the form of Pakistan. But his was a lonely voice. Nobody in the Congress listened to him. On the other hand, the British never cared for Hindu–Muslim unity for it was not in their interests if they were united.

The British were ruling the world for several centuries. Naturally while retreating from India, they had to safeguard their strategic, imperialist, capitalist, and geopolitical interests. On the one hand, there was Russian communism, which might spread to Afghanistan and India. That had to be stopped. On the other hand, there was the oil of the Middle-east. The Russians had to be stopped there too. That game which started in the nineteenth century is known as the Great Game. Neither the Congress leaders nor Jinnah seemed to have been worried about all that. The British always had an eye on their interests and were never really bothered about the rift between the Hindus and Muslims. If Jinnah asked for Pakistan, it was because of the British. If we go into the records of the British Cabinet during that period, their main worries were about how to protect their geopolitical, strategic, and other interests in the Indian subcontinent and the entire Indian Ocean region including the Middle-east and south-east Asia.[13]

They needed uninterrupted oil supply and air communication between the UK and the Middle-east, India, Malaysia, and Australia. They needed to safeguard the shipping lanes. They also had to keep the Russians under check. So for the British, it was not a question of giving Pakistan because Jinnah asked for it. The British wanted to maintain control over that part of the world. Indian leaders never really thought about all that; nor did Jinnah think. He thought that if he gets Pakistan, he can become the undisputed leader of a nation and liberate all Muslims from the Hindus.[14]

At the high level meetings of the British Cabinet several ideas were mooted to safeguard British interests. One of them was to give a 'full Pakistan' to Jinnah. If that was not possible, a 'small Pakistan' must be given. It was thought that Pakistan in whatever shape will be favourable to the British. According to the British geo-strategist Olaf Caroe, if a 'full Pakistan' on the basis of Muslim-majority provinces plus Assam was given, then the British would have easy access to Afghanistan and China. At the same time, south Asia and the Indian Ocean region will be under control. That was necessary for world capitalist economy. So in order to safeguard all that, India had to be divided. If they left India united, it may become a superpower overnight. It can also ally with the Russians and challenge the British.[15] To prevent that, they made use of Jinnah. Jinnah was never aware of all these implications. But Jaswant Singh, Ayesha Jalal, and some others hold that Jinnah was extremely intelligent; they don't go into any further details. We are not sure if Nehru, Rajagopalachari, and Gandhi thought on similar lines.

For the British, Pakistan must be created as a counterpoise to Hindustan. That was not because Jinnah asked for Pakistan. The British wanted Pakistan to counter India. But the British could not give a 'full Pakistan' to Jinnah, because the Hindus were a majority in East Punjab and West Bengal. Attempts were made during the Viceroyalty of Lord Mountbatten, which would have ended up in a full Pakistan or even in a full and independent Bengal and West Pakistan. Besides, Sir Stafford Cripps was, till the end, of the view that the princely states had the right to become independent on the lapse of paramountancy. Prime Minister Attlee waited till the last moment to make Bengal independent and integrate it in the British Commonwealth. Jinnah then told the British 'Give us a full Pakistan, we also will join the Commonwealth'. The creation of the British Commonwealth itself seemed to be a ploy to maintain British/western imperialism.[16] One could say along with R.J. Moore that division assisted imperialism before Independence. Given the preceding, it is difficult to accept that division would not assist imperialism after Independence. Strangely Mountbatten wanted everyone to believe that the British were no more in need of the 'divide and rule' policy as they were leaving and if India was split it was because the Congress and the Muslim League could not see eye-to-eye.[17]

The Second World War had weakened Britain very much. America had stepped into its shoes. Agreement was reached to divide Punjab and Bengal on religious basis. A small Pakistan was thus created. But that Pakistan was nearly one-third of the size of India. One had to just imagine what would have happened to India if a 'full Pakistan' had been given. Through that division, Britain/America obtained a foothold in south Asia.

India was a new nation. Pakistan was a new nation. Both needed western help. In the beginning, Nehru did not want to join the Commonwealth. But later, listening to Krishna Menon, he joined the Commonwealth. He told he will join the Commonwealth if Punjab and Bengal were divided. Both India and Pakistan became members of the Commonwealth. As members of Commonwealth, they were safeguarding British/Western interests which included their capitalist interests in the world. That was the greatest victory of British diplomacy.

When Pakistan was to be created, the question arose about how to keep the Pathans quiet. The Pathans and Baluchis were not of Indian stock like the Sindhis and Punjabis. The last Viceroy Lord Mountbatten told Jinnah that he had to spend three and half crores annually to keep the Pathans quiet. But Jinnah thought that all were Muslims and they can live together. Today to keep the Pathans and their cousins in Afghanistan quiet, several million of rupees/dollars are being spent, not just by Pakistan but also by the western powers. Besides, army, navy, and air forces are being used, including western forces, causing innumerable deaths and destruction in Pakistan itself.

If we take a closer look at the region's past history, it will become quite obvious that there can be no permanent military solution to the Pathan/Afghan problem of Pakistan and Afghanistan. Afghanistan has been demanding the reunification of the Pathan-dominated areas in Pakistan for quite sometime. If this would have been done by the British at the time of Partition, leaving the whole of Punjab and Sind to be with India, much bloodshed and strife could have been avoided. Indians, both Hindus and Muslims, would have taken care of the northwestern frontier and would have saved the western powers from the evil that they are facing today, arising from the Afghanistan–Pakistan region. But that was not to be. The intention of the British at that time seemed to not allow India to emerge as a great power in the region, which in future could ally with Russia or China and probably keep the western powers out of the region. So they decided to split India, to cut down the power of India, to keep Pakistan under control, and to assure western presence in the region. In the late nineteenth century, the British split Afghanistan to serve their geopolitical interests and in the twentieth century, they did the same with India to serve those interests, in the process locking parts of Afghanistan within Pakistan. They created a strange and unnatural Pakistan State which was in two parts, divided from one another by hundreds of kilometres of Indian Territory. That was done with the concurrence of the Quaid-e-Azam.

It is also naive to think that the British split India for they were unable to quell Hindu–Muslim riots. It is impossible to believe that in the light of the fact Britain had just quelled the most formidable of their organized and ferocious opponents in the world, Germany and Japan. To think that Britain was not in a position to quell some unruly and unorganized Hindu–Muslim mobs in some parts of India and therefore they had to split India is one of those mythologies being floated by those leaders, who had accepted the Partition of India, as proposed by the British, probably wanting to taste absolute power at a very short notice.

At the time of Partition, the population of Muslims of India was about 25 per cent. Today there may be about 450 million Muslims in the subcontinent. What is their strength and power in south Asia? When Jinnah demanded Pakistan, it was with the objective of saving the interests of all Indian Muslims and Islam. But Jinnah's achievement was nothing more than splitting the Muslims between India and Pakistan. Naturally, in India, Muslims have become subordinated and dependent. Later, Bangladesh split away from Pakistan. The myth that Muslims constituted a nation by themselves, cultivated by Jinnah was blown apart due to this separation. With that another myth floated by Jinnah that Islam would prosper in Pakistan was also laid to rest. Bangladesh is an economic disaster. In what remains of Pakistan, Baluchistan was asking for Independence. There were the never-ending problems with the Pathans, Talibans, and the *Al Qaida*, not to speak of the problems with the *Mohajir*s (those who went to Pakistan from India) and the Sindhis, and the problems between minority Shias and majority Sunnis. Are these problems not part of Jinnah's achievements and legacy?

Jinnah himself remained always a Shia. There are no records to attest that Jinnah converted to Sunni Islam. He being a Gujarati also became a *Mohajir* in Pakistan. Wanting to save the Muslims from the Hindus and Islam from Hinduism, Jinnah steeped the Muslims of the subcontinent in a deep identity crisis. He demanded Pakistan without paying the least attention to those intra-Muslim problems. Neither did he understand the changing geopolitical and strategic interests of Britain and America. Had Muslims remained united within a close-knit India, heeding to the desperate calls of Maulana Abul Kalam Azad, they would have been a force to be reckoned with today. But that was not to be.

India escaped somewhat, although it was reduced to a 'struggling power'. As 'small Pakistan' was created on the basis of the Lahore Resolution, India lost west Punjab, Sind, and East Bengal. Baluchistan and North-West Frontier Province were never part of India. It was towards the end of the nineteenth century that Britain amalgamated them with British India.

Hindus lost very less. But that was more than enough to reduce India into a 'struggling power' and pin it down as a power without consequence at the international stage. The British knew this more than anyone else. On the other hand, Muslims lost the most. Sikhs also lost much. They were driven away from west Punjab. The British never showed genuine interest about the welfare of the Sikhs in the event of Partition. That is the reason behind the barbarous riots and killings that took place during Partition. In 1857, the British used the same Sikhs to quell the Indian rebellion, but now they were abandoned. This is pragmatic British politics.

Today some writers like Jaswant Singh, following Indian scholars like Mushirul Hasan and A.G. Noorani as well as Pakistani scholars like Ayesha Jalal, claim that the British were only acting as a midwife between Hindus and Muslims. They also claim that Jinnah was a nationalist, a secularist, and an outstanding leader, who made some miscalculations. In doing so, they never took into consideration the high level meetings of the British Cabinet with regard to the Partition of India. They never pondered over the fact that Jinnah hardly spoke of secularism during his agitations for Pakistan since 1940. Instead he was using the Islamic card all throughout to get what he wanted, because he knew that brandishing the godless secular card like the Congress will never work to gain the support of the Muslim masses. Jinnah launched the demand for Pakistan in 1940 in order to safeguard Islam and the interests of the Indian Muslims, both elite and non-elite. Although Jinnah had never come out with a statement that his Pakistan would be an Islamic State, he stood steadfastly for the maintenance of Shariat laws for Muslims.

Pakistan was needed by the British to protect their imperial interests. It is certainly not because Jinnah demanded Pakistan and the Congress opposed it or that they could not agree upon the Cabinet Mission Plan that the British decided to split India. Instead, the split was necessary in order to serve the interests of the British and the Anglo-Saxon dominated west, reduce the power of India, split the Indian Muslims, and render Pakistan dependent on the west, and eventually gain a permanent foothold in south Asia. It was also done with the objective of creating a Muslim block running from Pakistan to west Asia who would be partners in an Anglo-American alliance. Jinnah unskillfully played into British hands, while both the Congress and Muslim League leaders were oblivious to the geopolitical and strategic interests of the west in Asia and the Indian Ocean region, which pushed the British finally to divide India and quit. One could say that the British had achieved almost all their geopolitical and strategic objectives while retreating from India, whereas Jinnah and the Congress leaders kept haggling and squabbling till the last, leaving the British to preside over the division of India and the Indians.[18]

ACKNOWLEDGEMENTS

I have to thank a great number of people who were helpful to me directly and indirectly while writing this book. Above all, my gratitude is due to the staff of the India Office Library and Records and the British Library in London, the library of the Centre of South Asian Studies of Cambridge University, the National Archives of India and the Nehru Memorial Museum & Library of New Delhi, the Tamil Nadu Archives, Chennai, the libraries of the *Centre d'Etudes de l'Inde*, the *Bibliothèque François Mitterand*, the *Bibliothèque de Documentation Contemporaine* and the *Institut National des Langues et Civilisations Orientales* of Paris, without whose cooperation, advice, and guidance, it would have been immensely difficult in locating the various relevant materials and documents, on which this book is based. Among the staff, I am particularly grateful to Dr Nalini Persad of the India Office Library, London, Dr Kevin Greenbank, Archivist at the Centre of South Asian Studies of Cambridge University, Mrs Muhammad and Mrs Gobalkichenane Sundari of the *Institut National des Langues et Civilisations Orientales library*, Paris.

It is a privilege for me to have known Professor Francis Robinson, President of Royal Asiatic Society, London and former Vice-Principal of Royal Holloway College (University of London) since the 1980s when I was preparing for my PhD in Paris. He is recognized as a leading expert of Islam and Muslims in South Asia. He had off and on shared with me his views on Muslims in India and also about the Partition of India, which I have put to good use in the writing of this book on Jinnah. I am grateful to him for this. Professor Pokker of the Calicut University, Professor K.S. Mathew, former Head of the Department of History of the University of Pondicherry and Dr V. Rajesh, Assistant Professor at the Indian Institute for Science Education and Research, Mohali, Punjab, were also helpful to me in this respect with their views, comments, and remarks.

I am greatly indebted to the late Mohamed Raza Khan, former member of the All-India Muslim League and delegate from Madras to the Lahore Muslim League conference in the year 1940, for his views and comments not only on the Partition of India, but also on various personalities involved in the Partition including Muhammad Ali Jinnah. Mr Abdul Latif, lawyer, Moulvi, and former general secretary of the Tamil Nadu Muslim League, is another person to whom I address my gratitude for his views on C. Rajagopalachari, who played a great role in the Partition. My special thanks is due to the veteran Madras historian and chronicler, S. Muthiah. My wife, Dr Leena More as usual had been a great source of encouragement and cooperation.

NOTES

INTRODUCTION

1. Tara Chand, *History of the Freedom Movement*, 3 vols, New Delhi, 1972; C.H. Philips and M.D. Wainwright (eds), *The Partition of India: Policies and Perspectives, 1935–1947,* London, 1970, pp. 18, 36
2. Aga Khan, *The Memoirs of the Aga Khan*, London, 1954, pp. 292, 298; Khalid Bin Sayeed, 'The Personality of Jinnah and his Political Strategy', in C.H. Philips and M.D. Wainwright (eds), *The Partition of India: Policies and Perspectives, 1935–1947*, London, 1970, p. 276
3. Khalid Bin Sayeed, *Pakistan: the Formative Phase, 1857–1948,* London, 1968, pp. 8, 24, 86
4. Stanley Wolpert, *Jinnah of Pakistan*, New York, 1984; Francis Robinson, Review of Stanley Wolpert's *Jinnah of Pakistan*, New York, 1984 and Ayesha Jalal's 'The Sole Spokesman: Jinnah, the Muslim League and the Demand for Pakistan', Cambridge, 1985, *Modern Asian Studies*, vol. XX, 3 July 1985, pp. 611–18; Rafiq Zakaria, *The Man who Divided India: An Insight into Jinnah's leadership and its Aftermath*, Bombay, 2004, p. xi; Sharif al Mujahid, *Quaid-I-Azam Jinnah: Studies in Interpretation*, Delhi, 1985, p. 22; A.G. Noorani, *Jinnah and Tilak*, Oxford, 2010; Sir Percival Griffiths, *The British Impact on India,* London, 1952, p. 340; Mushirul Hasan, *Nationalism and Communal Politics, 1885–1930*, New Delhi, 1994, p. 283; Venkat Dhulipala, *Creating a New Medina: State Power, Islam and the Quest for Pakistan*, Cambridge, 2014
5. H.M. Seervai, *Partition of India: Legend and Reality*, New Delhi, 2005 (reprint)
6. Abul Kalam Azad, *India Wins Freedom: The Complete Version*, Hyderabad, 1989, p. 197; Ayesha Jalal, *The Sole Spokesman: Jinnah, the Muslim League and Demand for Pakistan,* Cambridge, 1985, p. 33
7. Francis Robinson, *op. cit.*; Cf. also Rafiq Zakaria, 'Jinnah did not want Pakistan', *The Times of India, Sunday Review*, 22 September 1985; Asim Roy, 'The High Politics of India's Partition: The Revisionist Perspective', *Modern Asian Studies*, vol. 24, Part 2, May 1990, pp. 385–6
8. Jaswant Singh, *Jinnah: India–Partition, Independence*, New Delhi, 2009
9. Ayesha Jalal, *The Sole Spokesman: Jinnah, The Muslim League and the Demand for Pakistan*, Cambridge, 1985
10. Paul Brass, *Language, Religion and Politics in North India*, Cambridge, 1974, p. 79; Hayat Sikandar, *The Charismatic Leader: Quaid-i-Azam Mohammad Ali Jinnah and the Creation of Pakistan*, Oxford, 2008

11. Anil Seal, *The Emergence of Indian Nationalism*, Cambridge, 1971; C.J. Baker and Gordon Johnson (eds), *Power, Profit and Politics: Essays on Imperialism, Nationalism and Change in the Twentieth Century India*, Cambridge, 1981; John Gallagher, Gordon Johnson and Anil Seal (eds), *Locality, Province and Nation: Essays on Indian Politics, 1870–1940*, Cambridge, 1973); C.J. Baker and David Washbrook, *South India: Political Institution and Political Change, 1880–1940*, New Delhi, 1975; C.J. Baker, *The Politics of South India, 1920–1937*, Cambridge, 1976

HISTORICAL BACKGROUND

1. Imtiaz Ahmad (ed.), *Caste and Social Stratification among the Muslims*, Delhi, 1973; Mubarak Ali, *Pakistan in Search of Identity*, Karachi, 2009
2. W.W. Hunter, *The Indian Empire: Its People, History and Products*, London, 1886, p. 317; Khalid Bin Sayeed, *Pakistan: The Formative Phase, 1857–1948,* London, 1968, pp. 3–4; K.A. Nizami (ed.), *Shah Waliullah Ke Siyasi Maktuba (Political Letters of Shah Waliullah)*, Aligarh, 1951, p. 106; J.B.P. More, *Religion and Society in South India: Hindus, Muslims and Christians*, Nirmalagiri, 2006, Chapters 1 and 2
3. William Dalrymple, *The Last Mughal: The Fall of a Dynasty: Delhi, 1857,* London, 2006; David Saul, *The Indian Mutiny*, London, 2003; Sekhar Bandyopadhay, *From Plassey to Partition: A History of Modern India*, New Delhi, 2004
4. A.B. Keith (ed.), *Speeches and Documents on Indian Policy, 1750–1921*, vol. 1, London, 1922, p. 384; Report of the Hunter Education Commission, 1882, p. 22
5. W.W. Hunter, *The Indian Mussalmans*, Lahore, 1968, second edition; Resolution No. 300, Shimla, 14 August 1871, *Report of the Hunter Education Commission*, 1882, p. 484; J.B.P. More, 'Muslim Specificities in French India during the Nineteenth Century', *Journal of the Institute for Research in Social Sciences and Humanities*, vol. 2, no. 1, January–June 2007, p. 120; Hugh Tinker, *The Foundations of Local Government in India, Pakistan and Burma*, London, 1968, pp. 49–50; Sumit Sarkar, *Modern India, 1885–1947*, Delhi, 1983, p. 21; Peter Hardy, *The Muslims of British India*, Cambridge, 1972, pp. 116, 125; Sir John Strachey, *India: Its Administration and Progress*, London, 1888, p. 4; Sir John R. Seeley, *The Expansion of England*, London, 1883, p. 92; V.P. Menon, *The Transfer of Power in India*, Madras, 1968, p. 33
6. S.A. Khan, *An Essay on the Causes of the Indian Revolt,* Calcutta, 1860; S.A. Khan, *The Causes of the Indian Revolt*, Oxford, 2000; G.F.I. Graham, *The Life and Works of Sir Syed Ahmed Khan,* London, 1885; A.B. Rajput, *Muslim League Yesterday and Today*, Lahore, 1948, p. 16; Y.V. Gankovsky and L.R. Gordon–Polonskaya, *A History of Pakistan*, Moscow, 1964, p. 16

7. G.F.I. Graham, *op. cit.*, p. 185; Dorothy Norman, *Nehru: The First Sixty Years*, vol. I, Bombay, 1965, p. 301
8. Paul Brass, *Language, Religion and Politics in North India*, Cambridge, 1974; Khalid Bin Sayeed, *Pakistan: The Formative Phase, 1857–1948*, London, 1968, p. 19; Nikki Keddie, *An Islamic Response to Imperialism*, Los Angeles, 1968, p. 59; F.E. Keay, *A History of Hindi Literature*, Calcutta, 1920, p. 88
9. G.F.I. Graham, *op. cit.*, pp. 1, 72; Rafiq Zakaria, *Rise of Muslims in Indian Politics*, Bombay, 1980, Appendix C; K.A. Nizami, *op. cit.*, p. vii; N. Keddie, *An Islamic Response to Imperialism: Political and Religious Writings of Syed Jamal-al-Din al-Afghani*, California, 1968, pp. 55–6; Sumit Sarkar, *op. cit.*, 1984, pp. 77, 79; F. Robinson, *The Ulama of Farangi Mahall and Islamic Culture in South Asia*, Delhi, 2001, p. 197
10. S.A. Khan, *The Causes of the Indian Revolt*, Benares, 1873, p. 35
11. S.A. Khan, *op. cit.*, 2000, p. xii
12. Peter Hardy, *op. cit.*, p. 127; D.G. Tendulkar, *Mahatma: Life of Mohandas Karamchand Gandhi*, vol. I, New Delhi, pp. 10–11; R. Coupland, *The Indian Problem: Report on the Constitutional Problem in India, 1833–1935*, vol. I, London, 1942, p. 33
13. Rafiq Zakaria, *op. cit.*, Appendix B; A. Appadorai, *Documents of Political Thought in Modern India*, vol. I, London, 1973, p. 37; Cf. also S. Sen, *The Birth of Pakistan*, Calcutta, 1955, p. 42; F. Robinson, *Separatism among Indian Muslims: The Politics of the United Provinces' Muslims, 1860–1923*, Cambridge, 1974, p. 131
14. K.A. Nizami, *op. cit.*, pp. vii, 31–2, 46–7
15. Peter Hardy, *op. cit.*, pp. 116, 125; Sir John Strachey, *op. cit.*, p. 4; John Seeley, *op. cit.*, p. 92
16. Sumit Sarkar, *op. cit.*, 1983, pp. 22–4; B.R. Ambedkar, *Pakistan or the Partition of India*, Bombay, 1946, pp. 240–6; M.V. Pylee, *Constitutional History of India, 1600–1950*, London, 1967, pp. 46–7
17. Peter Hardy, *op. cit.*, pp. 130, 137–8; Rafiq Zakaria, *op. cit.*, 1980, Appendix E; Jaswant Singh, *Jinnah: India–Partition, Independence*, New Delhi, 2009, p. 30; R. Coupland, *op. cit.*, p. 33; Gankovsky and Gordon–Polonskaya, *op. cit.*, pp. 15–18; S. Sen, *op. cit.*, p. 42; V.P. Menon, *The Transfer of Power in India*, Bombay, 1957, p. 9
18. Justin Jones, *Shia Islam in Colonial India: Religion, Community and Sectarianism*, New York, 2012, p. 6; S. Virani, *The Ismailis in the Middle Ages: A History of Survival, A Search for Salvation*, New York, 2007, p. 102
19. Anne Edwards, *Throne of Gold: The Lives of the Aga Khans*, New York, 1995, p. 22
20. Anne Edwards, *Ibid.*, pp. 23, 63, 66; Farhad Daftary, *The Ismailis: Their History and Doctrines*, Cambridge, 1990, pp. 510–12

21. Anne Edwards, *Ibid.,* pp. 3, 8, 19; Lokhandwalla, 'Islamic Law and Ismaili Communities, Khodjas and Bohras', *Indian Economic and Social History Review*, vol. IV, no. 2, pp. 155–76; Gankovsky and Gordon–Polonskaya, *op. cit.,* p. 23; Rafiq Zakaria, 'Jinnabhai', *The Asian Age*, 18 November 2001; Cf. also Rafiq Zakaria, *The Man who Divided India: An Insight into Jinnah's Leadership and its Aftermath*, Bombay, 2001; Aga Khan, *The Memoirs of the Aga Khan*, London, 1954; S. Blanchy, *Karana et Banian: Les Communautés Commerçantes d'Originie Indienne à Madagascar*, Paris, 1995, pp. 206–9

FROM JINNAHBHAI TO JINNAH

1. Sarojini Naidu (ed.), *Mohammad Ali Jinnah, An Ambassador of Unity: His Speeches and Writings, 1912–1917*, Madras, 1918; Stanley Wolpert, *Jinnah of Pakistan*, New York, 1984, pp. 4, 5, 170; Akbar Ahmed, *Jinnah, Pakistan and Islamic Identity: The Search for Saladin*, London, 1997, pp. 3–4; Jaswant Singh, *Jinnah: India–Partition Independence*, New Delhi, 2009, p. 62; Fatima Jinnah, *My Brother: Mohammad Ali Jinnah (1876–1948)*, Karachi, 1987, pp. 44–52; Rafiq Zakaria, 'Jinnabhai', *The Asian Age*, 18 November 2001; Saleem Qureshi, 'Iqbal and Jinnah', in C.M. Naim (ed.), *Iqbal, Jinnah and Pakistan*, Lahore, 1984, p. 11; A. Jawed, *Secular and Nationalist Jinnah*, New Delhi, 1998, p. 265; Aziz Beg, *Jinnah and His Times*, Islamabad, 1986, pp. 89–90, 92; G. Allana, *Quaid-e-Azam Jinnah,* Lahore, 1988, p. 7, Hector Bolitho, *Jinnah: Creator of Pakistan*, London, 1954, pp. 5–14
2. Stanley Wolpert, *Ibid.,* p. 5; Rafiq Zakaria, *Ibid.*; Sarojini Naidu, *Ibid.;* Fatima Jinnah, *Ibid.,* pp. 54–60
3. Rafiq Zakaria, *Ibid.*; Anne Edwards, *Throne of Gold: The Lives of the Aga Khans,* New York, 1995, p. 9; Cf. also Stanley Wolpert, *Jinnah of Pakistan*, New York, 1984, p. 9; Jaswant Singh, *op. cit.,* pp. 63–4; Fatima Jinnah, *Ibid.,* pp. 75, 77; 'Interview with Miss Fatima Jinnah', in K.H. Khurshid, *Memories of Jinnah*, Karachi, 1990, p. 85; E. Wrench, *Immortal Years*, London, 1945, p. 132
4. Rafiq Zakaria, *Ibid.*; Hector Bolitho, *Jinnah: Creator of Pakistan*, London, 1954, p. 9; Fatima Jinnah, *Ibid.,* p. 74; Lincoln Inn's Admission Register, 1893, in Saleem Qureshi (ed.), *Jinnah: The Founder of Pakistan*, Karachi, 1998, p. 61; Rafiq Zakaria, *The Man who Divided India,* Mumbai, 2004, p. 6; J. Ahmad, *Quaid-e-Azam as Seen by his Contemporaries*, Lahore, 1976, Appendix I; *Dawn*, 26 January 1948; G. Allana, *Quaid-e-Azam Jinnah,* Lahore, 1988, p. 18; Angela Holdsworth (ed.), *A Portrait of Lincoln's Inn*, London, 2007, p. 119
5. Stanley Wolpert, *op. cit.,* p. 4; Rafiq Zakaria, *Ibid.*; 'Note from Jinnah to the Librarian', 7 January 1995 and 'Jinnah's declaration regarding Age', in Saleem Qureshi (ed.), *Ibid.,* pp. 65, 67, 71; Aziz Beg, *op. cit.,* p. 90

6. Rafiq Zakaria, *Ibid.*; Hector Bolitho, *op. cit.*, p. 14; Jaswant Singh, *op. cit.*, pp. 65, 74; Fatima Jinnah, *op. cit.*, p. 77; Cf. also K.H. Khurshid, *Memories of Jinnah*, for a photograph of Jinnah with his wealthy Parsi friend Pestonjee Rustomjee driving in Victoria Gardens, Bombay
7. 'Petition for Call to Bar, Lincoln's Inn', 1896, in Saleem Qureshi (ed.), *op. cit.*, p. 73
8. Rafiq Zakaria, *Ibid.*; Jaswant Singh, *Ibid.*, pp. 74, 601f; I.B. Wells, *Ambassador of Hindu–Muslim Unity: Jinnah's Early Politics*, New Delhi, 2005, p. 18; Peter Hardy, *The Muslims of British India*, Cambridge, 1972, p. 127; Fatima Jinnah, *Ibid.*, pp. 82–6; Saleem Qureshi, *op. cit.*, p. 16; Rafiq Zakaria, *op. cit.*, pp. 8–15
9. John Hollister, *The Shia of India*, London, 1953; Justin Jones, *Shia Islam in Colonial India: Religion, Community and Sectarianism*, New York, 2012; Moojan Momen, *An Introduction to Shi'i Islam: The History and Doctrines of Twelver Shi'ism*, New York, 1985; Nasr Vali, *The Shia Revival: How Conflicts within Islam will Shape the Future*, Norton, 2006, pp. 88–90
10. Akbar Ahmed, *op. cit.*, p. 64

ENTRY INTO POLITICS

1. I.B. Wells, *Ambassador of Hindu–Muslim Unity: Jinnah's Early Politics*, New Delhi, 2005, p. 18; Riaz Ahmad, *Quaid-i-Azam Mohammad Ali Jinnah*, Islamabad, 1988, p. 69; 1994, p. 18; Jaswant Singh, *Jinnah: India–Partition Independence*, New Delhi, 2009, pp. 75, 81; Rafiq Zakaria, 'Jinnabhai', *The Asian Age*, 18 November 2001; H.P. Mody, *Sir Pherozeshah Mehta: A Political Biography*, Bombay, 1921, pp. 252–3; T.V. Parvate, *Bal Gangadhar Tilak*, Ahmedabad, 1958, p. 161; Rafiq Zakaria, *Rise of Muslims in Indian Politics*, Bombay, 1970, p. 103; B.R. Nanda, *Gokhale: The Indian Moderates and the British Raj*, Delhi, 1998, p. 187; Hector Bolitho, *Jinnah: Creator of Pakistan*, London, 1954, p. 20; Hector Bolitho doubts very much about Jinnah's participation in the deliberations of the Conference– Cf. Hector Bolitho, p. 27
2. Ian Stephen, *Pakistan*, London, 1967, p. 150; Saad Khairi, *Jinnah Reinterpreted*, Karachi, 1995, p. 72
3. Rafiq Zakaria, 'Jinnahbhai', *The Asian Age*, 18 November 2001; Anne Edwards, *Throne of Gold: The Lives of the Aga Khans*, New York, 1995, p. 58; Sumit Sarkar, *Modern India, 1885–1947*, Delhi, 1984, p. 121; D.G. Tendulkar, *Mahatma: Life of Mohandas Karamchand Gandhi*, vol. I, p. 16
4. Anne Edwards, *Throne of Gold: The Lives of the Aga Khans*, New York, 1995, p. 58; Sumit Sarkar, *Ibid.*, p. 99; H. Mukherjee and U. Mukherjee, *'Bande Mataram' and Indian Nationalism (1906–1908)*, Calcutta, 1957, pp. 93–4; J.B.P. More, *Puducheri Valartha Bharathiar* (Tamil), Pondicherry, 2010, p. 35; T.V. Parvate, *op. cit.*, pp. 115–38
5. Anne Edwards, *Ibid.*, pp. 62–3

6. C. Dobbin, *Basic Documents in the Development of Modern India and Pakistan, 1835–1947,* London, 1970, pp. 66–70; F. Robinson, *Separatism Among Indian Muslims: The Politics of the United Provinces' Muslims, 1860–1923*, Cambridge, 1974, p. 48; Matiur Rahman, *From Consultation to Confrontation: A Study of the Muslim League in British Indian Politics, 1906–1912*, London, 1970, pp. 52–60; Mubarak Ali, *Pakistan in Search of Identity*, Karachi, 2009, pp. 2–6; Cf. also Imtiaz Ahmad (ed.), *Caste and Social Stratification among the Muslims*, Delhi, 1973
7. Farzana Shaik, *Community and Consensus in Islam, Muslim Representation in Colonial India, 1860–1947,* Cambridge, 1989, pp. 135–41; Mubarak Ali, *Ibid.;* Rafiq Zakaria, *Rise of Muslims in Indian Politics,* Bombay, 1980, Appendix F; M.R. Khan, *What Price Freedom*, Madras, 1969, pp. 4–5; K.A. Nizami (ed.), *Shah Waliullah Ke Siyasi Maktuba (Political Letters of Shah Waliullah)*, Aligarh, 1951, p. 129; Francis Robinson, Introduction to *The Causes of the Indian Revolt,* by Syed Ahmad Khan, Oxford, 2000, pp. xi, xii
8. S.S. Pirzada (ed.), *Foundation of Pakistan*, vol. I, Karachi, 1969, pp. xxxiv, xxxvi–xxxvii; Jaswant Singh, *op. cit.,* p. 51; Sumit Sarkar, *op. cit.,* p. 141; D. Norman, *The First Sixty Years*, vol. I, Bombay, 1965, p. 302; V.P. Menon, *The Transfer of Power in India*, Madras, 1968, p. 10; Cf. also Valentine Chirol, *Indian Unrest*, London, 1910; Sharif al Mujahid (ed.), *Muslim League Documents*, Karachi, 1990, pp. 11–117, 119
9. Jaswant Singh, *Ibid.,* pp. 50–2; M.R. Khan, *op. cit.,* pp. 4–5; Anne Edwards, *op. cit.,* p. 3
10. *India* (Tamil), 6 October 1906 (reproduced from *Advocate of India*, Bombay); Aga Khan, *The Memoirs of the Aga Khan*, London, 1954, pp. 124–5
11. M.R. Khan, *op. cit.,* pp. 2–5; Rafiq Zakaria, *op. cit.,* Appendix F; Cf. also Aga Khan, *Ibid.,* pp. 94, 124–5
12. Rafiq Zakaria, *Ibid.,* Appendix G; Aga Khan, *Ibid.,* pp. 124–5
13. Farzana Shaikh, *op. cit.,* p. 159; Matiur Rahman, *op. cit.,* p. 38; Rafiq Zakaria, *Ibid.*; Peter Hardy, *The Muslims of British India*, Cambridge, 1972, p. 165; C.H. Philips (ed.), *The Evolution of India and Pakistan, 1858–1947: Select Documents*, London, 1962, p. 144; J.S. Grewal, *Muslim Rule in India: The Assessment of British Historians*, Calcutta, 1970, p. 168; Saad Khairi, *op. cit.,* p. 78; Matiur Rahman, *From Consultation to Confrontation*, London, 1973, pp. 303–4, Sharif al Mujahid, *op. cit.,* pp. 160–9, 225
14. M.R. Khan, *op. cit.,* pp. 26, 73, 74
15. S.S. Pirzada (ed.), *The Collected Works of Quaid-e-Azam Mohammad Ali Jinnah*, vol. I Karachi, pp. 32–5; Jaswant Singh, *op. cit.,* pp. 75–6; B.R. Nanda, *Gokhale*, Delhi, 1998, p. 283; Hector Bolitho, *Jinnah Creator of Pakistan*, London, 1954, p. 20
16. *Ibid.;* M.C. Chagla, *Roses in December*, 1973, pp. 14–5; Stanley Wolpert, *Tilak and Gokhale*, Berkeley, 1962, p. 220; T.V. Parvate, *Bal Gangadhar Tilak*, Ahmedabad, 1958, p. 91; Aziz Beg, *op. cit.,* p. 203; Hector Bolitho, *Ibid.,* p. 46

17. Pattabhi Sitaramayya, *History of the Indian National Congress*, vol. I, 1885–1935, Bombay, 1935, p. 27
18. S.M. Burke and Salim-al-Dui-Quraishi, *Quaid-I-Azam Mohammad Ali Jinnah: His Personality and his Politics*, Oxford, US, 1997, p. 96; Jaswant Singh, *op. cit.,* pp. 81, 83, 92; Rafiq Zakaria, *The Man who divided India*, Mumbai, 2004, p. 13; A.G. Noorani, *Jinnah and Tilak*, Oxford, 2010, p. 13
19. I.B. Wells, *op. cit.,* p. 19; Jaswant Singh, *Ibid.,* p. 84; Saad Khairi, *op. cit.,* p. 84; M. Umar, *Quaid-i-Azam Mohammad Ali Jinnah*, Karachi, 1973, pp. 20–30
20. Sumit Sarkar, *op. cit.,* p. 143; S.S. Pirzada, *Foundations of Pakistan,* vol. I, Karachi, 1969, p. 250
21. *Ibid.;* Mubarak Ali, *op. cit.,* p. 9
22. Francis Robinson, *Separatism Among Indian Muslims: The Politics of the United Provinces' Muslims, 1860–1923*, Cambridge, 1974, p. 204; Gail Minault, *The Khilafat Movement: Religious Symbolism and Political Mobilisation in India*, New York, 1982, p. 52; D.G. Tendulkar, *op. cit.,* p. 90; B.N. Pandey, *The Break-up of British India*, London, 1969, p. 96
23. Francis Robinson, *Ibid.,* p. 177; Sumit Sarkar, *op. cit.,* p. 143
24. Riaz Ahmed, *Jinnah: The Formative Years, 1892–1920*, Islamabad, 1988, pp. 92–3; R. Coupland, *The Indian Problem: Report on the Constitutional Problem in India, 1833–1935*, vol. I, London, 1942, pp. 46–7; M. Umar (ed.), *Quaid-i-Azam Mohammad Ali Jinnah: Rare Speeches, 1910–1918,* Karachi, 1973, pp. 55–60, 95; Stanley Reed (ed.), *The Indian Year Book*, Bombay, 1915, p. 476; Jaswant Singh, *op. cit.,* pp. 88–9; Saad Khairi, *op. cit.,* p. 86; Stanley Wolpert, *Jinnah of Pakistan,* Delhi, 1985, p. 33; Hector Bolitho, *op. cit.,* pp. 48, 51, 52, 53; A.M. Zaidi (ed.), *Sectarian Nationalism and Khilafat: Documents*, Delhi, 1975, vol. I, pp. 402–3, 424
25. I.B. Wells, *op. cit.,* pp. 13–60; Cf. also Sarojini Naidu (ed.), *Mohammad Ali Jinnah, An Ambassador of Unity: His Speeches and Writings, 1912–1917*, Madras, 1918, p. 11; Saad Khairi, *op. cit.,* pp. 83–4; G. Allana, *Quaid-e-Azam Jinnah,* Lahore, 1988, p. 21; Mushirul Hasan (ed.), *Mohammad Ali Jinnah in Indian Politics: Select Writings*, New Delhi, 1982, pp. 164–5
26. Saad Khairi, *Ibid.,* pp. 87–9; Jaswant Singh, *op. cit.,* pp. 94, 101; M. Umar, *op. cit.,* pp. 99–107
27. Dorothy Norman, *The First Sixty Years*, vol. I, Bombay, 1965, p. 302
28. Sumit Sarkar, *op. cit.,* p. 144; Francis Robinson, *The Ulama of Farangi Mahall and Islamic Culture in South Asia*, Delhi, 2001, pp. 154–5
29. S.K. Majumadar, *Jinnah and Gandhi*, Calcutta, 1966, p. 29; Jaswant Singh, *op. cit.,* pp. 100–1; Stanley Wolpert, *op. cit.,* pp. 36–8; *CWMG*, XIII, 1964, p. 9

30. D.G. Tendulkar, *op. cit.,* p. 185; Anthony Parel (ed.), *Hind Swaraj and Other Writings*, Cambridge, 1997
31. M. Umar, *op. cit.,* pp. 121–38
32. Sumit Sarkar, *op. cit.,* p. 179; Riaz Ahmed, *op. cit.,* pp. 120–1; S.R. Bakshi, *Struggle for Independence: Ali Brothers*, New Delhi, 1992, p. 132; S.S. Pirzada (ed.), *Foundations of Pakistan,* vol. I, pp. 353–4; Mushirul Hasan, *op. cit.,* p. 225; Mohammad Umar, *Quaid-i-Azam Mohammad Ali Jinnah*, Karachi, 1973, pp. 113–4; H. Owen, 'Negotiating the Lucknow Pact', *Journal of Asian Studies*, 31 March 1972, p. 575
33. T.V. Parvate, *op. cit.,* pp. 91, 334, 343–4, 367–8, 378, 383, 388–90, 539; Jaswant Singh, *op. cit.,* pp. 611f, 612f; Cf. also Hugh Owen, 'Negotiating the Lucknow Pact', *Journal of Asian Studies*, 31 March 1972, pp. 561–87; Stanley Wolpert, *Tilak and Gokhale*, Berkeley, 1962, pp. 273–4, 280; S.K. Majumdar, *Jinnah and Gandhi,* Calcutta, 1966, pp. 40–3; Aziz Beg, *Jinnah and His Times,* Islamabad, 1986, p. 23; S.M. Burke and Salim Al-Din Qurashi, *Quaid-i-Azam Mohammad Ali Jinnah*, Karachi, 1997, pp. 110–1; M. Umar, *Ibid.,* pp. 185–8; A.G. Noorani, *Jinnah and Tilak,* Oxford, 2010, pp. 26–33; Riaz Ahmad, *The Works of Quaid-i-Azam Mohammad Ali Jinnah*, vol. IV, 1917–1918, Islamabad, 1999, pp. 6, 31–3, 403–4, 418, 593
34. B.R. Ambedkar, *Pakistan or the Partition of India,* Bombay, 1946; T.V. Parvate, *Ibid.,* p. 348; Cf. Sarojini Naidu (ed.), *op. cit.*; M. Umar, *op. cit.,* pp. 121–38
35. R. Coupland, *Indian Partition: Report on the Constitutional Problem in India, 1936– 1942,* vol. II, London, 1943, pp. 27–8; Khalid Bin Sayeed, *Pakistan: The Formative Phase, 1857–1948,* London, 1968, p. 40; T.V. Parvate, *Ibid.,* pp. 351–2; Stanley Wolpert, *op. cit.,* p. 152; Mushirul Hasan (ed.), *op. cit.,* pp. 225, 307–8, 307f; A.G. Noorani, *op. cit.,* pp. 15–7
36. M.R. Khan, *op. cit.,* pp. 7–9; C. Dobbin, *op. cit.,* pp. 71–3
37. Peter Hardy, *op. cit.,* p. 187; Sumit Sarkar, *op. cit.,* p. 151
38. M. Umar, *op. cit.,* p. 116; D.G. Tendulkar, *op. cit.,* vol. I, p. 191; Hector Bolitho, *Jinnah: Creator of Pakistan*, London, 1954, p. 166; S. Naidu (ed.), *Mohammad Ali Jinnah, An Ambassador of Unity: His Speeches and Writings, 1912–1917*, Madras, 1918, pp. x, xii, 13–37; S.S. Pirzada (ed.), *The Collected Works of Quaid-e-Azam Mohammad Ali Jinnah*, vol. I, p. 252
39. Mushirul Hasan, *Nationalism and Communal Politics in India*, New Delhi, 1979, p. 90; Hugh Owen, 'Negotiating the Lucknow Pact', *Journal of Asian Studies*, 31 March 1972, p. 581
40. Mushirul Hasan, *Ibid.,* pp. 94, 223–5; G. Allana, *Pakistan Movement: Historic Documents*, Lahore, 1977, p. 40
41. R. Coupland, *op. cit.,* vol. I, p. 72; Rafiq Zakaria, *op. cit.,* 2004, pp. 18, 29; Cf. also M.C. Chagla, *Roses in December*; Rafiq Zakaria 'Jinnabhai', *The Asian Age*, 18 November 2001

42. Dorothy Norman, *op. cit.,* p. 37
43. S.S. Pirzada, *op. cit.,* I, p. 354; M. Umar, *op. cit.,* pp. 145–50; Cf. also Farzana Shaikh, *op. cit.,* p. 161
44. S. Wolpert, *Jinnah of Pakistan*, New York, 1984, pp. 43–53, 170; Akbar Ahmed, *Jinnah, Pakistan and Islamic Identity: The Search for Saladin*, London, 1997, pp. 11–5; M.C. Chagla, *op. cit.,* p. 120; Gail Minault, *op. cit.,* p. 72; Kanji Dwarkadas, *Ruttie Jinnah: The Story of a Great Friendship*, Bombay, n.d.; S. Yasmeen, *Ruttie Jinnah, Life and Love*, Islamabad, 1997; K.R. Haider, *Ruttie Jinnah*, Karachi, 2010; Aziz Beg, *Jinnah and His Times: A Biography*, Islamabad, 1986, p. 300; A. Jawed, *Secular and Nationalist Jinnah*, New Delhi, 1998, pp. 20, 22; Kanji Dwarkadas, *India's Freedom Struggle, 1913–1937*, pp. 38, 112; S.M. Edwardes, *Memoir of Sir Dinshaw Manockjee Petit*, Oxford, 1923; G. Allana, *Quaid-e-Azam Jinnah*, Lahore, 1988, p. 166; Hector Bolitho, *op. cit.,* pp. 75, 88
45. S.S. Pirzada, *Some Aspects of Quaid-i-Azam's Life*, Islamabad, 1978, pp. 49–50; A.G. Noorani, *Jinnah and Tilak, Comrades in Freedom Struggle*, Oxford, 2010, p. 47

BIDDING ADIEU TO CONGRESS

1. Riaz Ahmad, *The Works of Quaid-i-Azam Mohammad Ali Jinnah*, *1917–1918*, vol. IV, Islamabad, 1999, pp. 40, 42; T.V. Parvate, *Bal Gangadhar Tilak: A Narrative and Interpretative Review of his Life, Career and Contemporary Events*, Ahmedabad, 1958, p. 143; Jaswant Singh, *Jinnah: India–Partition–Independence.* New Delhi, 2009, pp. 612f, 613f; V. Montagu (ed.), *Edwin S. Montagu: An Indian Diary*, London, 1930, pp. 57–8; Hector Bolitho, *Jinnah: Creator of Pakistan*, London, 1954, p. 76
2. Aga Khan, *India in Transition: A Study of Political Evolution*, London, 1918, p. 45
3. V.P. Menon, *The Transfer of Power in India*, Madras, 1968, pp. 20–6; Sumit Sarkar, *Modern India, 1885–1947*, Delhi, p. 153
4. Sumit Sarkar, *Ibid.,* pp. 188–9; Jaswant Singh, *op. cit.,* pp. 125–8; S. Wolpert, *Tilak and Gokhale: Revolution and Reforms in the Making of Modern India,* Berkeley, 1962, p. 287; G. Minault, *The Khilafat Movement: Religious Symbolism and Political Mobilisation in India*, New York, 1982, pp. 60–2; T.V. Parvate, *Bal Gangadhar Tilak, op. cit.,* p. 405
5. M.H. Saiyid, *Mohammad Ali Jinnah: A Political Study*, Lahore, 1970, p. 82
6. Sumit Sarkar, *op. cit.,* pp. 195–96; S. Wolpert, *op. cit.,* p. 282; Peter Hardy, *The Muslims of British India*, Cambridge, 1972, p. 189; S. Ghose, *Mahatma Gandhi,* Bombay, 1991, pp. 124–5; B.R. Nanda, *The Nehrus: Motilal and Jawaharlal,* New York, 1963, p. 171
7. Ahmad, Riaz, *The Works of Quaid-i-Azam Mohammad Ali Jinnah*, vol. V, 1919–1920, Islamabad, 2002, pp. 250–1; 255–56; Burke and Salim-al-Din-Quraishi, *Quaid-I-Azam Mohammad Ali Jinnah: His Personality and his Politics*, New York, 1997, pp. 127–30

8. B.R. Ambedkar, *Pakistan or the Partition of India,* Bombay, 1946, p. 312; A.G. Noorani, *Jinnah and Tilak, Comrades in Freedom Struggle*, Oxford, 2010, p. 48; Ahmad Riaz, *op. cit.,* pp. 326, 361, 363, 429–34; I.B. Wells, *Ambassador of Hindu–Muslim Unity: Jinnah's Early Politics*, New Delhi, 2005, pp. 117–19; S.S. Pirzada, *Foundations of Pakistan: Documents of the All India Muslim League,1906–1947*, vol. I, 1970, pp. 541–4; S.S. Pirzada, *The Collected Works of Quaid-e-Azam Mohammad Ali Jinnah*, Karachi, vol. I, pp. 389–90, 395–6
9. B.R. Ambedkar, *Ibid.,* p. 144; S. Ghose, *op. cit.,* p. 129; Raza Khan, *What Price Freedom*, Madras, 1969, pp. 11–2; B.B. Misra, *The Indian Political Parties: An Historical Analysis of Political Behaviour up to 1947*, Oxford, 1976, p. 181
10. Jaswant Singh, *op. cit.,* pp. 124, 613f; S. Ghose, *op. cit.,* pp. 138–9; S.S. Pirzada, *The Collected Works of Quaid-e-Azam Mohammad* Ali *Jinnah*, Karachi, vol. I, p. 400; Ahmad Riaz, *op. cit.,* pp. 436–41, 457–66; H. Bolitho, *op. cit.,* pp. 83–4
11. Ahmad Riaz, *Ibid.,* pp. 481–4
12. Shiva Rao, *India's Freedom Movement, Some Notable Figures*, New Delhi, 1972, p. 126; Burke & Salim-al-Din-Quraishi, *op. cit.,* pp. 127–30; H. Bolitho, *op. cit.,* pp. 84–5; S.S. Pirzada, *op. cit.,* vol. I, pp. 404–6; Ahmad Riaz, *op. cit.,* pp. 484–9
13. G. Minault, *op. cit.,* pp. 72–84; S.K. Majumdar, *Jinnah and Gandhi: Their Role in India's Quest for Freedom*, Lahore, 1976, p. 70; D.G. Tendulkar, *Mahatma: Life of Mohandas Karamchand Gandhi*, vol. II, p. 48; Jayakar, *The Story of My Life,* vol. I, p. 388; S.S. Pirzada, *Ibid.,* pp. 386–7; Dorothy Norman, *Nehru, The First Sixty Years*, vol. I, Bombay, 1965, p. 63
14. Anne Edwards, *Throne of Gold: The Lives of the Aga Khans,* New York, 1995, p. 8; Rafiq Zakaria, *The Man who Divided India: An Insight into Jinnah's Leadership and its Aftermath*, Bombay, 2004, pp. 22, 24; H. Bolitho, *op. cit.,* pp. 83, 85; Aga Khan, *The Memoirs of the Aga Khan*, London, 1954, p. 135; Aziz Beg, *Jinnah and His Times: A Biography*, Islamabad, 1986, p. 24; Rafiq Zakaria, *Iqbal: Poet and Politician*, New Delhi, 1993, p. 77
15. Bandyopadhyay, *Quaid-i-Azam Mohammad Ali Jinnah and the Creation of Pakistan*, New Delhi, 1991, p. 81
16. F. Shaikh, *Community and Consensus in Islam, Muslim Representation in Colonial India, 1860–1947,* Cambridge, 1989, p. 180
17. F. Sheikh, *Ibid.,* p. 177; M.H. Saiyid, *op. cit.,* p. 130; A. Ahmad, *Islamic Modernism in India and Pakistan, 1857–1964*, London, 1967, pp. 123–31, 133
18. S. Ghose, *op. cit.,* p. 143; Sumit Sarkar, *op. cit.,* p. 205; *The Times*, 29 June 1921; Ahmad Riaz, *op. cit.,* p. 308; David Page, *Prelude to Partition: The Indian Muslims and the Imperial System of Control, 1920–1932,* Delhi, 1982, p. 106; A.G. Noorani, *Jinnah and Tilak, Comrades in Freedom Struggle*, Oxford, 2010, pp. 59–60
19. Sumit Sarkar, *op. cit.,* pp. 216–7; Bamford, *Histories of the Non-Cooperation and Khilafat Movements*, Delhi, 1974, pp. 78–9, 174–5

20. David Page, *op. cit.,* p. 108; Allana, *Quaid-e-Azam Jinnah: The Story of a Nation*, Lahore, 1980, p. 163
21. Sumit Sarkar, *op. cit.,* p. 233; Raza Khan, *op. cit.,* p. 12
22. David Page, *op. cit.,* p. 114f; Saad Khairi, *Jinnah Re-interpreted: Journey from Indian Nationalism to Muslim Statehood*, Karachi, 1995, pp. 191–2; Mushirul Hasan, *A Nationalist Conscience, M.A. Ansari, The Congress and the Raj*, New Delhi, 1987, p. 179; Mushirul Hasan (ed.), *My Life A Fragment: An Autobiographical Sketch of Maulana Mohammad Ali*, New Delhi, 1999, p. 207
23. Mushirul Hasan, *Ibid.,* 1999, pp. 36–7; David Page, *Ibid.,* p. 100
24. Jaswant Singh, *op. cit.,* pp. 130, 617f; Rafiq Zakaria, *op. cit.,* 2004, pp. 30, 33–6; B.R. Nanda, *op. cit.,* pp. 227–8; *The Times of India*, 22 November 1923; V.P. Menon, *op. cit.,* p. 30; A.M. Zaidi, *Sectarian Nationalism and Khilafat: Documents*, vol. II, Delhi, 1975, p. 21; S.S. Pirzada, *op. cit.,* 1970, vol. II, pp. 363–8
25. B.R. Nanda, *Ibid.,* pp. 234, 239; Bandyopadhyay, *op. cit.,* pp. 52–3
26. Shiva Rao, 'India, 1935–47', in Philips and Wainwright (eds), *The Partition of India: Policies and Perspectives, 1935–1947*, London, 1970, p. 418
27. *The Times of India*, 20 June 1924, 10 March 1925; *The Times*, 11 March 1925; Riaz Ahmad, *Quaid-i-Azam Mohammad Ali Jinnah. Second Phase of His Freedom Struggle, 1924–1934*, Islamabad, 1994, pp. 32–5; S.S. Pirzada, *op. cit.,* 1970, vol. II, pp. 101–2; S.S. Pirzada, *op. cit.,* vol. III, 1986, p. 20; Jayakar, *The Story of My Life*, vol. II, p. 569
28. Sumit Sarkar, *op. cit.,* p. 235; S.S. Pirzada, *Ibid.,* 1970, vol. I, pp. 575–7; R. Coupland, *The Indian Problem: Report on the Constitutional Problem in India, 1833–1935*, vol. I, London, 1942, p. 74
29. S.S. Pirzada, *Foundations of Pakistan: Documents of the All India Muslim League, 1906–1947*, vol. I, pp. 678–9; A.M. Zaidi, *op. cit.,* p. 22
30. David Page, *op. cit.,* pp. 119–20; S.S. Pirzada, Some *Aspects of Quaid-i-Azam's Life*, pp. 49–50; A.G. Noorani, *op. cit.,* p. 491; Wells, *op. cit.,* pp. 143–4
31. S. Wolpert, *Jinnah of Pakistan*, New York, 1984, p. 87
32. Ambedkar, *op. cit.,* p. 328; Jaswant Singh, *op. cit.,* p. 136; David Page, *op. cit.,* pp. 114, 120; B.R. Nanda, *op. cit.,* p. 242
33. C. Khaliquzzaman, *Pathway to Pakistan*, Lahore, 1961, pp. 138–9; V.P. Menon, *op. cit.,* p. 41; Mushirul Hasan, *Nationalism and Communal Politics in India, 1885–1930,* New Delhi, 1994, p. 289
34. V.P. Menon, *op. cit.,* pp. 33–4
35. A.M. Mustafa, 'My Happy Recollections', in K. Miles (ed.), *Liaquat: The Man of Destiny*, Karachi, 1953, p. 39; R.D. Long, *'Dear Mr. Jinnah': Selected Correspondence and Speeches of*

Liaquat Ali Khan, 1937–1947, Oxford, 2004, pp. xv, xvi, xix, xx; Griffin and Massey, *Chiefs and Families of Note in the Punjab,* vol. I, Lahore, 1901, pp. 29–30

36. Rafiq Zakaria, *op. cit.,* 1993, p. 84; V.L. Joshi (ed.), *Lala Lajpat Rai: His Writings and Speeches*, vol. II, Delhi, 1966, pp. 175–8
37. M.C. Chaudhuri, *The Emergence of Pakistan,* New York, London, 1967, p. 25; A. Hamid, *Muslim Separatism in India, 1858–1947,* Karachi, 1967, pp. 176–7, 205; I.H. Qureshi, *The Muslim Community of the Indo-Pakistan Sub-continent,* The Hague, 1962, p. 295
38. Jayakar, *op. cit.,* p. 535; *The Times of India*, 22 March 1927; Wells, *op. cit.,* p. 146; Riaz Ahmad, *op. cit.,* vol. V, 2002, p. 366
39. Khairi, *op. cit.,* p. 197; H. Bolitho, *op. cit.,* p. 89; S. Wolpert, *op. cit.,* p. 88; R. Afzal, *Quaid-i-Azam M.A. Jinnah: Speeches in the Legislative Assembly of India,1924–1930*, Lahore, 1980, second edition, p. 117
40. Shan Muhammad (ed.), *Writings and Speeches of Sir Syed Ahmed Khan,* Bombay, 1972, p. 165; Riaz Ahmad, *op. cit.,* 1994, p. 23; *The Times of India*, 15 and 25 October 1926
41. Ambedkar, *op. cit.,* p. 111; S. Wolpert, *op. cit.,* p. 89; S.S. Pirzada, *Foundations of Pakistan: Documents of the All India Muslim League,1906–1947*, I, pp. 556–63
42. *The Times of India*, 30 March 1927
43. Riaz Ahmad, *op. cit.,* 1994, pp. 93, 206–7; *The Times of India*, 15 July 1927
44. *The Times of India*, 24 September 1927
45. Sumit Sarkar, *op. cit.,* pp. 262–3; *Indian Quarterly Register*, vol. I, 1927, pp. 36–7; R.J. Moore, *The Crisis of Indian Unity, 1917–1940*, Oxford, 1974, p. 24
46. Jaswant Singh, *op. cit.,* pp. 140–2; S. Wolpert, *op. cit.,* p. 100; *The Times of India*, 3 May 1927; S.S. Pirzada, *op. cit.,* vol. II, pp. 107–27
47. A. Jawed, *Secular and Nationalist Jinnah*, New Delhi, 1998, p. 248; Riaz Ahmad, *op. cit.,* 1994, p. 108; Khairi, *op. cit.,* pp. 204, 208; Sumit Sarkar, *op. cit.,* p. 262; Gankovsky and L.R. Gordon–Polonskaya, *A History of Pakistan*, Moscow, 1964, p. 35
48. *The Times of India*, 17 November and 8 December 1927
49. Sumit Sarkar, *op. cit.,* p. 262; V.P. Menon, *op. cit.,* p. 35; Khairi, *op. cit.,* p. 204; *The Times of India*, 2 January 1928 and 23 June 1928; Gankovsky and Pooanskaya, *Ibid.,* p. 54
50. Raza Khan, *op. cit.,* pp. 12–3; Jaswant Singh, *op. cit.,* p. 155
51. Sumit Sarkar, *op. cit.,* pp. 262–3
52. *Ibid.,* pp. 262–3; Ambedkar, *op. cit.,* pp. 280–1; Jaswant Singh, *op. cit.,* p. 619f; V.P. Menon, *op. cit.,* p. 36; Rafiq Zakaria, *op. cit.,* 1993, pp. 85–6; S.S. Pirzada (ed.), *The Collected Works of Quaid-e-Azam Mohammad Ali Jinnah*, Karachi, vol. III, pp. 316–9
53. Mushirul Hasan, *op. cit.,* p. 299; Jaswant Singh, *op. cit.,* p. 139; V.P. Menon, *op. cit.,* pp. 35–6; A.G. Noorani, *op. cit.,* pp. 65, 67, 87

54. Mushirul Hasan, *Ibid.*, pp. 272–3; A.G. Noorani, *Ibid.*, pp. 87–8, 90–1
55. Rafiq Zakaria, *op. cit.*, 2004, pp. 43–4

EXILE IN LONDON

1. S. Wolpert, *Jinnah of Pakistan*, New York, 1984, pp. 100–1; Jaswant Singh, *Jinnah: India–Partition, Independence*, New Delhi, 2009, pp. 146–8, 150
2. Dorothy Norman, *The First Sixty Years*, vol. I, Bombay, 1965, p. 506
3. K.K. Aziz, *The All India Muslim Conference, 1928–1935: A Documentary Record*, Karachi, 1972, pp. 44–7, 53–6; Bandyopadhyay, *Quaid-i-Azam Mohammad Ali Jinnah and the Creation of Pakistan*, New Delhi, 1991, p. 70; Rafiq Zakaria, *The Man who Divided India: An Insight into Jinnah's Leadership and its Aftermath*, Bombay, 2004, p. 47; H. Bolitho, *Jinnah: Creator of Pakistan*, London, 1954, p. 47; Rafiq Zakaria, *Iqbal: Poet and Politician*, New Delhi, 1993, pp. 78–9
4. *The Times of India*, 4 and 5 March 1928; C. Dobbin, *Basic Documents in the Development of Modern India and Pakistan, 1835–1947*, London, 1970, pp. 93–4; P. Hardy, *The Muslims of British India*, Cambridge, 1972, p. 212; V.P. Menon, *The Transfer of Power in India*, Madras, 1968, pp. 36–7
5. C.H. Philips, *The Evolution of India and Pakistan, 1858–1947, Select Documents*, London, 1962, pp. 135, 236–7
6. *Ibid.*, pp. 239–40; *IQR*, vol. 2, 1930, pp. 337–40; S.S. Pirzada (ed.), *Foundations of Pakistan: Documents of the All India Muslim League,1906–1947*, vol. I, Dacca, 1970, pp. 153–70; C.M. Naim (ed.), *Iqbal: Jinnah and Pakistan*, Lahore, 1984, p. 172; *Madras Mail*, 29 December 1930
7. C.H. Philips, *Ibid.*, p. 239; H. Bolitho, *op. cit.*, pp. 98–9; B.R. Ambedkar, *Pakistan or the Partition of India*, Bombay, 1946, p. 109; Khalid Bin Sayeed, *Pakistan: The Formative Phase, 1857–1948*, London, 1968, pp. 104, 109; M. Raza Khan, *What Price Freedom*, p. 20; C. Khaliquzzaman, *Pathway to Pakistan*, Lahore, 1961, p. 50
8. Rafiq Zakaria, *op. cit.*, 2004, pp. 50–1; B.B. Misra, *The Indian Political Parties: An Historical Analysis of Political Behaviour up to 1947*, Oxford, 1976
9. H. Bolitho, *op. cit.*, pp. 91, 92, 95; Chaman Lal, 'The Quaid-i-Azam as I knew him', in J. Ahmad, *Quaid-e-Azam as seen by his Contemporaries*, Lahore, 1976, p. 175
10. V.P. Menon, *op. cit.*, p. 42; *IQR*, vol. 2, 1929, p. 300; S. Ghose, *op. cit.*, pp. 190, 198; *The Times of India*, 24 April 1930; R.J. Moore, *The Crisis of Indian Unity, 1917–1940*, Oxford, 1974, pp. 172, 241–2; C.H. Philips, *op. cit.*, pp. 236–7; R. Coupland, *The Indian Problem*, vol. I, 1942, p. 111
11. M. Raza Khan, *op. cit.*, p. 15; Rafiq Zakaria, *op. cit.*, pp. 54, 59; H. Bolitho, *op. cit.*, pp. 54, 55, 59; S.S. Pirzada, *The Collected Works of Quaid-e-Azam Mohammad Ali Jinnah*, vol. III, p. 50

12. Sumit Sarkar, *Modern India, 1885–1947*, Delhi, 1984, p. 308; S. Ghose, *op. cit.*, p. 198; Jaswant Singh, *op. cit.*, p. 172
13. *The Times of India*, 31 July 1930; Jaswant Singh, *Ibid.*, p. 173
14. R.J. Moore, *op. cit.*, pp. 155, 163; S. Wolpert, *op. cit.*, p. 120; V.P. Menon, *op. cit.*, pp. 44–5; David Page, *Prelude to Partition: The Indian Muslims and the Imperial System of Control, 1920–1932*, Delhi, 1982, p. 229; *The Times of India*, 20 November 1929 and 2 December 1929; Tomlinson, *The Indian National Congress and the Raj, 1929–1942*, London, 1976, pp. 27–8; Aga Khan, *The Memoirs of the Aga Khan*, London, 1954, pp. 230–4
15. H. Bolitho, *op. cit.*, p. 101; Jaswant Singh, *op. cit.*, p. 93
16. *The Times of India*, 1 August, 3, 5 and 6 September 1931
17. V.P. Menon, *op. cit.*, p. 46; Rafiq Zakaria, *op. cit.*, 2004, p. 61; Rafiq Zakaria, *op. cit.*, 1993, p. 88; A. Edwards, *Throne of Gold: The Lives of the Aga Khans*, New York, 1995, p. 123
18. *The Times of India*, 8 December 1930; M. Raza Khan, *op. cit.*, pp. 21, 22; V.P. Menon, *Ibid.*, p. 47; Riaz Ahmad, *Quaid-i-Azam Mohammad Ali Jinnah: Second Phase of His Freedom Struggle, 1924–1934*, Islamabad, 1994, pp. 131–2, 136, 147
19. Aga Khan, *op. cit.*, pp. 217–8; Dorothy Norman, *op. cit.*, pp. 251, 256; A. Edwards, *op. cit.*, pp. 8, 87, 95; Rafiq Zakaria, *op. cit.*, 2004, p. 60 ; R.J. Moore, *op. cit.*, p. 219; Sumit Sarkar, *op. cit.*, p. 319; Jaswant Singh, *op. cit.*, p. 191; Farzana Shaikh, *Community and Consensus in Islam: Muslim Representation in Colonial India, 1860–1947*, Cambridge, 1989, pp. 188–9
20. Communal Decision, Parliamentary Paper, 1932, Cmd. 4147, IOL; C. Dobbin, *op. cit.*, pp. 115–7, S.C. Bose, *The Indian Struggle, 1920–1942*, London, 1962, p. 269
21. Farzana Shaikh, *op. cit.*, pp. 188–9
22. A. Edwards, *op. cit.*, pp. 142–3
23. V.P. Menon, *op. cit.*, p. 50; A.G. Noorani, *Jinnah and Tilak: Comrades in Freedom Struggle*, Oxford, 2010, p. 92
24. Monica Felton, *I meet Rajaji*, London, 1962, pp. 181–2; *Madras Mail*, 21 November 1932; R.K. Murthi, *Rajaji: Life and Work*, New Delhi, 1979, p. 77
25. *CWMG*, vol. 66, pp. 451–4; S. Ghose, *op. cit.*, 1991, pp. 222–3, 235; C. Dobbin, *op. cit.*, pp. 118–9; R. Gandhi, *The Rajaji Story*, vol. I, 1978, pp. 239–40; K.H. Nehru and A. Hatch, *We Nehrus*, New York, 1967, p. 109; D.G. Tendulkar, *Mahatma: Life of Mohandas Karamchand Gandhi*, vol. II, p. 174
26. Shiva Rao, *India's Freedom Movement*, 1972, pp. 14, 238; *Madras Mail*, 24 April 1933; S. Ghose, *op. cit.*, 1991, p. 307; *Minutes of Evidence given before the Joint Committee on Indian Constitutional Reforms* (sessions 1932–1933), vol. II, London, 1934, p. 1496; Shiva Rao, 'India 1935–47', in Philips and Wainwrigh (eds), *The Partition of India: Policies and Perspectives,1935–1947*, London, 1970, p. 416

BACK TO INDIAN POLITICS

1. V.P. Menon, *The Transfer of Power in India*, Madras, 1968, pp. 50, 51; Riaz Ahmad, *Quaid-i-Azam Mohammad Ali Jinnah: Second Phase of His Freedom Struggle, 1924–1934*, Islamabad, 1994, p. 173
2. M. Raza Khan, *What Price Freedom*, Madras, 1969, p. 24; Jaswant Singh, *Jinnah: India–Partition, Independence*, New Delhi, 2009, pp. 204–5; R.D. Long, *'Dear Mr. Jinnah', Selected Correspondence and Speeches of Liaquat Ali Khan, 1937–1947*, Oxford, 2004, pp. xix, xx; S.S. Pirzada, *Foundations of Pakistan: Documents of the All India Muslim League, 1906–1947*, vol. II, Karachi, 1970, pp. 229–33; IAR, 1934, vol. I, pp. 317–9; H. Bolitho, *Jinnah: Creator of Pakistan*, London, 1954, pp. 99, 104, 114
3. I.B. Wells, *Ambassador of Hindu–Muslim Unity: Jinnah's Early Politics*, New Delhi, 2005, p. 235; Jaswant Singh, *Ibid.*, p. 205; M. Raza Khan, *Ibid.*, p. 24; Riaz Ahmad, *op. cit.*, pp. 176–7
4. *The Times of India*, 3 March 1934 and 8 November 1934; 7 January 1935; V.P. Menon, *op. cit.*, p. 51; Ambedkar, *Pakistan or the Partition of India*, Bombay, 1946, p. 250; Jaswant Singh, *op. cit.*, p. 205; M. Raza Khan, *Ibid.*, pp. 23–4; Rafiq Zakaria, *The Man who Divided India: An Insight into Jinnah's Leadership and its Aftermath*, Bombay, 2004, p. 65
5. Ambedkar, *Ibid.*, p. 40
6. R.J. Moore, *Escape from Empire, The Attlee Government and the Indian Problem*, London, 1983, pp. 3, 4; C.H. Philips, *The Evolution of India and Pakistan, 1858–1947, Select Documents*, London, 1962, p. 318; C. Dobbin, *Basic Documents in the Development of Modern India and Pakistan, 1835–1947*, London, 1970, pp. 119–21; S.R. Mehrotra, 'The Congress and the Partition of India', in C.H. Philips and M.D. Wainwright (eds), *The Partition of India: Policies and Perspectives, 1935–1947*, London, 1970, p. 188; S. Ghose, *Mahatma Gandhi*, Bombay, 1991, pp. 257–9; Khalid Bin Sayeed, *Pakistan: The Formative Phase, 1857–1948*, London, 1968, p. 80
7. C.H. Philips, *The Partition of India, 1947*, Leeds, 1967, p. 1; P. Moon, *Divide and Quit*, London, 1962, p. 13; R.J. Moore, *op. cit.*, p. 6
8. S. Ghose, *op. cit.*, pp. 343–4; C. Dobbin, *op. cit.*, pp. 119–21; Letter No. 42 from Viceroy Linlithgow to His Majesty, 19 October 1939, Linlithgow Papers, IOL; K.H. Nehru and A. Hatch, *We Nehrus*, New York, 1967, p. 109; J. Nehru, *A Bunch of Old Letters*, Delhi, 1986, pp. 188–91
9. A.G. Noorani, *Jinnah and Tilak: Comrades in Freedom Struggle*, Oxford, 2010, pp. 18, 364–5; Mushirul Hasan, *A Nationalist Conscience: M.A. Ansari, The Congress and the Raj*, New Delhi, 1987, pp. 239–43; B. Metcalf, 'Iqbal: Ideology in Search of an Audience', in C.M. Naim (ed.), *Iqbal, Jinnah and Pakistan: The Vision and the Reality*, Lahore, 1984, p. 132; R. Prasad, *India Divided*, Bombay, 1946, p. 155; J. Nehru, *A Bunch of Old Letters*,

Delhi, 1986, p. 278; S.C. Bose, *Crossroads being the Works of Subhas Chandra Bose, 1938–40*, Calcutta, 1962, pp. 43–4; Zaidi and Zaidi, *The Encyclopaedia of Indian National Congress*, vol. 11, New Delhi, 1980, pp. 106–9, 487–9; V.N. Pyarelal, *Mahatma Gandhi: The Last Phase*, vol. I, Ahmedabad, 1956, p. 83

10. M. Raza Khan *op. cit.,* pp. 26–7; A. Saeed (ed.), *Quaid-i-Azam Mohammad Ali Jinnah: A Bunch of Rare Letters*, Lahore, 1999, pp. 21–2; Azim Husain, *Fazl-i-Husain: A Political Biography*, Bombay, 1946, pp. 309, 310
11. M.C. Chagla, *Muslim and the Nehru Report*, Bombay, 1972, pp. 103–4; Ayesha Jalal, *The Sole Spokesman: Jinnah, the Muslim League and Demand for Pakistan*, Cambridge, 1985, p. 20; D. Pandey, 'Congress–Muslim League Relations, 1937–39: The Parting of Ways', *Modern Asian Studies*, vol. 12, no. 4, 1978
12. Sumit Sarkar, *Modern India, 1885–1947*, Delhi, 1984, pp. 353–4; D. Gilmartin, *Empire and Islam: Punjab and the Making of Pakistan*, Berkeley, 1988, p. 165; Sharif al Mujahid, *Quaid-i-Azam and His Times*, Karachi, 1985, pp. 482–7; M. Raza Khan, *op. cit.,* p. 26
13. Sumit Sarkar, *Ibid.,* pp. 353–4; D. Gilmartin, *Ibid.,* p. 165; *Letters of Iqbal to Jinnah* (with a Foreword by M.A. Jinnah), s.l, n.d., pp. 6, 10
14. Ayesha Jalal, *op. cit.,* p. 20
15. S. Wolpert, *Jinnah of Pakistan*, New York, 1984, pp. 212–6; H. Bolitho, *op. cit.,* p. 113
16. M.H. Raza Khan, *op. cit.,* pp. 26, 27, 30; Sharif al Mujahid, *op. cit.,* p. 26
17. A.G. Noorani, 'The House that Jinnah Built', *Frontline*, 25 October–7 November 2003; S. Wolpert, *op. cit.,* p. 159
18. Rafiq Zakaria, *op. cit.,* 2004, p. 71; Shiva Rao, *India's Freedom Movement: Some Notable Figures*, New Delhi, 1972, p. 129
19. *Statesman*, 4 January 1937; Sharif al Mujahid, *op. cit.*
20. S. Wolpert, *Nehru: A Tryst with Destiny*, Oxford, 1996, pp. 206, 212–4, 222–6; *SWJN*, vol. 7, pp. 179–80; S. Ghose, *op. cit.*, pp. 256–7; C. Dobbin, *op. cit.,* pp. 124–8
21. Returns showing the results of the elections in India, 1937, Cmd. 5589; Gankovsky, Gordon–Polonskaya, *A History of Pakistan*, Moscow, 1964, p. 64; Sumit Sarkar, *op. cit.,* p. 349; D. Gilmartin, *op. cit.,* p. 165
22. H. Bolitho, *op. cit.,* p. 113
23. *Letters of Iqbal, op. cit.,* pp. 11, 12, 14
24. M. Raza Khan, *op. cit.,* pp. 34, 35; Sumit Sarkar, *op. cit.,* pp. 353, 354; *Leader,* 4 August 1937; Abul Kalam Azad, *India wins Freedom*, Madras, 1959, pp. 160–61; Khaliquzzaman, *Pathway to Pakistan*, Lahore, 1961, pp. 160–63; R. Coupland, *Indian Partition, Report on the Constitutional Problem in India, 1936–1942*, vol. II, London, 1943, pp. 110–12; A.W. Khan, 1961, pp. 78–81

25. Shiva Rao, *op. cit.,* p. 129; Tomlinson, *The Indian National Congress and the Raj, 1929–1942*, London, 1976, p. 104
26. *Leader*, 19 May, 5 June and 25 July 1937; *Pioneer*, 27 March 1937; M. Raza Khan, *op. cit.,* pp. 32–5; Nanda, 'Nehru and the Partition of India', in C.H. Philips and M.D. Wainwright (eds), *The Partition of India: Policies and Perspectives, 1935–1947*, London, 1970, p. 156; Percival Griffiths, *The British Impact on India*, London, 1952, p. 340
27. P. Moon, *op. cit.,* 1962, p. 16; J. Nehru, *op. cit.,* p. 265; S. Wolpert, *op. cit.,* 1996, pp. 223, 250; Abul Kalam Azad, *India Wins Freedom*, 1959, pp. 160–3; Khaliquzzaman, *op. cit.,* pp. 152–3; Tomlinson, *op. cit.,* pp. 103–4; *Madras Mail,* 13 October 1937; File No. B-9-1938, Proposals of Hindu–Muslim Understanding, AICC Papers, NMML
28. Nanda, *op. cit.,* p. 158; IAR, 1939, p. 435; A. Jalal, *op. cit.,* p. 43; *Report of the Enquiry Committee appointed by the Council of AIML to inquire into the Muslim Grievances in the Congress provinces*, Delhi, 1938; Letter No. 28 from Lord Linlithgow to His Majesty, 10 February 1938, Linlithgow Papers, IOL; S.S. Pirzada, *op. cit.,* vol. II, 1970, pp. 264–73, 300–9

RADICALIZATION OF THE MIND

1. Gankovsky and Gordon–Polonskaya, *A History of Pakistan*, Moscow, 1964, p. 67
2. Ambedkar, *Pakistan or the Partition of India*, Bombay, 1946, p. 255; *CWMG*, pp. 66, 257, 468–9; IAR, 1937, II, pp. 403–5, 470; V.P. Menon, *The Transfer of Power in India*, Madras, 1968, pp. 56–7; Penderel Moon, *Divide and Quit*, London, 1962, p. 18; C.H. Philips, *The Evolution of India and Pakistan, 1858–1947, Select Documents*, London, 1962, p. 347; C.H. Philips, *The Partition of India 1947*, Leeds, 1967, pp. 15–7; S.S. Pirzada, *Foundations of Pakistan*, vol. II, *pp.* 264–73; M. Raza Khan, *What Price Freedom*, Madras, 1969, pp. 40–3; S. Ghose, *Mahatma Gandhi*, Bombay, 1991, p. 308
3. Cf. M. Raza Khan, *Ibid.,* pp. 46–7
4. Shiva Rao, *India's Freedom Movement, Some Notable Figures*, New Delhi, 1972, p. 130; Khalid Bin Sayeed, *Pakistan: The Formative Phase, 1857–1948,* London, 1968, p. 93; David Gilmartin, *Empire and Islam: Punjab and the Making of Pakistan*, Berkeley, 1988, p. 74; S. Wolpert, *Nehru: A Tryst with Destiny*, Oxford, 1996, pp. 151–2; Penderel Moon, *op. cit.,* p. 17
5. David Gilmartin, *Ibid.,* pp. 168, 175, 177–8; Griffin and Massey, *Chiefs and Families of Note in the Punjab*, vol. I, Lahore, 1901, pp. 205–9; Rafiq Zakaria, *Iqbal: Poet and Politician*, New Delhi, 1993, pp. 93, 134–5; *Letters of Iqbal to Jinnah* (with a Foreword by M.A. Jinnah), s.l, n.d., pp. 27–32; Ghulam Rasul Khan, *The Punjab Provincial Muslim League: Its Past and Present*, Lahore, pp. 8, 15, 16
6. Rafiq Zakaria, *Ibid.,* pp. 135–6

7. S.S. Pirzada (ed.) *Quaid-i-Azam Jinnah's Correspondence*, Karachi, 1966, p. 159; M. Hasan (ed.), *Towards Freedom*, 1939, New Delhi, 2007, p. xvii
8. Rafiq Zakaria, *op. cit.,* pp. 141, 144–5, 149; *Letters of Iqbal to Jinnah*, pp. 1–4, 14–24; H. Bolitho, *Jinnah: Creator of Pakistan*, London, 1954, p. 115
9. Rafiq Zakaria, *The Man who Divided India: An Insight into Jinnah's Leadership and its Aftermath*, Bombay, 2004, p. 77; *Letters of Iqbal to Jinnah*, pp. 1–4
10. S.S. Pirzada (ed.), *Foundations of Pakistan: Documents of the All India Muslim League, 1906–1947*, vol. I, Karachi, Dacca, 1970, pp. 282–8; Mihir Bose, *The Lost Hero: A Biography of Subhas Chandra Bose*, London, 1982, p. 124; S.C. Bose, *Crossroads being the Works of Subhas Chandra Bose, 1938–40*, Calcutta, 1962, p. 356; Tomlinson, *The Indian National Congress and the Raj, 1929–1942*, London, 1976, p. 125; Khaliquzzaman, *Pathway to Pakistan*, Lahore, 1961, pp. 255–6; C.H. Philips and M.D. Wainwright (eds), *The Partition of India: Policies and Perspectives, 1935–1947*, London, 1970, p. 28; R. Coupland, *Indian Partition: Report on the Constitutional Problem in India, 1936–1942*, vol. II, London, 1943, pp. 27–9; L.A. Gordon, *Bengal: The Nationalist Movement, 1876–1940*, New York, 1974, pp. 279–88; IAR, 1938, I, pp. 377–357; Jawaharlal Nehru, *A Bunch of Old Letters*, Delhi, 1986, pp. 329, 340–2
11. R. Coupland, *op. cit.,* pp. 56–9
12. *Ibid.,* pp. 65–8, 74–5; *Hindustan Times*, 9 October 1942; *The Times of India*, 13 October 1942
13. R. Coupland, *op. cit.,* p. 112
14. A.R. Copley, *The Political Career of C. Rajagopalachari, 1937–1954*, Delhi, 1978, pp. 54–60; J.B.P. More, *The Political Evolution of Muslims in Tamilnadu and Madras, 1930–1947*, pp. 151–62; Rajmohan Gandhi, *The Rajaji Story: I, A Warrior from the South*, Madras, 1978, pp. 54–60
15. J.B.P. More, *Ibid.,* pp. 173–4; Rajmohan Gandhi, *Ibid.,* p. 144
16. A. Jalal, *The Sole Spokesman: Jinnah, the Muslim League and Demand for Pakistan*, Cambridge, 1985, p. 41
17. Jawaharlal Nehru, *op. cit.,* pp. 276–7; R. Coupland, *op. cit.,* p. 189
18. Jawaharlal Nehru, *Ibid.,* pp. 278–9; *IAR*, vol. I, 1938, pp. 369–75; Zaidi and Zaidi, *The Encyclopedia of Indian National Congress*, vol. 11, New Delhi, 1980, pp. 96–109, 183–96, 487–9; S. Wolpert, *op. cit.,* p. 234; *SWJN*, vol. 8, pp. 214–6; S.C. Bose, *op. cit.,* pp. 43–4; V.N. Pyarelal, *Mahatma Gandhi: The Last Phase*, vol. I, Ahmedabad, 1956, p. 83; B.N. Pandey, *The Break-up of British India*, London, 1969, pp. 149–50; J. Ahmad (ed.), *Historic Documents of the Muslim Freedom Movement*, Lahore, 1970, pp. 207–8
19. Jawaharlal Nehru, *Ibid.,* p. 285; *CWMG*, vol. 66, pp. 349–50, 387, 395–6, 449, 479–81; vol. 67, pp. 22, 37, 56, 70, 90; vol. 68, p. 208; vol. 70, pp. 212–4; vol. 71, pp. 132, 352, 371

20. Ambedkar, *op. cit.,* p. 253; Pandey, *op. cit.,* p. 150
21. A. Jalal, *op. cit.,* p. 45; S.C. Bose, *op. cit.,* pp. 37–46; Zaidi and Zaidi, *op. cit.,* pp. 487–9, 500
22. S.S. Pirzada, *op. cit.,* pp. 290–5
23. *Report of the Enquiry Committee Appointed by the Council of AIML to inquire into the Muslim Grievances in the Congress Provinces,* Delhi, 1938; Sumit Sarkar, *Modern India, 1885–1947,* Delhi, 1984, p. 355; *Manchester Guardian,* 12 January 1940; S. Ghose, *op. cit.,* p. 266; Fazlul Huq, *Muslim Sufferings under Congress Rule,* Calcutta, 1939; Abul Kalam Azad, *India Wins Freedom: The Complete Version,* Hyderabad, 1989, p. 16
24. Sumit Sarkar, *Ibid.,* pp. 352–3, 356–7; B.N. Pandey, *The Indian Nationalist Movement, 1885–1947, Select Documents,* London, 1979, p. 118
25. C.H. Philips, *op. cit.,* pp. 350–1; S.S. Pirzada, *op. cit.,* vol. I, pp. 300–4; II, pp. 300–9
26. *The Times of India,* 5, 10 and 11 October 1938; *Leader,* 11 October 1938; *Statesman,* 11 October 1938; *Pioneer,* 15 October 1938; Mohammad Ali Chaudhuri, *The Emergence of Pakistan,* New York, London, 1967, p. 31
27. S.S. Pirzada, *op. cit.,* vol. II, p. 343; *The Times of India,* 10 and 12 October 1938; Syed Abdul Latif, *The Muslim Problem in India,* Bombay, 1939, pp. v–vii; Penderel Moon, *Divide and Quit,* London, 1962, pp. 18–9; Sir Sikandar Hayat Khan, *Outlines of a Scheme of Indian Federation,* Lahore, 1939
28. S. Wolpert, *op. cit.,* pp. 370–1; M.C. Chagla, *Roses in December: An Autobiography,* Bombay, 1973, p. 120
29. Gwyer and Appadorai (eds), *Speeches and Documents on the Indian Constitution, 1922–47,* vol. II, Oxford, 1957, pp. 444–5, 455–62; R. Coupland, *op. cit.,* vol. II, pp. 203–4; Khalid Bin Sayeed, *op. cit.,* p. 111; Lal Bahadur, *The Muslim League: Its History, Activities and Achievements,* Agra, 1954, pp. 205–10; Rahmat Ali, *The Millat of Islam and the Menace of Indianism,* s.l., 1940
30. Gwyer and Appadorai, *op. cit.,* pp. 464–5; Khaliquzzaman, *op. cit.,* p. 115; Khalid Bin Sayeed, *op. cit.,* pp. 108–11, 113; A. Saeed (ed.), *Quaid-i-Azam Mohammad Ali Jinnah: A Bunch of Rare Letters,* Lahore, 1999, p. 43; S.S. Pirzada, *Ibid.,* pp. xx–xxi, vol. 2; Karim Rezaul, *Pakistan Examined,* Calcutta, 1941, pp. 131–47; David Gilmartin, *op. cit.,* p. 182; A. Jalal, *op. cit.,* p. 56; Mian Kifayat Ali, *Confederacy of India,* Lahore, 1935; Letter from Lord Linlithgow to Lord Zetland, 12 March 1940, Mss.Eur.F. 125/9, Sl No. 13, vol. V, pp. 169–76, IOL
31. Mushirul Hasan (ed.), *Towards Freedom Movement: Documents on the Movement for Independence in India,* 1939, New Delhi, 2000, pp. 1239, 1244, 1252, 1281, 1415, 1928; *Hindustan Times,* 3 March 1939
32. S. Wolpert, *Jinnah of Pakistan,* New York, 1984, p. 170
33. V.P. Menon, *op. cit.,* pp. 59–60

34. *Ibid.,* p. 60; S. Wolpert, *op. cit.,* p. 171; S. Wolpert, *op. cit.,* 1996, p. 256; Jaswant Singh, *Jinnah: India–Partition, Independence*, New Delhi, 2009, pp. 261–2
35. V.P. Menon, *op. cit.,* pp. 63–4; Letter from Lord Linlithgow to Lord Zetland, 27 February 1940, Zetland Collections, IOL; Tomlinson, *op. cit.,* p. 139; *IAR*, 1939, vol. II, pp. 243–5; D.G. Tendulkar, *Mahatma: Life of Mohandas Karamchand Gandhi*, vol. V, New Delhi, 1961–63, p. 163
36. D.G. Tendulkar, *Ibid.,* vol. V, p. 164; V.P. Menon, *Ibid.,* pp. 63–4; B.B. Misra, *The Indian Political Parties: An Historical Analysis of Political Behaviour up to 1947*, Oxford, 1976, pp. 332, 334
37. D.G. Tendulkar, *Ibid.,* p. 184; *CWMG*, vol. 70, pp. 410–14; *Hindustan Times*, 18 October 1939; Letter No. 42 from Lord Linlithgow to His Majesty, 19 October 1939, Linlithgow Papers, IOL
38. V.P. Menon, *op. cit.,* pp. 64, 65, 66, 67
39. *Hindustan Times*, 18 October 1939 and 5 November 1939; *CWMG*, vol. 70, pp. 362–4, 430–3; *IAR*, 1939, vol. II, pp. 411–3
40. D.G. Tendulkar, *op. cit.,* p. 184; S. Wolpert, *op. cit.,* p. 224
41. S.S. Pirzada (ed.), *Quaid-i-Azam Jinnah's Correspondence*, Karachi, 1966, p. 363; Pandey, 1979, pp. 137–8; *Madras Mail*, 29 September 1939; Letter dated 12 November 1939 from Rajendra Prasad to Jawaharlal Nehru, AICC Papers, NMML; Ambedkar, *op. cit.,* pp. 254–5; B.B. Misra, *op. cit.,* pp. 132–5; S. Ghose, *op. cit.,* p. 311
42. M. Raza Khan, *op. cit.,* pp. 49–50
43. Jawaharlal Nehru, *op. cit.,* pp. 278, 413–9; Jamil-ud-din Ahmad (ed.), *Historic Documents of the Muslim Freedom Movement*, Lahore, 1970, p. 363
44. V.P. Menon, *op. cit.,* pp. 68, 72; *CWMG,* vol. 70, pp. 426, 429; *IAR*, 1939, vol. II, p. 40; B.B. Misra, *op. cit.,* pp. 335–7; *Pioneer*, 4–6 November 1939; Letter No. 49 from Lord Linlithgow to His Majesty, 5 February 1940, Linlithgow Papers, IOL
45. Ambedkar, *op. cit.,* pp. 250, 256
46. *CWMG*, vol. 70, p. 335; Letter No. 24 from Lord Linlithgow to His Majesty, 9 August 1937, Linlithgow Papers, IOL; S. Ghose, *op. cit.,* p. 279; A. Jalal, *op. cit.,* p. 49
47. S. Wolpert, *Jinnah of Pakistan*, New York, 1984, p. 176; Sukhbir Choudhary, *Encyclopedia of Indian Nationalism*, New Delhi, 1994, vol. IV, pp. 1, 57, 157; Penderel Moon, *op. cit.,* p. 25
48. Jawaharlal Nehru, *op. cit.,* p. 414
49. *Ibid.,* pp. 417, 419; *SWJN*, vol. 10, pp. 401–3, 413–4; S. Wolpert, *op. cit.,* 1996, pp. 266–7; D.G. Tendulkar, *op. cit.,* vol. V, p. 217
50. *Indian Review*, January 1940, p. 28; *CWMG*, vol. 71, pp. 109, 117–8, 132–3; C.H. Philips, *op. cit.,* 1962, pp. 352–3; *Manchester Guardian*, 2 January 1940; 8 February 1940;

V.P. Menon, *op. cit.,* pp. 68–9; V.N. Pyarelal, *op. cit.,* p. 80; Kudiarasu, 7 and 14 January 1940; Z.H. Zaidi, 'Aspects of the Development of Muslim League Policy, 1937–47', in C.H. Philips and M.D. Wainwright (eds), *The Partition of India: Policies and Perspectives, 1935–1947*, London, 1970, p. 262

51. Jawaharlal Nehru, *op. cit.,* pp. 429, 432
52. *Manchester Guardian*, 3 and 5 January 1940; R. Coupland, *The Future of India*, vol. III, London, 1945, p. 77; Letter No. 35 from Lord Linlithgow to His Majesty, 4 October 1938, Linlithgow Papers, IOL; Letter No. 42 from Lord Linlithgow to His Majesty, 19 October 1939, Linlithgow Papers, IOL
53. David Gilmartin, *op. cit.,* p. 208; Khaliquzzaman, *op. cit.,* p. 201
54. Note of Interview between Lord Linlithgow and Jinnah, 4 September 1939; Enclosure 2, Lord Linlithgow to Lord Zetland, 5 September 1939, vol. 18, Zetland Papers, IOL; Khaliquzzaman, *Ibid.,* pp. 205–8, 211; Zetland, *Essayez*, London, 1956, pp. 148, 248; S. Ghose, *op. cit.,* p. 311; *Hindustan Times,* 5 November 1939; *CWMG*, vol. 70, pp. 327, 341–2, 382; Anita Inder Singh, *The Origins of the Partition of India 1936–1947*, Oxford, 1987, p. 56
55. Ahmad Aziz, *Islamic Modernism in India and Pakistan, 1857–1964*, London, 1967, p. 165
56. Sumit Sarkar, *op. cit.,* p. 377; R.J. Moore, *Escape from Empire: The Attlee Government and the Indian Problem*, London, 1983, pp. 8, 17; E. Estorick, *Stafford Cripps: The Master Statesman*, London, 1949, pp. 195–205
57. B.B. Misra, *op. cit.,* pp. 337–9
58. Anita Inder Singh, *op. cit.,* pp. 56–7; Lord Linlithgow to the Secretary of State, 16 March 1940, vol. 19, Linlithgow Papers, IOL; S. Ghose, *op. cit.,* p. 311; *The Times of India*, 13 and 19 February 1940; A. Jalal, *op. cit.,* p. 56
59. V.P. Menon, *op. cit.,* pp. 80–2; *The Times of India*, 13 and 19 February 1940
60. *CWMG*, vol. 71, pp. 337–9, 371; B.B. Misra, *op. cit.,* p. 340; V.P. Menon, *Ibid.,* p. 84; Zaidi and Zaidi, *op. cit.,* vol. 12, pp. 358–65
61. R.J. Moore, *The Crisis of Indian Unity, 1917–1940*, Oxford, 1974, pp. 312, 316

FINAL CALL FOR PAKISTAN

1. A.G. Noorani, Review article, 'Punjab and Pakistan', *Frontline*, 25 March 2005
2. M. Raza Khan, *What Price Freedom*, Madras, 1969, pp. 57, 58; M.H. Saiyid, *Mohammad Ali Jinnah: A Political Study*, Lahore, 1945, pp. 663–7; Khaliquzzaman, *Pathway to Pakistan*, Lahore, 1961, p. 234
3. H. Bolitho, *Jinnah: Creator of Pakistan*, London, 1954, p. 128
4. M. Raza Khan, *op. cit.,* pp. 60–3; Interview with M. Raza Khan, Madras delegate at Lahore conference

5. *Ibid.*, pp. 62–3; Interview with M. Raza Khan
6. *Ibid.*, pp. 63–5; S.S. Pirzada, *Foundations of Pakistan: Documents of the All India Muslim League,1906–1947*, vol. I, Karachi, Dacca, 1970, pp. 327–39; S.S. Pirzada, *Foundations of Pakistan: All India Muslim League Documents, 1906–1947*, vol. II, *1924–1947*, Islamabad, 2007, pp. 303–7; Sarwar Hasan, *Jinnah: Transfer of Power,* Karachi, 1966, p. 3; S. Ghose, *Mahatma Gandhi,* Bombay, 1991, p. 312
7. Aziz Ahmad, *Islamic Modernism in India and Pakistan, 1857–1964*, London, 1967, p. 165; Letter No. 51 from Lord Linlithgow to His Majesty, 13 June 1940, Linlithgow Papers, IOL; V.P. Menon, *The Transfer of Power in India*, Madras, 1968, p. 79; A.G. Noorani, 'The Partition of India' Review Article in *Frontline*, vol. 18, 4 January 2002; C.H. Philips, *The Evolution of India and Pakistan, 1858–1947: Select Documents*, London, 1962, p. 253
8. H. Bolitho, *op. cit.,* p. 137
9. M. Raza Khan, *op. cit.,* pp. 76–7; Interview with M. Raza Khan
10. *Ibid.,* p. 78; Interview with M. Raza Khan
11. *The Mail,* 23, 24 and 25 March 1940; A. Appadorai, *Documents of Political Thought in Modern India*, vol. I, London, 1973, pp. 267–71; *IAR*, Jan–June 1940, vol. I, pp. 311–12; See also, Mohamed Raza Khan, *What Price Freedom*, Madras, 1969
12. Y.V. Gankovsky and L.R. Gordon–Polanskaya, *A History of Pakistan*, Moscow, 1964, pp. 73–4; R. Coupland, *The Future of India: Report on the Constitutional Problem in India,* vol. III, London, 1945, p. 85
13. C.H. Philips, *op. cit.,* pp. 353–4
14. Statement of Jinnah on Lahore Resolution, 31 March 1940, in Sarwar Hasan, *op. cit.,* pp. 20–2; R. Coupland, *op. cit.,* p. 85
15. R.G. Casey, *An Australian in India*, London, 1947, pp. 72, 73
16. A.G. Noorani, 'Punjab and Pakistan', *Frontline*, 25 March 2005, pp. 78–82; V.P. Menon, *The Transfer of Power in India*, Madras, 1968, p. 463; M.R.T., *Pakistan and Muslim India*, Bombay, 1943, p. 52; David Gilmartin, *Empire and Islam: Punjab and the Making of Pakistan*, Berkeley, 1988, pp. 182–3; Khalid Bin Sayeed, *Pakistan: The Formative Phase, 1857–1948*, London, 1968, pp. 113, 115; C. Khaliquzzaman, *Pathway to Pakistan*, Lahore, 1961, p. 234
17. Cf. A. Jalal, *The Sole Spokesman: Jinnah, the Muslim League and Demand for Pakistan,* Cambridge, 1985, pp. 59–60; Jaswant Singh, *Jinnah: India–Partition, Independence*, New Delhi, 2009, pp. 273, 276
18. S. Ghose, *op. cit.,* p. 312; A. Jalal, *Ibid.,* pp. 50, 57–9
19. Rahmat Ali, *The Millat and the Mission*, Cambridge, 1944, pp. 2, 13, 17; Ahmed Khan, *The Founder of Pakistan through Trial and Triumph*, s.l., 1942, pp. 6–7, 20

20. M. Raza Khan, *op. cit.,* pp. 67–8; David Gilmartin, *op. cit.,* p. 183; Letter from H.D. Craik to Lord Linlithgow, March 1941, vol. 90, Linlithgow Papers, IOL; S.S. Pirzada, *op. cit.,* vol. II, 1970, pp. 423–6
21. David Gilmartin, *op. cit.,* pp. 183–4; Lal Bahadur, *The Muslim League: Its History, Activities and Achievements*, Agra, 1954, p. 191; A. Jalal, *op. cit.,* p. 4; Ambedkar, *Thoughts on Pakistan*, Bombay, 1947, pp. 367–8, 411; Rizwan Ahmad (ed.), *The Quaid-i-Azam Papers, 1941–42*, Karachi, 1976, pp. 63–4
22. *The Times of India*, 20 April 1940
23. Letter No. 51 from Lord Linlithgow to His Majesty, 13 June 1940, Linlithgow Papers, IOL
24. Khaliquzzaman, *op. cit.,* p. 257; Hugh Tinker, *Experiment with Freedom: India and Pakistan, 1947,* London, 1967, p. 24
25. Hugh Tinker, *Ibid.;* Khaliquzzaman, *Ibid., CWMG*, vol. 71, p. 371
26. *CWMG*, vol. 71, p. 345; D.G. Tendulkar, *Mahatma: Life of Mohandas Karamchand Gandhi*, vol. 5, New Delhi, p. 271
27. Sankar Ghose, *op. cit.,* pp. 312–3
28. *CWMG*, vol. 71, p. 412
29. D.G. Tendulkar, *op. cit.,* p. 264; *Statesman*, 5 May 1940; C.H. Philips and M.D. Wainwright (eds), *The Partition of India: Policies and Perspectives, 1935–1947*, London, 1970, p. 26; *CWMG*, vol. 71, p. 412; See also Proceedings of Congress Working Committee, Wardha, 16 and 17 April 1940, G.32/1940, AICC Papers, NMML
30. *CWMG*, vol. 71, pp. 27, 46–8; S. Ghose, *op. cit.,* p. 314
31. *Leader,* April 15, 1940; *SWJN*, vol. 11, p. 17; S. Wolpert, *Nehru: A Tryst with Destiny*, Oxford, 1996, p. 272; See also Mehrotra, 'The Congress and the Partition of India', in C.H. Philips and M.D. Wainwright (eds), *The Partition of India: Policies and Perspectives,1935–1947*, London, 1970
32. V.P. Menon, *The Transfer of Power in India*, Madras, 1968, p. 83
33. Ambedkar, *Pakistan or the Partition of India*, Bombay, 1946 (1940 first edition)
34. See for example, *Kudiarasu*, 31 March 1940
35. M.H. Shahid, *The Quaid-i-Azam on Important Issues*, Lahore, 1989, pp. 19–22; *The Mail,* 1 and 11 April 1940; S.S. Pirzada, *op. cit.,* vol. II, pp. 331–2; *The Hindu*, 27 March 1940; Sarwar Hasan (ed.), *Jinnah: Transfer of Power*, Karachi, 1966, pp. 22–3
36. S. Ghose, *op. cit.,* pp. 2, 9; S. Gopal, *Jawaharlal Nehru: A Biography*, New Delhi, 1989, pp. 132–3; S.S. Pirzada, *Ibid.,* vol. II, p. 369; D.G. Tendulkar, *op. cit.,* vol. V, pp. 299–313, 327–33; Letter from C. Rajagopalachari to M.R. Jayakar, 23 January 1942, Jayakar Papers, NAI; Letter from M.R. Jayakar to C. Rajagopalachari, 21 January 1942,

Jayakar Papers, NAI; *Manchester Guardian*, 24 July, 8 and 9 August, 13 November 1940; B.N. Pandey, *The Break-up of British India*, London, 1969, pp. 149–50

37. Tel R., 'From Lord Erskine, Governor of Madras to Lord Linlithgow', No. 181-C, 25 December 1939, Erskine Papers, IOL; Report dated 18 January 1940 from Lord Erskine to Lord Linlithgow, L/P&J/5/202, IOL
38. *The Indian Review*, May, 1940, pp. 292, 314; *The Hindu*, 17 April 1940; R. Coupland, *Indian Partition: Report on the Constitutional Problem in India, 1936–1942*, vol. II, London, 1943, p. 67; R. Coupland, *The Future of India: Report on the Constitutional Problem in India*, vol. III, London, 1945, p. 40; *Tribune*, 24 March, 29 April 1940; Anita Inder Singh, *The Origins of the Partition of India, 1936–1947*, Oxford, 1987, p. 58
39. R. Coupland, *op. cit.*, p. 238
40. V.P. Menon, *op. cit.*, pp. 78–9, 87
41. A. Waheed (ed.), *Jinnah–Linlithgow Correspondence, 1939–1943*, Lahore, 1976, pp. 34–5
42. Hanif Shahid, *The Quaid-i-Azam on Important Issues*, Lahore, 1989, pp. 23–5
43. V.P. Menon, *op. cit.*, p. 89
44. *Ibid.*, pp. 90–1; *Indian Annual Register*, 1940, vol. II, pp. 252–4
45. M. Raza Khan, *op. cit.*, pp. 81–2
46. S. Ghose, *op. cit.*, pp. 280–1; R.J. Moore, *Escape from Empire: The Attlee Government and the Indian Problem*, London, 1983, p. 9; C.H. Philips, *op. cit.*, 1962, pp. 370–1; Khalid Bin Sayeed, *op. cit.*, pp. 118–19
47. M. Raza Khan, *op. cit.*, p. 84; B.B. Misra, *The Indian Political Parties: An Historical Analysis of Political Behaviour up to 1947*, Oxford, 1976, p. 434; V.P. Menon, *op. cit.*, pp. 94, 99, 100; Sumit Sarkar, *Modern India, 1885–1947*, Delhi, 1984, p. 380
48. V.P. Menon, *op. cit.*, p. 95
49. Sumit Sarkar, *op. cit.*, p. 281; V.P. Menon, *op. cit.*, p. 98; Letter No. 54 from Lord Linlithgow to His Majesty, 15 October 1940, Linlithgow Papers, IOL; Letter No. 56 from Lord Linlithgow to his Majesty, 20 February 1941, Linlithgow Papers, IOL
50. Letter No. 56 from Lord Linlithgow to His Majesty, February 1941, Linlithgow Papers, IOL
51. *Manchester Guardian*, 4 and 23 April 1941; Letter No. 59 from Lord Linlithgow to His Majesty, 7 July 1941, Linlithgow Papers, IOL

EPILOGUE

1. R.G. Casey, *An Australian in India*, London, 1947, pp. 54–5
2. *Ibid.*
3. *Ibid.*

4. Note on the proceedings of the AIML at Delhi, 24–26 April 1943, *Transfer of Power Papers* (TP) vol. III, pp. 919–22; R.G. Casey (Bengal) to Lord Wavell, Tel. Calcutta, 3 December 1945, TP, vol. VI, p. 591
5. *The Modern Review*, July 1945, p. 2; Lal Bahadur, *Struggle for Pakistan: Tragedy of the Triumph of Muslim Communalism in India 1906–1947*, London, 1988, p. 231
6. Letter from Nawab of Bhopal to Lord Mountbatten and Liaquat Ali Khan, 10 April 1947, TP, X, pp. 330–1; Record of Interview between Lord Mountbatten and Liaquat Ali Khan, 10 April 1947, TP. X, pp. 330–1; *Dawn*, 6 August 1946; Letter from Nawab of Bhopal to Lord Mountbatten, 27 March 1947 and Minutes of Viceroy's Fourth Meeting, TP. X, pp. 34–6
7. J.B.P. More, *Partition of India: Players and Partners*, Tellicherry, 2008, pp. 109–67
8. *Ibid.*, pp. 71, 80; Gwyer and Appadorai (eds), *Speeches and Documents on the Indian Constitution, 1922–37*, vol. II, Oxford, 1957, p. 525; Mohamed Raza Khan, *What Price Freedom,* Madras, 1969, p. 99; *Indian Annual Register*, 1942, vol. I, pp. 294–5; *The Mail*, 14 April 1943; *Hindustan Times*, 16 June 1947; *National Herald*, 16 June 1947
9. J.B.P. More, *op. cit.*, pp. 109–67
10. Jawaharlal Nehru, *The Discovery of India*, Delhi, 1985, p. 536
11. *Manchester Guardian*, 5 October 1943; Gopal Sarvepalli, *Jawaharlal Nehru: A Biography, 1947–56*, vol. II, Delhi, 1979, p. 258
12. Abul Kalam Azad, *India wins Freedom*, Hyderabad, 1989, p. 209
13. See Peter Brobst, *The Future of the Great Game, Sir Olaf Caroe: India's Independence and the Defense of India*, Akron, Ohio, 2005; R.J. Moore, *op. cit.*, p. 11; Eric Estorick, *Stafford Cripps, The Master Statesman*, London, 1949, p. 332; Olaf Caroe, *Wells of Power: A Challenge to Islam, A Study in Contrasts*, London, 1951, pp. 64, 67, 121; Note on the Results to British Commonwealth of the Transfer of Political Power in India, TP VIII, pp. 50–2
14. Olaf Caroe, *Ibid.*, pp. 32, 33, 88, 96, 97, 121, 147, 164, 166; Brobst, *op. cit.*, pp. xiv; Future Relations between India and adjacent countries: Memo of the Secretary of state, India Office, 22 March 1947, TP X, pp. 2–3; Sir G. Spire to Mr. Weightman, Kabul, 5 April 1947, TP X, pp. 135–6; Appreciation of the Strategic Value of India to the British Commonwealth of Nations (final paper), TP VIII, pp. 53–4
15. R.G. Casey, Letter from Governor of Bengal to Viscount Wavell, 11 November 1944, Political Series, vol. I, part I, Wavell Collections; *Hindustan Times*, 28 March 1947; see also R.G. Casey, *An Australian in India*, London, 1947; see also Indian Conference in London: Record of Meeting, 1 December 1946, TP IX, p. 276; Note on the results to British Commonwealth of the Transfer of Political Power in India and Appreciation of the Strategic Value of India to the British Commonwealth of Nations (Final

Paper), TP VIII, pp. 50–3, 56; Staff, Ministry of Defence, 13 June 1947, TP XI, p. 344; Appreciation of the Strategic Value of India to the British Commonwealth of Nations (Final Paper), TP, VIII, p. 57; Draft Memorandum to the Chiefs of staff to the Minister of Defence India: Strategic Requirement, TP XI, pp. 957–60; Chief of Staff's Committee C.O.S. (47) 62nd meeting, 12 May 1947, TP X, p. 791; Letter from Mr. Turnbull to Mr. Harris, 19 June 1947, TP XI, pp. 517–8; B. Shiva Rao, *India's Freedom Movement: Some Notable Figures*, New Delhi, 1972, p. 213; R.J. Moore, op. cit., pp. 61, 62, 81

16. J.B.P. More, *op. cit.,* p. 308; Chief of Staff's Committee. C.O.S. (47) 62nd meeting, 12 May 1947, TP X, p. 789; Fraser to Attlee, 26 May 1947, TP X, pp. 989–90, TP XI, p. 945; *Le Populaire*, 8 May 1948; Note by Field Marshall Sir C. Auchinleck, 11 May 1946, TP XII, pp. 800–1; *Hindustan Times*, 20 July 1946, 21 July 1946, 7 October 1946, 18 January 1947; Sir Stafford Cripps to Rajagopalachari, Milbank, 23 June 1947, TP XI, pp. 565–6
17. Minutes of Viceroy's Fourth Miscellaneous Meeting, New Delhi, 18 April 1947, TP X, p. 315; Record of Interview between Lord Mountbatten and Liaquat Ali Khan, 10 April 1947, TP X, pp. 330–1; Krishna Menon to Lord Mountbatten, 12 April 1947, TP X, p. 372; Lord Wavell to Lord Pethick Lawrence, New Delhi, 17 September 1946, TP VIII, p. 536; R J Moore, *op. cit.,* p. 81
18. For more details regarding all this and the events leading to partition from 1940 to 1947, Cf. J.B.P. More, *Partition of India: Players and Partners*, Tellicherry, 2008

BIBLIOGRAPHY

INDIA OFFICE LIBRARY, LONDON

Erskine Papers

Linlithgow Papers

Private Office Records, L/PO/48; L/PO/49

Rahmat Ali Papers

Wavell Collections

Zetland Papers

NATIONAL ARCHIVES OF INDIA, NEW DELHI

Home Department Files: Public, Judicial and Political

Rajagopalachari Papers

NEHRU MEMORIAL MUSEUM & LIBRARY, NEW DELHI

All India Congress Committee Papers

Jayakar Papers

Satyamurti Papers

Tej Bahadur Sapru Papers

LIBRARIES

London and Cambridge

British Library

Centre of South Asian Studies Library, Cambridge

Colindale Newspaper Library

India Office Library and Records

School of Oriental and African Studies Library

Paris

Bibliothèque Internationale de Documentation Contemporaine

Bibliothèque Nationale de France

Centre d'Etudes de l'Inde Library

Institut National des Langues et Civilisations Orientales Library

New Delhi

Jawaharlal Nehru University Library

Nehru Memorial Museum & Library

Chennai

Adyar Library

Connemara Public Library

Madras University Library

Tamil Nadu Archives Library

NEWSPAPERS AND PERIODICALS

Civil and Military Gazette (Lahore)

Dawn, New Delhi (Muslim League paper)

Deccan Times, Madras (Muslim League paper)

Harijan (Gandhian paper, Ahmedabad)

Hindustan Times (nationalist, Delhi)

India (nationalist, Pondicherry)

Kudi Arasu (Dravida Kazhagam official press organ)

Leader (Allahabad paper)

Madras Mail (loyalist paper, Madras)

The Hindu (nationalist, Madras)

The Mail (loyalist, Madras)

The Pioneer (Allahabad paper)

The Statesman (loyalist, Calcutta)

The Star of India (Calcutta paper)

The Times of India (nationalist, Bombay)

The Tribune (Lahore)

Viduthalai (Dravida Kazhagam paper)

OFFICIAL PUBLICATIONS

Census of India, 1941

Communal Decision, 1932. Cmd. 4147

Government of India Act, 1935, Delhi, 1936

Indian Round Table Conference Proceedings, London, 1931, 1932, 1933. Cmd. 3738, 3997, 4238

Indian Statutory Commission, London, 1929–1930

India and the War: Communiqué issued by the Governor General and resolutions by the Indian National Congress, the All India Muslim League, and the Chamber of Princes, London, 1940. Cmd. 6196

Minutes of Evidence given before the Joint Committee on Indian Constitutional Reforms, Sessions 1932–33, vol. II, London, 1934

Report of the Enquiry Committee, appointed by the council of the All India Muslim League to Inquire into the Muslim Grievances in Congress provinces, Delhi, 1938 (*Pirpur Report*)

Report of the Joint Committee on Indian Constitutional Reform, 1933–34, London, 1934

Report by S.M. Shareef on Muslim Grievances, 2 vols, Patna, 1940

Returns showing the Results of Elections in India, 1937. Cmd. 5589

Returns showing the results of the general election to the Legislative Assembly in India, 1934–35, Cmd. 4939

BOOKS

Adhikari, G.M., *Pakistan and Indian National Unity*, London, 1943

Afzal, M.R., *Selected Speeches and Statements of the Quaid-i-Azam Mohammad Ali Jinnah (1911–34 and 1947–48)*, Lahore, 1966

Afzal, Rafique, *Malik Barkat Ali—His Life and Writings*, Lahore, 1969

___, *Quaid-i-Azam M.A. Jinnah: Speeches in the Legislative Assembly of India, 1924–1930*, Lahore, 1980, second edition

Ahmad, Aziz, *Islamic Modernism in India and Pakistan, 1857–1964*, London, 1967

Ahmad, Imtiaz (ed.), *Caste and Social Stratification among the Muslims*, Delhi, 1973

Ahmad, Jamil-ud-din, *Through Pakistan to Freedom*, Lahore, 1944

___, (ed.), *Some Recent Speeches and Writings of Mr. Jinnah*, vols I and II, Lahore, 1960, 1964

___, (ed.), *Historic Documents of the Muslim Freedom Movement*, Lahore, 1970

___, (ed.), *Quaid-i-Azam as Seen by his Contemporaries*, Lahore, 1976

Ahmad Riaz, *Jinnah and Jauhar*, Islamabad, 1979

Ahmad, Riaz, *Quaid-i-Azam Mohammad Ali Jinnah—The Formative Years: 1892–1920*, Islamabad, 1988

___, *Quaid-i-Azam Mohammad Ali Jinnah—Second Phase of His Freedom Struggle: 1924–1934*, Islamabad, 1994

___, *The Works of Quaid-i-Azam Mohammad Ali Jinnah, 1917–1918*, Vol. IV, Islamabad, 1999; Vol. V, 1919–1920, Islamabad, 2002

Ahmad, Rizwan (ed.), *The Quaid-i-Azam Papers, 1941–42*, Karachi, 1976

Ahmad, Waheed (ed.), *Letters of Mian Fazl-i-Husain*, Lahore, 1976

___, (ed.), *Jinnah–Linlithgow Correspondence*, Lahore, 1978

Ahmed, S., Akbar, *Jinnah, Pakistan and Islamic Identity: The Search for Saladin*, London, 1997

Ahmed, Rafiuddin, *The Bengal Muslims, 1871–1906: A Quest for Identity*, Delhi, 1981

Ahsan, Aitzaz, *The Indus Saga and the Making of Pakistan*, Karachi, 1996

Akbar, M.J., *The Making of India*, London, 1988

Albiruni, A.H., *Makers of Pakistan and Modern Muslim India*, Lahore, 1950

Ali, Kifayat, Mian (A Punjabi), *Confederacy of India*, Lahore, 1935

Ali, Mubarak, *Pakistan in Search of Identity*, Karachi, 2009

Allana, G., *Pakistan Movement—Historic Documents*, Lahore, 1977

___, *Quaid-i-Azam Jinnah: The Story of a Nation*, Lahore, 1980

Almeida, Prakash, *Jinnah: Man of Destiny*, New Delhi, 2001

Alva, Joachim, *Men and Supermen*, Bombay, 1943

Ambedkar, B.R., *Pakistan or the Partition of India,* Bombay, 1946 (1940 first edition)

___, *Ranade, Gandhi and Jinnah*, Bombay, 1943

___, *What Congress and Gandhi have done to the Untouchables*, Bombay, 1946, second edition

___, *Ambedkar's Attack or the Fight against Untouchability*, Delhi, 1946

___, *Thoughts on Pakistan*, Bombay, 1947 (first published 1941)

Amery, L.S., *India and Freedom*, London, 1942

___, *My Political Life*, 4 vols, London, 1953–55

Appadurai, A., *Documents of Political Thought in Modern India,* vol. I, London, 1973

Azad, A.K., *India's Choice*, London, 1940

Azad, Abul Kalam, Moulana, *India Wins Freedom*, Madras, 1964, first printed 1959

___, *India Wins Freedom: The Complete Version*, Hyderabad, 1989

Aziz, Kursheed Kamal, *Aga Khan III: Selected Speeches and Writings of Sultan Muhammad Shah.* London, 1958

___, *Britain and Muslim India*, London, 1963

___, *The Making of Pakistan: A Study in Nationalism*, London, 1967

___, *History of Partition of India: Origin and Development of the Idea of Pakistan, 1931–1940*, New Delhi, 1968

___, (ed.), *Ameer Ali: His Life and Work.* Lahore, 1968

___, (ed.), *The All India Muslim Conference, 1928–1935: A Documentary Record,* Karachi, 1972

___, *Rahmat Ali: A Biography*, Lahore, 1987, 2008

Baker, C.J. and David Washbrook, *South India: Political Institution and Political Change, 1880–1940*, New Delhi, 1975

Baker, C.J. *The Politics of South India, 1920–1937*, Cambridge, 1976

Baker, C.J., Johnson Gordon, and Anil Seal (eds), *Power, Profit and Politics: Essays on Imperialism, Nationalism and Change in the Twentieth Century India*, Cambridge, 1981

Bakshi, Ilahi, *With the Quaid-i-Azam during his Last Days*, Karachi, 1978

Bakshi, S.R., *Struggle for Independence: Ali Brothers*, New Delhi, 1992

Bamford, P., *Histories of the Non-Cooperation and Khilafat Movements*, Delhi, 1974

Bandopadhya, Sailesh Kumar, *Quaid-i-Azam Mohammad Ali Jinnah and the Creation of Pakistan*, New Delhi, 1991

Bandyopadhay, Sekhar, *From Plassey to Partition: A History of Modern India*, New Delhi, 2004

Banerjea, Surinder Nath, *The Man and the Vision*, Madras, n.d.

Banerjea, Surinder Nath, *A Nation in the Making*, London, 1925

Bayly, C.A., *The Local Roots of Indian Politics, Allahabad, 1880–1920*, Oxford, 1975

___, *Indian Society and the Making of the British Empire (The New Cambridge History of India)*, Cambridge, 1990

Beck, Theodore, *Essays on Indian Topics*, Allahabad, 1888

Becker, M.L., *The All India Muslim League: 1906–1947*, Cambridge, 1957

Beg, Aziz, *Jinnah and His Times: A Biography*, Islamabad, 1986

Benedict, Anderson, *Imagined Communities: Reflections on the Origin and Spread of Nationalism*, London, 1983

Birla, G.D., *In the Shadow of the Mahatma: A Personal Memoir*, Calcutta, 1953

Blanchy, Sophie, *Karana et Banian: Les Communautés Commerçantes d'Originie Indienne à Madagascar*, Paris, 1995

Bolitho, Hector, *Jinnah–Creator of Pakistan*, London, 1954

Bose, Mihir, *The Lost Hero—A Biography of Subhas Chandra Bose*, London, 1982

Bose, Subhas Chandra, *Crossroads being the works of Subhas Chandra Bose, 1938–40*, Calcutta, 1962

___, *The Indian Struggle, 1920–42*, London, 1964

Brailsford, H.N., *Subject India*, London, 1943

Brass, Paul, *Factional Politics in an Indian State: The Congress Party in Uttar Pradesh*, Berkeley, 1965

___, *Language, Religion and Politics in North India*, Cambridge, 1974

Brecher, Michael, *Nehru—A Political Biography*, London, 1959

Bright, J.S. (ed.), *Before and After Independence: Collection of Nehru's Speeches, 1922–1950,* New Delhi, 1950

Brown, J.M., *Gandhi's Rise to Power: Indian Politics 1915–1922*, Cambridge, 1972

Burke, S.M. and Salim-al-Din-Quraishi, *Quaid-i-Azam Mohammad Ali Jinnah: His Personality and his Politics*, New York, 1997

Carr, E.H. *What is History?* New York, 1961

Caroe, Olaf, Sir, *The Pathans*, London, 1948

Carter, Lionel (ed.), *Punjab Politics 1936–1939: The Start of Provincial Autonomy, Governor's Fortnightly Reports*, New Delhi, 2005

Casey, R.G., *An Australian in India*, London, 1947

___, *Personal Experience—1939–46*, London, 1962

Chagla, Mohammad Carim, *Muslim and the Nehru Report*, Bombay, 1972

___, *Roses in December—An Autobiography*, Bombay, 1973

Chand, Tara, *History of the Freedom Movement*, 3 vols, New Delhi, 1972

Chandra, K., *The Tragedy of Jinnah*, Lahore, 1943

Chatterji, Joya, *Bengal Divided: Hindu Communalism and Partition*, Cambridge, 1994

Chirol, Valentine, *Indian Unrest*, London, 1910

Chaudhuri, Mohammad Ali, *The Emergence of Pakistan*, New York, London, 1967

Choudhry, Nirad, C., *The Autobiography of an Unknown Indian*, New York, 1951

Choudhary, Rahmat Ali, *The Millat of Islam and the Menace of Indianism*, s.l., 1940

___, *The Millat and the Mission*, Cambridge, 1942

___, *The Millat of Islam and the Menace of 'Indianism'*, 1942 (first published in 1940)

___, *What does the Pakistan National Movement stand for?* Cambridge, 1942

___, *The Millat and the Mission*, Cambridge, 1944 (first issued, 1942)

___, *Pakasia: The Historic Orbit of the Pak Culture*, Cambridge, 1946

___, *Pakistan. The Fatherland of the Pak Nation*, Cambridge, 1947

___, *The Greatest Betrayal: How to Redeem the Millat?*, Cambridge, 9 June 1947

Choudhary, Sukhbir, *Encyclopaedia of Indian Nationalism*, New Delhi, 1994

Chopra, P.N., *Role of Indian Muslims in the Struggle for Freedom*, New Delhi, 1979

Copley, A.R., *The Political Career of C. Rajagopalachari, 1937–1954: A Moralist in Politics*, Delhi, 1978

___, *Gandhi against the Tide*, Calcutta, 1993

Coupland, Reginald, *The Indian Problem—Report on the Constitutional Problem in India, 1833–1935*, I, London, 1942

___, *Indian Partition, Report on the Constitutional Problem in India, 1936–1942*, II, London, 1943

___, *The Future of India, Report on the Constitutional Problem in India, III*, London, 1945

Craddock, Reginald, Sir, *Dilemma in India*, London, 1929

Daftary, Farhad, *The Ismailis—Their History and Doctrines*, Cambridge, 1990

Dalrymple, William, *The Last Mughal: The Fall of a Dynasty: Delhi, 1857,* London, 2006

Dani, Ahmad Hasan (ed.), *World Scholars on Quaid-i-Azam Mohammad Ali Jinnah*, Islamabad, 1979

Das, Durga, *India from Curzon to Nehru and After*, Calcutta, 1973

Das, M.N., *Partition and Independence of India*, New Delhi, 1982

David, Saul, *The Indian Mutiny*, London, 2003

Davis, Kingsley, *The Population of India and Pakistan*, Princeton, 1951

Dobbin, Christine, *Basic Documents in the Development of Modern India and Pakistan, 1835–1947*, London, 1970

Dhulipala, Venkat, *Creating a New Medina: State Power, Islam and the Quest for Pakistan*, Cambridge, 2014

Dwarkadas, Kanji, *Ruttie Jinnah—The Story of a Great Friendship*, Bombay, n.d.

___, *India's Fight for Freedom, 1913–1917*, Bombay, 1966

Dutt, R.P., *A New Chapter in Divide and Rule*, Bombay, 1946

Edwards, Anne, *Throne of Gold: The Lives of the Aga Khans*, New York, 1995

Edwardes, S.M., *Memoir of Sir Dinshaw Manockjee Petit*, Oxford, 1923

Edwardes, Michael, *Nehru, A Political Biography*, London, 1971

Estorick, Eric, *Stafford Cripps: The Master Statesman*, London, 1949

Faruqi, Zia-ul-Hasan, *The Deoband School and the Demand for Pakistan*, Bombay, 1963

Fazlul, Huq, A.K., *Muslim Sufferings under Congress Rule*, Calcutta, 1939

Felton, Monica, *I Meet Rajaji*, London, 1962

Fischer, Louis, *The Life of Mahatma Gandhi*, London, 1982

French, Patrick, *Liberty or Death: Indian Journey to Independence and Division*, London, 1997

Frischauer, Willi, *The Aga Khan*, New York, 1971

Gallagher, John, Johnson Gordon, and Anil Seal (eds), *Locality, Province and Nation: Essays on Indian Politics, 1870–1940*, Cambridge, 1973

Gandhi, M.K., *Constructive Programme: The Meaning and its Place*, second revised edition, Ahmedabad, 1945

___, *An Autobiography: The Story of My Experiments with Truth*, London, 1949

___, *Communal Unity*, Ahmedabad, 1949

Gandhi, M.K., *Hind Swaraj and Other Writings* (ed.), by Anthony Parel, Cambridge, 1997

___, *The Collected Works of Mahatma Gandhi*, Vols 66–89, Ahmedabad, 1976–1983

Gandhi, Rajmohan, *The Rajaji Story: Vol. 1. A Warrior from the South*, Madras, 1978

___, *The Rajaji Story, 1937–1972*, vol. 2, Bombay, 1984

___, *Understanding the Muslim Mind*, New Delhi, 1988

___, *Ghaffar Khan: Non-violent Badshah of the Pakthuns*, New Delhi, 2004

Gankowsky, Y.V. and L.R. Gordon – Polanskaya, *A History of Pakistan*, Moscow, 1964

Ghose, Sankar, *Mahatma Gandhi*, Bombay, 1991

Gilmartin, David, *Empire and Islam: Punjab and the Making of Pakistan*, Berkeley, 1988

Glendevon, J., *The Viceroy at Bay: Lord Linlithgow in India, 1936–43*, London, 1971

Gopal, Madan, *Sir Chotu Ram, A Political Biography*, Delhi, 1977

Gopal, Ram, *Indian Muslims: A Political History*, Bombay, 1959

Gopal, Sarvepalli, *The Viceroyalty of Lord Irwin, 1926–1931*, Oxford, 1957

___, (ed.), *Selected Works of Jawaharlal Nehru*, First Series, vols 1 to 15, New Delhi, 1972–1982

___, *Jawaharlal Nehru: A Biography*, vol. I, 1889–1947, London, 1975

___, *Selected Works of Jawaharlal Nehru*, Second Series, vols 1 to 12, New Delhi, 1984–91

___, *Jawaharlal Nehru: A Biography*, Abridged edition, New Delhi, 1989

Gordon, L.A., *Bengal: The Nationalist Movement, 1876–1940*, New York, 1974

Graham, G.F.I., *The Life and Works of Sir Syed Ahmed Khan*, London, 1885

Greenwall, Harry, *The Aga Khan*, London, 1952

Grewal, J.S., *Muslim Rule in India: The Assessment of British Historians*, Calcutta, 1970

Griffin, L.H. and C.F. Massey, *Chiefs and Families of Note in the Punjab.* I, Lahore, 1901

Griffiths, Percival, Sir, *The British Impact on India*, London, 1952

Gupta, A.K., *North-West Province Legislature and Freedom Struggle, 1932–47*, New Delhi, 1947

Gwyer M. and Appadurai, A. (eds), *Speeches and Documents on the Indian Constitution, 1922–47*, 2 vols, Oxford, 1957

Haider, K.R., *Ruttie Jinnah*, Karachi, 2010

Halifax, The Earl of (Lord Irwin), *Fullness of Days*, London, 1957

Hamid, Abdul, *Muslim Separatism in India, 1858–1947*, Karachi, 1967

Handa, R.L., *History of Freedom Struggle in Princely States*, New Delhi, 1968

Haq, Mushirul, *Muslim Politics in Modern India, 1857–1947*, Meerut, 1970

Hardy, Peter, *The Muslims of British India*, Cambridge, 1972

Hasan, Khalid (ed.), *Quaid-i-Azam Mohammad Ali Jinnah: A Centenary Tribute, 1876–1976*, London, 1976

Hasan, Mushirul, *Mohamed Ali: Ideology and Politics*, New Delhi, 1981

___, (ed.), *Mohammad Ali Jinnah in Indian Politics: Select Writings*, New Delhi, 1982

___, (ed.), *Communal and Pan-Islamic Trends in Colonial India*, New Delhi, 1985

___, *A Nationalist Conscience: M.A. Ansari, The Congress and the Raj*, New Delhi, 1987

___, *Nationalism and Communal Politics in India, 1885–1930*, New Delhi, 1994

___, (ed.), *My Life A Fragment: An Autobiographical Sketch of Maulana Mohammad Ali*, New Delhi, 1999

___, *Towards Freedom Movement: Documents on the Movement for Independence in India*, 1939, New Delhi, 2000

___, *Towards Freedom: Documents on the Movement for Independence in India, Parts I and II*, New Delhi, 2008

Hasan, Sarwar (ed.), *Jinnah, Transfer of Power*, Karachi, 1966

Hasan, Syed Shamsul, *Plain Mr. Jinnah*, Karachi, 1976

Hasan, Syed Zafarul and Qadri Husain, *The Problem of Indian Muslims and Its Solution*, Aligarh, 1939

Hasnain, Nadeem, Husain Sheikh Abrar, *Shias and Shia Islam in India: A Study in Society and Culture*, Delhi, 1988

Hayat, Sikandar, *The Charismatic Leader: Quaid-i-Azam Mohammad Ali Jinnah and the Creation of Pakistan*, Oxford, 2008

Hodson, H.V., *Twentieth Century Empire*, London, 1948

___, *The Great Divide: Britain, India, Pakistan*, London, 1969

Holdsworth, Angela (ed.), *A Portrait of Lincoln's Inn*, London, 2007

Hollister, John, *The Shia of India*, London, 1953

Howarth, Toby, *The Twelver Shia as a Muslim Minority in India: Pulpit of Tears*, London, 2005

Hunter, W.W., *The Indian Mussalmans*, Lahore, 1968

___, *The Indian Empire: Its People, History and Products*, London, 1886, second edition

Huntington, Samuel, P., *The Clash of Civilisations and the Remaking of the World Order*, New York, 1996

Husain, Azim, *Fazl-i-Husain, A Political Biography*, Bombay, 1946

Iftihar-ul-Huq, *India's Problem of her Future Constitution* (Preface by M.A. Jinnah), Bombay, 1940

Ikram, S.M., *Modern Muslim India and the Birth of Pakistan*, Lahore, 1970

___, *Indian Muslims and Partition of India*, Delhi, 1995

Iqbal, Muhammad, *The Reconstruction of Religious Thought in Islam*, London, 1934

___, *Letters of Iqbal to Jinnah* (Foreword by M.A. Jinnah), s.l, n.d.

Ispahani, M.A.H., *Quaid-i-Azam Jinnah as I Knew Him*, Karachi, 1966

Jalal, Ayesha, *The Sole Spokesman: Jinnah, the Muslim League and Demand for Pakistan*, Cambridge, 1985

Jafar, Malik Muhammad (ed.), *Jinnah as a Parliamentarian*, Lahore, 1977

Jafri, Qasim (ed.), *Quaid-i-Azam's Correspondence with Punjab Muslim Leaders*, Lahore, 1977

Jamasji-Hirjikaka, Daleara and Qureshi Yasmin, *The Merchant Knight: Adamjee Haji Dawood*, Karachi, 2004

Jawed, Ajeet, *Secular and Nationalist Jinnah*, New Delhi, 1998

Jayakar, M.R., *The Story of My Life*, 2 vols, Bombay, 1958

Jinnah, Fatima, *My Brother: Mohammad Ali Jinnah (1876–1948)* (ed.), By Sharif al Mujahid, Karachi, 1987

Jinnah, Mahomed Ali, *An Ambassador of Unity: His Speeches and Writings, 1912–1917*, Madras, 1918

___, *Speeches and Statements as Governor–General of Pakistan, 1947–48*, Islamabad, 1989

Jinnah, M.A. (Foreword), *Pakistan and Muslim India* by M.R.T., Bombay, 1943

Joachim, Alva, *Leaders of India*, Bombay, 1943

Jones, K.W., *Arya Dharm*, Berkeley, 1976

Jones, Allen Keith, *Politics in Sindh 1907–1940, Muslim Identity and the Demand for Pakistan*, Oxford, 2002

Jones, Justin. *Shia Islam in Colonial India: Religion, Community and Sectarianism.* New York, 2012

Joshi, V.L. (ed.), *Lala Lajpat Rai: His Writings and Speeches*, Delhi, 1966

Jung, N.Y. (ed.), *The Pakistan Issue: Being the Correspondence between S.A. Latif and M.A. Jinnah on the one hand, and between him and Maulana A.K. Azad, Dr. Rajendra Prasad and Pandit Jawaharlal Nehru on the other and connected papers on the subject of Pakistan*, Lahore, 1943

Kabir, Humayun (ed.), *Azad Abdul Kalam: A Memorial Volume*, New York, 1959

___, *Muslim Politics 1906–47 and other Essays*, Calcutta, 1969

Kaura, Uma, *Muslims and Indian Nationalism: The Emergence of the Demand for India's Partition, 1928–1940*, Delhi, 1977

Kazimi, Mohammad Reza, *M.A. Jinnah. Views and Reviews*, Oxford, 2005

___, *Liaquat Ali Khan: His Life and Work*, Karachi, 2003

Keay, F.E., *A History of Hindi Literature*, Calcutta, 1920

Keddie, Nikki, *An Islamic Response to Imperialism—Political and Religious Writings of Syed Jamal-al-Din al'Afghani*, Los Angeles, 1968

Keith, A.B., *A Constitutional History of India, 1600–1935*, London, 1936

Kenneth, Jones, *Arya Dharm*, Berkeley, 1976

Khairi, Saad, R., *Jinnah Re-interpreted: Journey from Indian Nationalism to Muslim Statehood*, Karachi, 1995

Khaldun, Ibn, *The Muqaddimah: An Introduction to History*, 3 vols, Princeton, 1958

Khaliquzzaman, C., *Pathway to Pakistan*, Lahore, 1961

Khan, Abdul Ghaffar Khan, *My Life and Struggle: Autobiography of Badshah Khan* (trs. by B. Helen), New Delhi, 1969

Khan, Aga, *India in Transition: A Study of Political Evolution*, London, 1918

Khan, Aga, H.H., *The Memoirs of the Aga Khan*, London, 1954

Khan, A., Ahmad, *The Founder of Pakistan through Trial to Triumph*, London, 1942

Khan, Ghulam Rasul, *The Punjab Provincial Muslim League: Its Past and Present*, Lahore, 1939

Khan Medi Ali (Mohsin-ul-Mulk), *Causes of the Decline of the Muhammadan Nation*, Bombay, 1891

Khan, Mohamed Raza, *What Price Freedom*, Madras, 1969

Khan, M.Y., *The Glory of the Quaid-i-Azam*, Karachi, 1970

Khan, Nawab Sir Muhammad Shah Nawaz of Mamdot (publ.), 'A Punjabi', *Confederacy of India*, Lahore, 1939 (attributed to Mian Kifayat Ali)

Khan, Noon, Firoz, *From Memory*, Lahore, 1966

Khan, Shafique, *Mr. Jinnah as a Political Thinker*, Karachi, 1974

Khan, Syed Ahmed, *An Essay on the Causes of the Indian Revolt*, Calcutta, 1860

___, *The Causes of the Indian Revolt*, Benares, 1873

___, *The Causes of the Indian Revolt* (Introduction by Francis Robinson), Oxford, 2000

Khan, Sir, Sikandar Hayat, *Outlines of a Scheme of Indian Federation*, Lahore, 1939

Khan, Wali, *Facts are Facts—The Untold Story of India's Partition*, New Delhi, 1987

Khan, Yasmin, *The Great Partition: The Making of India and Pakistan*, Yale, 2007

Khosla, G.D., *Stern Reckoning: A Survey of the Events leading up to and following the Partition of India*, New Delhi, 1949

Khurshid, K.H., *Memories of Jinnah*, Karachi, 1990

Kumar, S., *Educational Philosophy in Modern India*, New Delhi, 2000

Lal Bahadur, *The Muslim League: Its History, Activities and Achievements*, Agra, 1954

___, *Struggle for Pakistan–Tragedy of the Triumph of Muslim Communalism in India, 1906–1947*, London, 1988

Lateef, S. Abdul, *The Great Leader*, Lahore, 1947

Latif, Syed Abdul, *The Muslim Problem in India*, Bombay, 1939

Latif, Nawab Abdul, *The Present Condition of Indian Muhammadans*, Calcutta, 1883

Lavan, Spencer, *The Ahmadiyah Movement*, Delhi, 1974

Lelyweld, David, *Aligarh's First Generation: Muslim Solidarity in British India*. Princeton, 1978

Linlithgow, Marquess of, *Speeches and Statements, 1936–43*, New Delhi, 1945

Lohia, Dr. R., *Mystery of Sir Stafford Cripps*, Bombay, 1942

Lohia, R.M., *Guilty Men of India's Partition*, Hyderabad, 1970

Long, Roger, D., *'Dear Mr. Jinnah', Selected Correspondence and Speeches of Liaquat Ali Khan, 1937–1947*, Oxford, 2004

___, *The Political Career of Mohammad Ali Jinnah*, Karachi, 2010

Macpherson, K., *The Muslim Microcosm: Calcutta 1918 to 1935*, Wiesbaden, 1974

Mahalanobis, P.C., *Distribution of Muslims in the Population of India*, Calcutta, 1946

Majumdar, S.K., *Jinnah and Gandhi: Their Role in India's Quest for Freedom*, Lahore, 1976

Malik, Iftikar Haider, *Sikandar Hayat Khan (1892–1942): A Political Biography*, Islamabad, 1985

Malik, Ikram Ali, *Muslim League Session 1940 and the Lahore Resolution*, Islamabad, 1990

Malik, Muhammad, *Allama Inayatullah Mashraqui: A Political Biography*, Karachi, 2000

Mansergh, N., E.W.R. Lumby, and Penderel Moon (eds), *Constitutional Relations Between India and Britain: The Transfer of Power*, London, 1970–83

Mansergh, N., *Prelude to Partition: Concepts and Aims in Ireland and India*, Cambridge, 1978

___, *The Commonwealth Experience 2: From British to Multi-racial Commonwealth*, Toronto, 1983

Mary, Countess of Minto, *India: Minto and Morley, 1905–10*, London, 1934

Masani, R.P., *Dadabhai Naoroji: The Grand Old Man of India*, London, 1934

Mathai, M.O., *Reminiscences of the Nehru Age*, New Delhi, 1978

___, *My Days with Nehru*, New Delhi, 1979

Mathews, Roderick, *Jinnah vs Gandhi*, New Delhi, 2012

McDonough, S. (ed.), *Mohammad Ali Jinnah: Maker of Modern Pakistan*, Massachusetts, 1970

McPherson, Kenneth, *Jinnah*, Brisbane, 1980

Mehrotra, S.R., *Towards India's Freedom and Partition*, New Delhi, 1979

Menon, V.P., *The Transfer of Power in India*, Madras, 1968

Merriam, A.H., *Gandhi vs Jinnah—The Debate over the Partition of India*, Calcutta, 1980

Metcalf, Barbara, *Islamic Revival in British India: Deoband, 1860–1900*, Princeton, 1982

Miles, K. (ed.), *Liaquat—The Man of Destiny*, Karachi, 1953

Minault, Gail, *The Khilafat Movement: Religious Symbolism and Political Mobilisation in India*, New York, 1982

Minto, M., *India, Morley and Minto, 1905–1910*, London, 1934

Mirza, Sarfaraz Hussain, *The Punjab Muslim Students Federation: An Annotated Documentary Survey, 1937–1947*, London, 1978

Misra, B.B., *The Indian Political Parties: An Historical Analysis of Political Behaviour up to 1947*, Oxford, 1976

———, *The Unification and Division of India*, Delhi, 1990

Mody, H.P., *Sir Pherozeshah Mehta: A Political Biography*, Bombay, 1921

Mohan, Ram, *Hindi against India*, New Delhi, 1968

Momen, Moojan, *An Introduction to Shi'i Islam: The History and Doctrines of Twelver Shi'ism*. New York, 1985

Montagu, V. (ed.), *Edwin S. Montagu: An Indian Diary*, London, 1930

Moon, Penderel, *Divide and Quit*, London, 1962

Moore, R.J., *The Crisis of Indian Unity, 1917–1940*, Oxford, 1974

___, *Churchill, Cripps and India, 1939–1945*, Oxford, 1979

___, *Escape from Empire: The Attlee Government and the Indian Problem*, London, 1983

Moraes, Frank, *Jawaharlal Nehru: A Biography*, New York, 1956

___, *Witness to an Era*, London, 1973

Moran, Lord, *Winston Churchill: The Struggle for Survival, 1940–65*, 1966

More, J.B.P., *The Political Evolution of Muslims in Tamil Nadu and Madras, 1930–47*, Hyderabad, 1997

___, *Freedom Movement in French India: The Mahé Revolt of 1948*, Tellicherry, 2001

___, *Muslim Identity, Print Culture and the Dravidian Factor*, Hyderabad, 2004

___, *Religion and Society in South India: Hindus, Muslims and Christians*, Nirmalagiri, 2006

___, *The Telugus of Yanam and Masulipatnam: From French Rule to Integration with India*, Pondicherry, 2007

___, *Puducheri Valartha Bharathiar* (Tamil), Pondicherry, 2010

M.R.T., *Pakistan and Muslim India*, Bombay, 1943

Muhammad, Shan, *The Indian Musalman: A Documentary Record*, New Delhi, 1985

Mujahid Sharif Al, *Quaid-i-Azam Jinnah: Studies in Interpretation*, Karachi, 1985

___, (ed.), *Quaid-i-Azam and His Times*, Karachi, 1990

___, (ed.), *Muslim League Documents 1900–1947 (vol.1 1900–1908)*, Karachi, 1990

Mujeeb, M., *The Indian Muslims*, London, 1967

Mukherjee, Haridas and Uma Mukherjee, *'Bande Mataram' and Indian Nationalism (1906–1908)*, Calcutta, 1957

Munshi, K.M., *Akhand Hindustan*, Bombay, 1942

___, (ed.), *Pilgrimage to Freedom*, Bombay, 1967

Murthi, R.K., *Rajaji—Life and Work*, New Delhi, 1979

Naidu, Sarojini (ed.), *Mohammad Ali Jinnah, An Ambassador of Unity: His Speeches and Writings, 1912–1917*, Madras, 1918

Naidu, Sarojini, *Muhammad Ali Jinnah: An Ambassador of Unity*, Lahore, 1989

Naim, C.M. (ed.), *Iqbal, Jinnah and Pakistan*, Lahore, 1984

Nanda, B.R., *Mahatma Gandhi: A Biography*, London, 1958

___, *The Nehrus: Motilal and Jawaharlal*, New York, 1963

___, *Gokhale, Gandhi and Nehrus: Studies in Indian Nationalism*, London, 1974

___, *Gokhale: The Indian Moderates and the British Raj*, Delhi, 1998

Naqvi, Mushtaq, *Partition: The Real Story*, Delhi, 1995

Narasimhan, C.R., *Rajagopalachari: A Biography*, London, 1993

Natesan, G.A., *Dadabhai Naoroji*, Madras, 1920

Nehru, Jawaharlal, *An Autobiography*, London, 1958

___, *A Bunch of Old Letters*, Delhi, 1986

___, *The Discovery of India*, Delhi, 1994

Nehru, Krishna Hutheesingh, Hatch, Alden, *We Nehrus*, New York, 1967

Nizami, K.A. (ed.), *Shak Waliullah Ke Siyasi Maktuba (Political Letters of Shah Waliullah)*, Aligarh, 1951

___, *Theodore Beck Papers from the Sir Syed Academy Archives*, Aligarh, 1991

Noman, Mohammed, *Muslim India: Rise and Growth of All India Muslim League*, Allahabad, 1942

___, (ed.), *Our Struggle, 1857–1947*, Karachi, n.d.

Norman, Dorothy, *The First Sixty Years*, I, Bombay, 1965

Noon, Feroz Khan, *From Memory*, Lahore, 1969

Noorani, A.G., *Jinnah and Tilak: Comrades in Freedom Struggle*, Oxford, 2010

Padamsee, Alex, *Representations of Indian Muslims in British Colonial Discourse*, Basingstoke, 2005

Page, David, *Prelude to Partition: The Indian Muslims and the Imperial System of Control, 1920–1932*, Delhi, 1982

Pal, J.J., *Jinnah and the Creation of Pakistan*, Delhi, 1983

Pandey, B.N., *The Break-up of British India*, London, 1969

___, (ed.), *The Indian Nationalist Movement, 1885–1947, Select Documents*, London, 1979

Panjabi, K.L., *Rajendra Prasad: First President of India*, London, 1960

___, *The Indomitable Sardar: A Political Biography*, Bombay, 1962

Panigrahi, D.N., *India's Partition: The Story of Imperialism in Retreat*, London, 2004

Parel, Anthony, *Hind Swaraj and Other Writings*, Cambridge, 1997

Parvate, T.V., *Bal Gangadhar Tilak: A Narrative and Interpretative Review of his Life, Career and Contemporary Events*, Ahmedabad, 1958

___, *Gopal Krishna Gokhale*, Ahmedabad, 1959

Philips, C.H. (ed.), *The Evolution of India and Pakistan, 1858–1947, Select Documents*, London, 1962

___, *The Partition of India 1947*, Leeds, 1967

Philips, C.H. and M.D. Wainwright (eds), *The Partition of India: Policies and Perspectives, 1935–1947*, London, 1970

Pichai, Alla, A.M., *Just a Peep into the Muslim Mind*, Madras, 1972

Pirzada, Syed Sharif-ud-din (ed.), *Foundations of Pakistan: Documents of the All India Muslim League, 1906–1947*, vols I and II, Karachi, Dacca, 1970

Pirzada, S.S. (ed.), *Quaid-i-Azam Jinnah's Correspondence*, Karachi, 1966

___, *Some Aspects of Quaid-i-Azam's Life*, Islamabad, 1978

___, (ed.), *The Collected Works of Quaid-e-Azam Mohammad Ali Jinnah*, Karachi, 3 vols, 1984–86

___, (ed.), *Foundations of Pakistan: All India Muslim League Documents, 1906–1947, II, 1924–1947*, Islamabad, 2007

Prakash, Indra, *Hindu Mahasabha: Its Contribution to Indian Politics*, New Delhi, 1966

Prasad, Bimal, *Pathway to India's Partition*, 3 volumes, New Delhi, 1999, 2000, 2003

___, (ed.), *Towards Freedom: Documents on the Movement for Independence in India, 1945*, New Delhi, 2005

Prasad, I., *Hindu–Muslim Problem*, Allahabad, 1974

Prasad, Rajendra, *India Divided*, Bombay, 1946

___, *At the Feet of the Mahatma Gandhi*, New York, 1955

Pyarelal, V.N. (ed.), *Gandhiji's Correspondence with the Government, 1942–44, 1944–47*, Ahmedabad, 1957–59

___, *Mahatma Gandhi: The Last Phase*, 2 vols, Ahmedabad, 1958

Pylee, M.V., *Constitutional History of India, 1600–1950*, London, 1967

Qureishi, F.H. (ed.), *Everyday with Quaid-i-Azam*, Karachi, 1976

Qureishi, I.H., *The Muslim Community of the Indo-Pakistan Sub-continent (1610–1947)*, Karachi, 1970 (first published in The Hague, 1962)

___, *The Struggle for Pakistan,* Karachi, 1965, 1980

Qureshi, Naeem, *Pan-Islamism in British India: The Politics of the Khilafat Movement 1918–1924*, Karachi, 2009

Qureishi, Saleem, *Jinnah and the Making of a Nation*, Karachi, 1969

___, (ed.), *Jinnah the Founder of Pakistan in the Eyes of his Contemporaries and His Documentary Records at Lincoln's Inn*, Karachi, 1998

Radhakrishnan, S., *The Hindu View of Life*, London, 1980

Rahman, Matiur, *From Consultation to Confrontation: A Study of the Muslim League in British Indian Politics, 1906–1912*, London, 1970

Rajagopalachari, C., *Chats behind Bars*, Madras, 1931

___, *Plighted Word*, Delhi, 1933

Rajput, A.B., *Muslim League Yesterday and Today*, Lahore, 1948

Ramgopal, *Indian Muslims—A Political History*, Bombay, 1959

Rao, Kodanda, P., *V.S. Srinivasa Sastri: A Political Biography*, Madras, 1963

Rao, Shiva, B. (ed.), *India's Constitution in the Making*, Bombay, 1960

___, *India's Freedom Movement, Some Notable Figures*, New Delhi, 1972

Rawoof, A.A., *Meet Mr. Jinnah*, Lahore, 1944

Rezaul, Karim, *Pakistan Examined*, Calcutta, 1941

Riddick, John, F., *Who was Who in British India?*, London, 1998

Rizvi, Gowher, *Linlithgow and India: A Study of British Policy and the Political Impasse in India, 1936–43*, London, 1978

Robinson, Francis, *Separatism among Indian Muslims: The Politics of the United Provinces' Muslims, 1860–1923*, Cambridge, 1974

___, *Islam and Muslim History in South Asia*, Delhi, 2000

___, *The Ulama of Farangi Mahall and Islamic Culture in South Asia*, Delhi, 2001

Saeed, Ahmad (ed.), *Quaid-i-Azam Mohammad Ali Jinnah: A Bunch of Rare Letters*, Lahore, 1999

Saiyid, M.H., *Mohammad Ali Jinnah: A Political Study*, Lahore, 1945, 1962, 1970

___, *The Sound of Fury: A Political Study of Mohammad Ali Jinnah*, New Delhi, 1981

Saiyidain, Hameeda, Syeda, *Islamic Seal on India's Independence, Abul Kalam Azad—A Fresh Look*, Karachi, 1998

Sampuranand, *Memories and Reflections*, Bombay, 1962

Sarkar, Sumit, *Modern India, 1885–1947*, Delhi, 1983, 1984 (reprint)

___, (ed.), *Towards Pakistan: Documents on the Movement for Independence in India*, New Delhi, 2007

Sastri, Srnivasa, V.S., *Life and Times of Sir Pherozeshah Mehta*, Bombay, 1975

Savarkar, V.D., *Hindutva: Who is a Hindu?*, Bombay, 1969

Sayeed, Khalid, Bin, *Pakistan: The Formative Phase, 1857–1948*, London, 1968

Sayeed, G.M., *Struggle for New Sind*, Karachi, 1949

Seal, Anil, *The Emergence of Indian Nationalism*, Oxford, 1971

Seeley, John, R., Sir, *The Expansion of England*, London, 1883

Seervai, H.M., *Partition of India: Legend and Reality*, Bombay, 1990, 2005 (reprint)

Sen, S., *The Birth of Pakistan*, Calcutta, 1955

Sen, S.P. (ed.), *Dictionary of National Biography*, 4 vols, Calcutta, 1972–74

Setalvad, C.H., *Recollections and Reflections*, Bombay, 1946

Shahid, Kamran, *Gandhi and the Partition of India: A New Perspective*, Lahore, 2005

Shahid, Mohammad Hanif, *The Quaid-i-Azam on Important Issues*, Lahore, 1989

Shaikh, Farzana, *Community and Consensus in Islam: Muslim Representation in Colonial India, 1860–1947*, Cambridge, 1989

Shaikh, A.Z and M.R. Malik (eds), *Quaid-i-Azam and the Muslim World: Selected Documents, 1937–1948*, Karachi, 1976

Shan, Muhammad (ed.), *Writings and Speeches of Sir Syed Ahmed Khan*, Bombay, 1972

___, *Khaksar Movement in India*, Meerut, 1973

Sharif al Mujadid, *Jinnah: Studies in Interpretation*, Karachi, 1981

Sheikh, N.A., *Quaid-i-Azam: Father of a Nation*, Karachi, 1996

Sherwani, L.A. (ed.), *Pakistan Resolution to Pakistan: A Selection of Documents Presenting the Case for Pakistan*, Karachi, 1969

___, *Speeches, Writings and Statements of Iqbal*, Lahore, 1977

___, *The Founder of Pakistan*, Karachi, 1996

Singh, Bhim Sen, *The Cripps Mission—A Handiwork of British Imperialism*, New Delhi, 1979

Singh, Anita Inder, *The Origins of the Partition of India, 1936–1947*, Oxford, 1987

Singh, Jaswant, *Jinnah: India–Partition Independence*, New Delhi, 2009

Sitaramayya, B., Pattabhi, *History of the Indian National Congress*, vol. I, 1885–1935, Bombay, 1935; vol. II, 1935–1947, Bombay, 1947

Smith, W.C., *The Muslim League, 1942–45*, Lahore, 1945

___, *Modern Islam in India*, London, 1946

Spate, O.H.K., *India and Pakistan*, London, 1960

Stephens, Ian, *Horned Moon*, London, 1953

___, *Pakistan*, London, 1967 (3rd edition)

Strachey, John, Sir, *India: Its Administration and Progress*, London, 1888

Swinson, Arthur, *North-West Frontier: People and Events 1839–1947*, London, 1967

Syed, Ameer Ali, *The Spirit of Islam*, London, 1922

Syed Wazir Hasan (comp.), *Proceedings of the Annual Session of the AIML Held at Bombay on 30th, 31st December 1915 and 1st January 1916*, Lucknow, 1916

Symonds, Richards, *The Making of Pakistan*, London, 1949

Tahmankar, D.V., *Sardar Patel*, London, 1970

Talbot, Ian, *Provincial Politics and the Pakistan Movement: The Growth of the Muslim League in the North-West and North-East, 1937–1947*, Karachi, 1988

Talbot, Ian and Gurharpal Singh, *Region and Partition: Bengal, Punjab and the Partition of the Subcontinent*, Oxford, 1999

Talha, Naureen, *Economic Factors in the Making of Pakistan, 1921–1947*, Oxford, 2001

Taylor, Anne, *Annie Besant: A Biography*, Madras, 1983

Tendulkar, D.G., *Mahatma: Life of Mohandas Karamchand Gandhi*, 8 vols, New Delhi, 1961–63

Tinker, Hugh, *Experiment with Freedom: India and Pakistan, 1947*, London, 1967

___, *The Foundations of Local Government in India, Pakistan and Burma*, London, 1968

Titus, Murray, T., *Indian Islam*, London, 1930

Thapar, R. (ed.), *Communalism and the Writing of Indian History*, New Delhi, 1969

Thatcher, Mary (ed.), *Cambridge South Asian Archives*, Cambridge, 1973

Thompson, Edward, *Enlist India for Freedom*, London, 1940

Tomlinson, B.R., *The Indian National Congress and the Raj, 1929–1942*, London, 1976

___, *The Political Economy of the Raj, 1914–1947: The Economics of Decolonization in India*, London, 1979

Toynbee, Arnold, *A Study of History*, 12 vols, Oxford, 1934–61

Tyabji, H.B., *Why Musalmans should oppose Pakistan*, Bombay, 1946

Tyabji, Husain, *Badruddin Tyabji: A Biography*, Bombay, 1952

Umar, Mohammad, Dr (ed.), *Quaid-i-Azam Mohammad Ali Jinnah: Rare Speeches, 1910–1918*, Karachi, 1973

___, *Quaid-i-Azam Mohammad Ali Jinnah: An Analysis of His Parliamentary Attributes*, Karachi, 1997

Vali, Nasr, *The Shia Revival—How Conflicts within Islam will Shape the Future*, Norton, 2006

Virani, Shafique, *The Ismailias in the Middle Ages: A History of Survival, A Search for Salvation*, New York, 2007

Waheed, Ahmad (ed.), *Jinnah–Linlithgow Correspondence, 1939–1943*, Lahore, 1976

Waheed-uz-Zaman, *Quaid-i-Azam Muhammad Ali Jinnah: Myth and Reality*, Islamabad, 1976

Wasti, S.R., *Lord Minto and the Indian Nationalist Movement, 1905–1910*, London, 1964

___, *At Quaid's Service: A Journey towards Discovery*, Lahore, 1996

Wells, Ian Bryant, *Ambassador of Hindu–Muslim Unity: Jinnah's Early Politics*, New Delhi, 2005

Wolpert, Stanley, *Tilak and Gokhale: Revolution and Reforms in the Making of Modern India*, Berkeley, 1962

___, *Jinnah of Pakistan*, New York, 1984
___, *Nehru: A Tryst with Destiny*, Oxford, 1996
Wrench, Evelyn, *Immortal Years*, London, 1945
Yasmeen, S., *Ruttie Jinnah, Life and Love*, Islamabad, 1997
Yong, Tan Tai, *The Garrison State: The Military, Government and Society in Colonial Punjab 1849–1947*, New Delhi, 2005
Yunus, Mohammad, *Frontier Speaks*, Bombay, 1997
___, *Persons, Passions and Politics*, Delhi, 1970
Yusuf, K.F. (ed.), *Politics and Policies of Quaid-i-Azam*, Islamabad, 1984
Zaidi, A.M., *From Syed to the Emergence of Jinnah*, New Delhi, 1975
___, (ed.), *Sectarian Nationalism and Khilafat: Documents*, Delhi, 1975
___, (ed.), *The Muslim School of Congress: Political Ideology of Muslim Congress Leaders from Mr. Badruddin Tyabji to Maulana Abul Kalam Azad, 1885–1943*, New Delhi, 1987
Zaidi, A.M. and S.G. Zaidi, *The Encyclopaedia of Indian National Congress*, XI, XII, XIII, New Delhi, 1980–1981
Zaidi, Z.H. (ed.), *M.A. Jinnah–Ispahani Correspondence*, Karachi, 1976
___, *Quaid-i-Azam Mohammad Jinnah Papers*, 5 volumes, Islamabad, 1994–2002
Zakaria, Rafiq, *Rise of Muslims in Indian Politics*. Bombay, 1970, 1980, third edition
___, *Iqbal, Poet and Politician*, New Delhi, 1993
___, *Sardar Patel and Indian Muslims*. Mumbai, 1996
___, *The Price of Partition*, Mumbai, 1998
___, *Gandhi and the Break-up of India*, Bombay, 1999
___, *The Man who Divided India: An Insight into Jinnah's Leadership and its Aftermath*, Bombay, 2004
Zetland, J. Lawrence, *Life of Lord Curzon*, London, 1928
Zetland, Marquess of, *'Essayez': The Memoirs of Lawrence, Second Marquess of Zetland*, London, 1956
Ziring, Lawrence, *Pakistan in the Twentieth Century: A Political History*, Karachi, 1997

ARTICLES

Ahmad, Imtiaz, 'The Ashraf–Ajlaf Distinction in Muslim Social Structure in India', *Indian Economic and Social History Review*, 3 September 1966, pp. 268–78
___, 'The Shia–Sunni Dispute in Lucknow, 1905–1980', in Milton Israel and Narendra Wagle (eds), *Islamic Society and Culture: Essays in Honour of Professor Aziz Ahmed*, Delhi, 1983, pp. 335–50
Anderson, Perry, 'Why Partition?', *London Review of Books*, vol. 34, no. 14, 19 July 2012, pp. 11–19

Bayly, C.A., 'The Pre-History of Communalism? Religious Conflict in India, 1700–1860', *Modern Asian Studies*, vol. 19, no. 2, 1985, pp. 177–203

Brass, Paul, R., 'Muslim Separatism in the United Provinces, Social Context and Political Strategy before Partition', *Economic and Political Weekly*, Annual Number, January 1970, pp. 167–86

___, 'A Reply to Francis Robinson', *Journal of Commonwealth and Comparative Politics*, vol. 15, no. 3, 1977, pp. 231–34

___, 'Elite Groups, Symbol Manipulation and Ethnic Identity among the Muslims of South Asia', in David Taylor and M. Yapp (eds), *Political Identity in South Asia*, London, 1979

Chaman Lal, Dewan, 'The Quaid-i-Azam as I knew him', in J. Ahmad, *Quaid-i-Azam as seen by His Contemporaries*, Lahore, 1976

Dillard, James, E. 'The Failure of Nehru's Mass Contact Campaign and the Rise of Muslim Separatism', *Journal of South Asian and Middle-eastern Studies*, vol. XXXI, no. 2, 2008

Friedmann, Yohanan, 'The Attitude of the Jami'yyat-i-ulama-i-Hind to the Indian National Congress and the Establishment of Pakistan', in Mushirul Hasan (ed.), *Inventing Boundaries: Gender, Politics and Partition of India*, Delhi, 2000, pp. 157–77

Ghosh, Papiya, 'Presenting the Southern Dimension of Partition', *The Hindu*, 27 December 1997, International Edition (Review of J.B.P. More's *The Political Evolution of Muslims in Tamil Nadu and Madras: 1930–47*), Hyderabad, 1997

Harrak, H., 'Sir Stafford Cripps as British Ambassador in Moscow, May 1940 to June 1941', *English Historical Review*, vol. xciv, 1979, pp. 48–70

Hasan, Mushirul, 'Sectarianism in Indian Islam: The Shia–Sunni Divide in the United Provinces', *Indian Economic and Social History Review*, vol. 27, no. 2, 1999, pp. 208–28

Jalal, Ayesha and Anil Seal, 'Alternative to Partition: Muslim Politics between Wars', *Modern Asian Studies*, vol. 15, no. 3, July 1981, pp. 415–54

Jalal, Ayesha 'Nation, Reason and Religion: Punjab's Role in the Partition of India', *Economic and Political Weekly*, 8 August 1998

___, 'Between Myth and History: The Lahore Resolution Revisited', *Dawn*, 23 March 2005

Jinnah, Fatima, 'A Sister's Recollections', in *Pakistan, Past and Present*, London, 1977

Jinnah, M.A., 'Two Nation-Theory', in *Time and Tide*, 9 March 1940

Lokhandwala, S.T., 'Islamic Law and Ismailia Communities, Khodjas and Bohras', *Indian Economic and Social History Review*, vol. IV, no. 2, pp. 155–76

Mahmudabad, Raja Muhammad Amir Akhtar Khan, 'Some Memories' in Mushirul Hasan (ed.), *India's Partition: Process, Strategy and Mobilisation*, Delhi, 1993, pp. 415–26

Mahmudabad, Raja, 'Of Some Memories', in C.H. Philips and M.D. Wainwright (eds), *The Partition of India: Policies and Perspectives, 1935–1947*, London, 1970

Metcalf, Barbara, 'Iqbal: Ideology in Search of an Audience', in C.M. Naim (ed.), *Iqbal, Jinnah and Pakistan: The Vision and the Reality*, Lahore, 1984

Mehrotra, S.R., 'The Congress and the Partition of India', in C.H. Philips and M.D. Wainwright (eds), *The Partition of India: Policies and Perspectives, 1935–1947*, London, 1970

Moore, R.J., 'The Mystery of the Cripps Mission', *Journal of Commonwealth Political Studies*, vol. XI, no. 3, November 1973, pp. 195–213

___, 'Jinnah and the Pakistan Demand', *Modern Asian Studies*, vol. 17, no. 4, 1983, pp. 529–61

More, J.B.P., 'Elite Manipulation, Islamic Solidarity and the Territorial Factor: The Southern Angle', in *Religion and Society in South India: Hindus, Muslims and Christians*, Nirmalagiri, 2006

___, 'Muslim Specificities in French India during the Nineteenth Century', *Journal of the Institute for Research in Social Sciences and Humanities*, vol. 2, no. 1, January–June 2007, pp. 117–32

___, 'Geo-political and Strategic Implications Related to the Emergence of the Indian and Pakistani Nation', Paper presented at the International Conference of 'The State in South Asia', organized by the Department of History, University of Hyderabad, India, 18 to 21 October 2010

Mustafa, A.M. 'My Happy Recollections', in K. Miles (ed.), *Liaquat—The Man of Destiny*, Karachi, 1953

Nanda, B.R., 'Nehru and the Partition of India', in C.H. Philips and M.D. Wainwright (eds), *The Partition of India: Policies and Perspectives, 1935–1947*, London, 1970

Oren, Stephen, 'The Sikhs, Congress and the Unionists in British Punjab', *Modern Asian Studies*, vol. 8, no. 3, 1974, pp. 397–418

Owen, Hugh, 'Negotiating the Lucknow Pact', *Journal of Asian Studies*, vol. 31, no. 3, 1972, pp. 561–87

Pandey, Deepak, 'Congress–Muslim League Relations, 1937–39: The Parting of Ways', *Modern Asian Studies*, vol. 12, no. 4, 1978

Rao, Shiva, B., 'India, 1935–47', in C.H. Philips and M.D. Wainwright (eds), *The Partition of India: Policies and Perspectives, 1935–1947*, London, 1970

Robinson, F., 'Islam and Muslim Separatism', in David Taylor and Malcolm Yapp (eds), *Political Identity in South Asia*, London, 1979, pp. 78–112

___, 'Islam and Muslim Society in South Asia', *Contributions to Indian Sociology*, vol. 7, no. 2, 1983

Robinson, Francis, 'Nation Formation: The Brass Thesis and Muslim Separatism', *Journal of Commonwealth and Comparative Politics*, vol. 15, no. 3, 1977, pp. 215–30

Sayeed, K.B., 'The Personality of Jinnah and His Political Strategy', in C.H. Philips and M.D. Wainwright (eds), *The Partition of India*, London, 1970, pp. 276–93

Skinner, Quentin, 'Some Problems in the Analysis of Political Thought and Action', *Political Theory*, vol. 2, no. 3, 1974, pp. 277–303

Stanely, Wolpert, 'Congress Leadership in Transition: Jinnah to Gandhi, 1914–20', in Dewitte C. Ellinwood and S.D. Pradhan (eds), *India and World War I*, New Delhi, 1978

Talbot, Ian, 'The Growth of the Muslim League in the Punjab, 1937–1946', *Journal of Commonwealth and Comparative Politics*, vol. 20, no. 1, March 1982

___, 'Deserted Collaborators: The Political Background to the Rise and Fall of the Punjab Unionist Party, 1923–1947', *Journal of Imperial and Commonwealth History*, vol. 11, no. 1, October 1982

Talbot, I., 'Jinnah and the Making of Pakistan', *History Today*, 34, February 1984

Zaidi, Z.H., 'Aspects of the Development of Muslim League Policy, 1937–47', in C.H. Philips and M.D. Wainwright (eds), *The Partition of India: Policies and Perspectives, 1935–1947*, London, 1970

Zakaria, Rafiq, 'Jinnah did not want Partition', *The Times of India*, Sunday Review, 22 September 1985

___, 'Jinnabhai', *The Asian Age*, 18 November 2001

MISCELLANEOUS

Archives of Freedom Movement (Muslim League Records) and List of Classified Volumes, Karachi, 1982

Census of India, 1921

Census of India, 1931

Encyclopaedie de l'Islam, Paris, 1927

Full and Authentic Report of Tilak Trial, 1908

Indian Annual Register, Calcutta, 1940 to 1947

Muthiah, Vellaiyan, 'Jaswant Singh's Unhistorical Work on Partition of India' (Tamil), Interview with J.B.P. More, published in *Puthiya Puthagam Pesuthu*, Chennai, October 2009

Nehru–Jinnah Correspondence, Allahabad, 1938

Noorani, A.G., Review Article, 'The Partition of India', *Frontline*, 4 January 2002

___, Review Article, 'The House that Jinnah Built', *Frontline*, 25 October–7 November 2003

___, Review Article, 'Punjab and Pakistan', *Frontline*, 25 March 2005

___, Review Article, 'Why Jinnah became Defiant', *Frontline*, 6 September 2013

Pakistan, Past and Present: A Comprehensive Study Published in Commemoration of the Centenary of the Birth of the Founder of Pakistan. London, 1977

Pirpur Report—Report of the Enquiry Committee appointed by the AIML to enquire into Muslim Grievances in Congress Provinces (Home Dept – F.31/30/39–Pub, NAI)

Reed, Stanley (ed.), *The Indian Year Book, 1914*, Bombay, 1915

Report of the Hunter Education Commission, 1882

Robinson, Francis, Review of Stanley Wolpert's *Jinnah of Pakistan* (New York, 1984) and Ayesha Jalal's *The Sole Spokesman: Jinnah, the Muslim League and the Demand for Pakistan* (Cambridge, 1985), *Modern Asian Studies*, vol. XX, no. 3, July 1986, pp. 611–18

Roy, Asim, Review Article, 'The High Politics of India's Partition: The Revisionist Perspective', *Modern Asian Studies*, vol. 24, Part 2, May 1990, pp. 385–408

The Constitution and Rules of the All-India Muslim League, Lahore, 1944

The International Who's Who, 1947, London

The International Who's Who, 1950, London

INDEX